VIOLENCE

VIOLENCE

Terrorism, Genocide, War

WOLFGANG SOFSKY

Translated from the German by Anthea Bell

Granta Books
London

Granta Publications, 2/3 Hanover Yard, Noel Road, London N1 8BE

First published in Great Britain by Granta Books 2003

A CIP catalogue record for this book is available from the British Library.

1 3 5 7 9 10 8 6 4 2

ISBN 1 86207 614 6

Typeset in Garamond by M Rules
Printed and bound in Great Britain
by Mackays of Chatham plc

Contents

I

Beyond the Border

II

Terror and Persecution

III
War

IV
The Aftermath

I

Beyond the Border

1

On killing

When the waters had gone down, the survivors left the Ark. We are not told what they saw on dry land: the bodies of animals, perhaps, driftwood, bloated human corpses. Noah built an altar from the stones lying around, chose some of the animals that had been saved and sacrificed them. Then Yahweh enjoyed the sweet savour of the burnt offerings and said in his heart: 'I will not again curse the ground any more for man's sake; for the imagination of man's heart is evil from his youth; neither will I again smite any more every thing living, as I have done.' And he told Noah: 'Be fruitful, and multiply, and replenish the earth. And the fear of you and the dread of you shall be upon every beast of the earth, and upon every fowl of the air, upon all that moveth upon the earth, and upon all the fishes of the sea; into your hand are they delivered. Every moving thing that liveth shall be meat for you; even as the green herb have I given you all things. But flesh with the life thereof, which is the blood thereof, shall ye not eat. And surely your blood of your lives will I require; at the hand of every beast will I require it, and at the hand of man; at the hand of every man's brother will I require the life of man. Whoso sheddeth man's blood, by man shall his blood be shed.'

The new age thus begins with an unexpected act of clemency and renunciation of violence. Yahweh had drowned the world in chaos not on a capricious divine whim, but in anger at the failure of his creation. Murder and wickedness had spread among Adam's descendants, who had offended their creator's pride and aroused his fury generation after generation. But now, appeased by the sweet smell of the burnt offering, Yahweh determines to tolerate evil. Human nature cannot be changed. It merits daily punishment with a new deluge, but Yahweh lifts the curse of annihilation and lays aside the bow of war. He promises mankind eternal life, immortality.

Divine grace is bought with another act of violence. A destructive fire is kindled at the beginning of the new age. The burnt sacrifice is a pious act of lavish wastefulness. It deprives the world's pure, edible animals of any useful function; there is no mention of their being eaten by human beings in a sacrificial feast. The shedding of blood is a sacred act, a tribute to the lord of life. After the holocaust, however, a time of endless terror begins for animals, who are delivered up defenceless to the intelligence and power of mankind. Peace among all creatures is finally at an end. Men can kill animals as they like, without remorse or pangs of conscience. The brute beasts are removed from the moral sphere of humanity from the outset. Armed with divine permission to slaughter, man learns from killing animals how to exercise violence without any sense of guilt. Other living creatures serve him as sacrifice and prey, draught animals and pets. He eats their flesh. And his appetite is boundless; man is a great destroyer of other forms of life, for his aim is to increase and multiply and bring the whole world under his command. Mankind stands on top of a great mound of dead animals, buying immortality at the price of their death en masse. Only blood is forbidden to human beings, who may eat the flesh of the animals but must leave the blood alone, since it belongs to God. It is shed on the altar during sacrifice, mollifying God with its savour.

Culture and society are founded on this licence to kill. The death of animals means life for mankind. Food is necessary to sustain life, and eating meat is the most effective way of warding off death. Yet Yahweh's promise goes hand in hand with the blood taboo, and man is strictly forbidden to do to his own kind what he does to animals. On no account must he eat the flesh of another human being; he must draw his strength only from the bodies of the beasts. He may not kill other human beings either. A taboo on cannibalism and murder is the first law imposed on mankind by God. He bans such violence, however, not on a sudden impulse of solicitude and goodwill. Human blood is taboo because it is God's property, and He alone has the right to shed it. The murderer, therefore, is God's arch-rival, claiming what is God's alone: power over life and death. Only He is the creator and destroyer. This monopoly is protected by the most stringent of all punishments, the death penalty. He who sheds another's blood shall have his own blood shed; he who extinguishes another's life has forfeited his own, and cannot buy redemption. The payment of compensation by one tribe to another no longer counts for anything; the murderer's guilt can be expiated only at the hands of the executioner, who enforces the sacred law. So that no one will usurp God's place, the right to kill is transferred to the secular authorities, who from now on threaten every subject with death.

So violence continued even after the cosmic chastisement which was the Flood. Slaughter and sacrifice, murder and execution, hunting and war are the fundamental forms of killing. Yahweh was under no illusions about mankind, which remains what it has always been. Since anyone can become an enemy, everyone must be prevented from committing murder; this is the basis of the law. Man must fear for his own life if he is to spare others. Civilization is therefore founded on the despotism of the fear of death.

Noah's covenant marks the transition from prehistory to civilization, but the myth says nothing about values and ideas, faith in God or the love of our neighbours. It speaks only of physical desires and perils: of eating and killing. Those are the basic facts of survival which validate the law. Yet the death penalty has hardly ever prevented a murderer from killing. Its deterrent value has always been slight; the law is powerless in the face of violent desires. Observing this, Yahweh soon lost interest in man and withdrew into omniscience, leaving the business of governing and punishing his creation to the earthly authorities. Mankind has been waiting in vain for further signs of His presence ever since. Humanity must bear its burdens alone: violence, the rigour of the law, fear and the knowledge of death.

For immortality was promised only to the species, not the individual. Survival is guaranteed not to men but to mankind, whose foreknowledge of death came with the expulsion from paradise. That certainty overshadows our lives. As far as we know, human beings are the only living creatures to feel not only acute panic in the face of death but also awareness of their own mortality. But though we all know we shall die, no one is ready to believe it, and one of the motive forces of cultural activity lies in preserving that illusion. Not for nothing does culture begin with the invention of funeral rites and burial customs to regulate the passing of the dead into the timeless ancestral world. The dead must be pacified and their appetites satisfied lest they return. They must leave the world of the living for ever, so they are washed and adorned, weapons and jewellery are placed in the tomb with them, they are given food and drink in a funeral feast celebrated by the living. Before they turn their backs on the world for ever, animals are killed for their pleasure. Torrents of blood flow round the funeral bier. Meat is for the living, blood for the dead. By sacrificing animals the survivors make death the instrument of their own will. They feel they have overcome death by slaughtering and eating together. The banquet brings peace to society and celebrates the triumph of life.

Culture is meant to guarantee survival. Its existence and justification consist in its postponement of the end. Its fundamental task is to safeguard life, on which the production and enjoyment of all other good things depend. The learned would like to persuade humanity that all is well with the world, or at least that it is on the way to improvement, but the ultimate test of cultural values is survival.

Where does our awareness of death come from? Death is not an incident within life, not life's goal or its closing chord of reconciliation, but its radical opposite. We cannot experience or learn from our own deaths. You cannot experience nothing. From a personal perspective, it is impossible to imagine non-existence, as impossible as imagining unconsciousness. No one can anticipate death; we can only anticipate that we shall die. And we all hope to go on living, even in death. Non-existence can be imagined only from an external viewpoint, through the eyes of others. Awareness of mortality therefore presupposes a position outside ourselves, not just existing but relating to ourselves: a self-relationship. Since it is in our nature not merely to exist but also to be constantly standing outside ourselves, awareness of our own death is inevitable. If we always lived inside ourselves we could not fear our end, but since we must always adopt an attitude of self-relationship we do not escape the fear of death.

The awareness of death has the same origin as the awareness of free will and of evil. If mankind were driven only by inclinations, wishes or desires we could not adopt any attitude towards ourselves. There would be no basis for any moral judgement of our actions. The question of guilt and responsibility would not arise. Supposing we acted only out of our own central being, not only would we be spared the fear of death, we would be relieved of the freedom to kill. Fear and violence do not, as has often been claimed, spring from our animal nature; no such insult should be offered to the animal kingdom, not even to beasts of prey. On the contrary: violence is the result of our specific humanity. As man is already outside himself, he is capable of any atrocity. Since he is not guided by instincts rising from his central nature, but relates to himself as an intellectual being, he can act worse than any animal, and as his behaviour is not predetermined he can commit any crime. Since he never lives entirely inside himself, he must fear his own death and the freedom of action of others. Freedom is a great good, if not the greatest, but it by no means guarantees moral virtue. The price of freedom is suffering and evil. The freedom of wolves means death to lambs.

Our fear of death engenders a need for security, durability, immortality. Human beings want to outlive themselves and everyone else. Plans for survival are devoted first to our own bodies, for it is the body that is threatened by death. The body is the natural adversary of all survival, an enemy that we can never escape. Admittedly it is the instrument of action, but also the organ of passivity, perception and suffering. It is threatened by infirmity, sickness, hunger, violence. It is delivered up practically defenceless to attack, vulnerable to any injury. We feel our own transience in it. Even pain that is not accompanied by any immediate danger of death announces what is to come. It is as if we anticipated our end in the pain, as a kind of presentiment of what ultimately cannot be experienced. The mortal body brings life to a definitive end. Although we feed and care for the body, keep it fit, adorn it, change its appearance or provide it with spare parts, although we keep a watch over it, maintaining it with discipline and close attention, we cannot outlive it. It is too powerful an enemy. It will have the last word.

The fact that human beings are particularly drawn to the moment in which they overcome fear is only the reverse side of that sense of danger. Like all the deeper experiences of life, the fascination of violence is ultimately physical in nature. The sight of it can become an obsession. It is not an avid desire for sensation that holds mankind spellbound but violence itself, the destruction of another body, the whimpering of a living being, the smell of blood. We feel conflicting reactions at first. Violence is repulsive, it induces nausea, it arouses fear and terror, but at the same time it is seductive and enthralling. We see what could happen to us. The shock hits us in the pit of the stomach; we feel a moment of sickness, dizziness, then a brief quivering of the nerves until at last relief soothes the fear. Whatever happens, the observer knows that he personally is safe. The pain he sees and hears is not his own. He increasingly relishes the mental strength gathering within him, the courage of his ability to defy and hold his own against such horrors. He stands erect at a safe distance, he rises above these events, he even feels a touch of sublimity.

Although violence leaves nothing behind but torn flesh, crushed bones, blood and filth, the observer cannot look away. Violence has the full force of immediacy. Because it affects the body directly, it breaks all the rules that usually hold humanity in check. Death is vividly, suddenly present. The screams, the crushed skull, the arm ripped off, the grimace of pain – these are death made visible. The observer wants to see death at work, tries to get close enough to touch it. Even those who at first were torn between attraction and repulsion fall under its spell. Suddenly the horror is gone, nausea and disgust turn to cheering, enthusiasm, euphoria. The desire for fear is a sensual pleasure too. The observer vents his feeling with cries of jubilation as he goes over to the side of the perpetrator of violence. He wants to share that restless energy, that power to kill. He celebrates the greatest victory that anyone can win, a victory over himself. Is it surprising that many people constantly thirst for the experience of survival, the sense of having overcome the fear of death entirely?

Two figures embody this conquest of the fear of death in its purest form: the martyr and the dead hero. The hero gives his life for the community, for his companions, for new life once the revolution has succeeded. He has defied the onslaught of fate to his last breath, sending countless enemies to their death. In return he gets a resplendent tomb close to a state, national or revolutionary memorial, a permanent monument in his honour, ensuring that he is remembered in word and deed on every appropriate occasion. The hero is the model for all warriors; he conquers death by scorning it. He gives his life for others, but he also spreads the terror of the firebrand who fears nothing. The hero moves in a place beyond good and evil, thus performing the highest of moral acts, self-sacrifice, with brutal ruthlessness. He stands firm until the enemy's superior power strikes him down. But at the moment of his death the lightning of eternal life strikes.

The hero personifies fearlessness in action, the martyr the

courage of pure suffering. He bears any kind of pain without resisting, and suffers what he is predestined to suffer. The hero fights countless enemies, the martyr fights only himself, the hardship of pain, a negative obsession with torment. He is a proud opponent of the spirit of his time, an incorrigible rebel against the ideas of those in power. Under torture, however, he is pitted only against himself. He steadfastly endures violence. The man who takes the part of hero for his faith is sure that he must follow his great vocation. To him, death is release from torture and the wickedness of the world. Pain is only an episode on the way to salvation. Once the defences of the self are broken down and all the body's resistance is over, fear and pain will disintegrate into nothing. Eternal life begins with death.

Heroes and martyrs win immortality by dying of their own free will. They survive in the memory of posterity and the bright realms of paradise. Here on earth, on the other hand, the craving for immortality has fatal consequences. The survivor not only wants to exist for ever but to exist when others do not. Survival means leaving others dead behind one. An old gentleman will study the obituaries in the paper every day, establishing to his own satisfaction that no one else in his age group is left. Survival requires the company of the dead, because only the death of others makes your own survival obvious. The illusion of immortality feeds on their death. There is a genuinely antisocial and extremely dangerous motive force at work here. The experience of existence is nowhere so evident as in the face of a great company of the dead. The survivor is still here, the dead are not. This is the moment of triumph over death. Whether the death is that of a friend who is mourned or an enemy who was feared, the satisfaction is the same. Elias Canetti put it briefly and cogently: 'Fear at the sight of death is resolved in the satisfaction of not being dead oneself. The dead man lies down, the survivor stands erect. It is as if there had just been a battle and you had struck down the dead yourself. Every man's hand is against others in the pursuit of survival. [. . .] The lowest form of survival is killing.'

Enthusiasm for survival is a destructive social power, and addictive. Those who are still alive while others are dead feel that they are *more* alive. Death, which threatens everyone, seems to have turned aside from them. But even stronger is the satisfaction of those who can provide themselves with the experience of survival by personally killing others. Killing has always been one of the greatest pleasures of the human species. Nothing gives you more vitality than having death in your hands. Those with the power to kill have subdued their worst enemies. They can feel invulnerable, revived, full of life. They think they know they will be among the last to die, perhaps the very last of all. Killing, then, is rooted in delusions of immortality. Man kills to survive others. Killing is far from being an act of self-defence or self-preservation. Men go to war to kill. They hunt down other human beings in order to elevate themselves safely above them. Inherent in the craving for survival is the potency of violence. Evil arises from freedom and mankind's desire to immortalize itself.

Yet the one thing the gods have allowed man in his attempt to overcome death is the chance of eternal fame. The laurel wreath was once awarded as the gift of heaven – for great deeds and words, for wisdom, generosity, courage and daring. To the individual, it is true, fame was never more than a poor substitute for the loss of eternal life, but it helped the species to survive. For fame confirms the social necessity of values and virtues. It reinforces the validity of our models and guides the individual's unedifying thirst for recognition into more desirable channels. A man crowned with laurels sets others an example, showing how they can make themselves immortal by their own efforts. The man of renown, the great king, the bold warrior, the inspired intellectual is seen as favoured by higher powers. His fame goes far and wide before him. His name must be on everyone's lips so that he is not forgotten. Not the gods, not the state, but Rumour proclaims a man's fame, and Rumour is an ugly creature, with thousands of eyes, tongues and ears concealed by its plumage as it moves swiftly between heaven and earth, growing with every move it makes.

No sooner has a witness heard of a massacre than he hurries to the scene to join in the celebration of slaughter. He longs to see the wounded and the dead and then go on his way strengthened and satisfied. He admires the showmen who make an exhibition of violence, the matadors in the arena, the heroes of killing. They demonstrate their sovereignty by muscular force, skill, the superiority of their bearing. A little turn of the wrist, a brief sideways glance, an elegant side-step – and the duel with the wild animal or the deadly enemy is over. They are masters of themselves; killing comes easily to them. Very seldom do they lose their air of honour and dignity. The gladiator who has survived all his fights wins undying fame. Other men meet such a great killer with timid awe, and most of all they idolize the man who can induce others to kill for him. Charisma of this kind still clings to the most bloodthirsty of despots. He sits unmoved on his throne among his subjects, proudly watching condemned men as they parade before him; a pointed finger, a glance one way or another, and his order to execute one of them is carried out. His followers are still expressing their admiration years later. They remember him with awe and long for his return, even when all his crimes have been revealed and condemned.

The struggle against death is always a struggle against the

course of time. The idols and institutions with which humanity lends form and meaning to life are intended to last for all eternity. Imaginary communities – the group, the people, the nation – are meant to guarantee safety, security and permanence. The changing generations cannot touch them. Society, the genuinely immortal, omnipresent god, survives all individuals. Yet the individual still longs for a state of ecstatic timelessness in which the loss of central meaning can be reversed, wishing for that oceanic sensation in which the ego and the world are united.

It begins with solitary rage: the individual slips away unnoticed, withdrawing from human company. By the time he returns, frenzy has changed him. His eyes stare straight ahead, his nose picks up every scent, his ears hear every sound. He mows down anything that stands in his way. A sense of such freedom as he has never known before spreads through him. His body expands, his release from himself is a dark joy, there are no more physical barriers dividing him from the world, the moral fetters separating him from his real being are broken. He is beside himself in the intoxication of his frenzy. Suddenly he can go in any direction he likes. He has forgotten death, the fears of a mortal creature, the burden of time, the toiling for immortality.

In a society that recognized the supremacy of death it would be easy to observe the old law against killing. No one would want to survive his fellows. As long as human beings rebel against death, however, they hunger and thirst for blood and relish killing. They want to be told how many others they have survived every day. It pleases them to see blood shed. And nothing fills them with greater pride than inflicting death with their own hands.

2

The paradise of cruelty

Two soldiers on a bridge have seized a man by his hands and feet and are about to throw him over the parapet into the water below. Another man is firing shots into the river, where a screaming figure tries to keep his head above water. A little way off a howling mob is dragging a charred corpse along the road. A crowd surrounds a young woman who is crouching on the ground. They are taking turns to step forward, dance up to her and jump on her ribcage to see how much it can stand. Bleeding heads with their ears cut off look through burning rings that resemble rubber tyres. Next to them a human being is confined in a wooden cage full of bug-like insects; a head pickled in murky liquid looks out of a tub. A huge clasp-knife is cutting a nailed-down body in half lengthwise. Bizarre monsters, half toad, half human, are at work on writhing bodies. A special torture is provided for each of the deadly sins. To the right, we see a firing squad. The city in the background is a wasteland of rubble glowing red and yellow. But the left-hand panel of the picture shows a peaceful, hilly landscape, a few trees and bushes, lush green meadows. There is not a living creature to be seen in these fields. As usual, paradise is empty of human beings.

We cannot tell how Hieronymus Bosch would have painted

hell in his triptych of the Last Judgement if he had been our contemporary in the new millennium, or indeed whether he would have reached for paintbrush and palette at all. He might simply have assembled pictures of real events into a collage. In the face of the worst that can be done, the arts lag behind reality, which seems to overload our powers of imagination and evaluation alike. The mind itself labours to survey the vast number of horrors, let alone to understand where the roots of cruelty lie, and what happens when it is unleashed.

Errors and illusions

There is no shortage of explanations. They range from the genetic inheritance of the species and the evildoer's state of mind to adverse circumstances and the general uncertainty of history. Discussion of violence is a battleground of ideologies and illusions. The point at issue is not so much establishing the facts as confirming those ancient articles of faith to which many still wish to cling. But a ban on thought inevitably entails a ban on perception. The usual kind of discourse leads straight to the loss of a sense of reality and denial of what may be expected of humanity.

Among the most comfortable hypotheses is the assumption that the legacy of evolution naturally predisposes us to violence. But the dictatorship of the genes does not govern natural history, any more than civilization is the realm of liberty. Even if such complex qualities as intelligence and aggression were inherited, the possession of a certain ability or inclination says nothing about the way in which it will be manifested. Theories cannot be tested by example unless opportunity presents itself. The genetic explanation blurs the distinction between incidents, conditions and dispositions, assuming that an act of violence implies a predisposition to commit it. But not everyone who commits violence has shown any suspect inclinations in advance, nor has everyone who stated at length that he was ready for anything eventually done what he so loudly proclaimed he would do.

The fact that there is no end to violence is not the result of the supposed wolfish nature of our species. It is an illusion to believe that those who commit violence are always impelled by rage or belligerence – as if we had only to wean humanity away from its savage lusts in order to master violence. Anger, hatred, rage or vengefulness can indeed induce people to commit violent acts, but how do aggressive inclinations account for the pleasure felt in enticing victims, the playful curiosity of experimentation, the obedient execution of orders, or the warrior's readiness to sacrifice himself? What does the recognition that violence is often the shortest and most efficient means to achieving an end have in common with passionate bellicosity?

The nature and extent of many atrocities mislead us into assuming that the perpetrators must have been motivated by particularly violent impulses. This intuition goes against all logic. Human beings can behave in very different ways for one and the same reason, or they can do exactly the same thing on widely different grounds. There is no essential connection between motives and actions. Murders can be committed out of love or hate, avarice or greed, jealousy or indifference. But not everyone who is tormented by jealousy, envies someone else's possessions, or has lost interest in the world inevitably becomes a murderer.

Nor is it very helpful to resort to the idea of rational connections. It is true that a number of acts of violence are the means to a personal or political end, and that suitable instruments are chosen and tried out for that end: weapons, accomplices, plans, scenes for committing a crime. However, the idea of rational action is no use for explaining violence. It not only ignores the sheer variety of emotions involved, it confuses purposes with causes and reasons. The connection between the means and the end is categorically different from the relationship between cause and effect. What people wish to achieve by violence tells us nothing about the causes or effects of their actions, unless we take will and purpose for the 'inner' causes of physical activities. Plans do not set an action in motion, but they do guide its course. Again, the means will often alter the end, steering an act in an unexpected direction.

Any instrumental concept of violence fundamentally fails to understand the dynamic of violent processes, which themselves engender their concomitant drives from the first. Violence does not obey the calculations of expediency, and cannot be reduced to the status of a means towards political, economic or ideological ends or interests. We shall not get a clear idea of most collective crimes if we think they can be ascribed to the purposes or reasons of individual criminals, manipulators or seducers.

A good many crimes are meticulously carried out, but it does not follow that they sprang from particularly fanatical convictions. Great crimes do not need grand ideas behind them. Lower instincts such as bloodlust, a desire for loot and resentment will be motive enough even for crimes against humanity. Politically, racist slogans or nationalist ideologies are more likely to serve as justification after the event than as the original motive for a crime. Utopian visions or travesties of religion, mythical tales or totalitarian blueprints for social order – such notions, invented by intellectuals, have seldom inspired those who carry out atrocities. Intellectuals are often inclined to great overestimation of the effect of ideas and ideologies. Hence, too, the widespread and erroneous belief that the perpetrators of violence are always blind and only require thorough enlightenment to desist from their activities. Faith and knowledge may lead to the adopting of a certain attitude, but there is a great gulf fixed between attitudes and behaviour. Cognitive explanations set their sights too high, overlooking all the actions that result from emotions, habit, or sheer thoughtlessness.

Many observers assume that there are pathological forces at work in acts of violence: mental derangement or outbreaks of frenzy. Apologists for the therapeutic society, moving sympathetically into reverse gear, customarily see the perpetrators as victims – 'victimized' by an unhappy childhood, inadequate parents or watching brutal horror films, as if there had been no atrocities before the advent of television. The list of unfortunate circumstances is truly comprehensive, including social disadvantage, economic crises, poverty and exploitation, political upheavals, the decline of the state monopoly of power or alternatively political repression, too much cultural tradition or cultural disorientation, no values or values fanatically held, lack of standards, a sense of anonymity, stress at work or unemployment, group pressures or isolation, poor family background or lack of discipline in the schools, drug-taking, trauma, depression, psychotic urges – all of these are held responsible for violence. According to this theory, the perpetrator of violence is part of the unfortunate society of the sick, the poor, the unemployed and the socially excluded, who can be helped only by such therapeutic methods as getting a job, special coaching at school, youth clubs, and an understanding of the thug's brutality. The point is only too obvious. These threadbare notions seek to eliminate the concept of guilt and free will. If the blame for violence is unloaded on psychological and social inadequacy, no one can ultimately be held responsible for a violent act and its consequences.

Yet most such pathological explanations will not even stand up to the simplest logical examination. How many others lead similar lives or exist in the same miserable conditions, and never dream of lifting a hand against anyone? Why are there not millions of violent criminals although there are millions of depressives, gun fanatics, horror-film fans, victims of broken marriages and unemployed people? Nothing forces anyone to attack a passer-by, jump on his ribcage when he is down or smash his skull in with an iron bar.

One element or other in a situation may affect the circumstances of a violent act, but how do the circumstances affect the act itself? The context is not a causal factor and is neither a sufficient nor an essential condition of violent behaviour. At most it favours or inhibits the use of violence. Determining the circumstances, whether they are biographical, social, political or historical, pinpoints significance and sometimes opportunity, but not causes. It may offer plausible stories, but not explanations. The context does not explain a single act of violence; at most it makes a connection between people's ideas of social conditions and the number of acts of violence committed: the social 'violence quota'. But obviously the multiplicity of alleged causes ultimately shows only that violence is not bound up with any particular cause or case history.

No society can be sure of preventing violence and ensuring peace for ever, but on the other hand infringements of the law derive from no social necessity. Even in environments where violence has become a way of life, not everyone takes the chances on offer. Although the risk of non-violence may be high, contempt for it great, and penalties draconian, there are wartime deserters, soldiers who load their guns but do not pull the trigger, firing squads who fail to fall in for duty. Even in the concentration camp, that place of institutionalized cruelty, there were overseers and guards who did not show brutality. It is only ever a minority who give not the slightest grounds for any hope at all. Individual cases show that there is a gulf between the situation which offers an opportunity and the deed itself. A small, unpredictable factor remains, defying explanation: the freedom to act with violence or to refrain.

Yet the analysis of violence has its point. In general people know perfectly well what they are doing and why they do it, but they know very little about the results of their actions. The preconditions and consequences of an action are beyond the horizon of those who perform it. Although ultimately it is individuals who carry out atrocities, violence is usually a social process. It takes time, it alters situations and it changes human beings.

An anthropological account of these changes tries to identify not the meaning but the form of social behaviour. Its approach is not cultural but universalist, and its theme is the dynamic inherent in social relations. It is more interested in social universals than individual cases, that is to say in those aspects of society that arise independently of one another and at times and places remote from each other. Historical events are not in the foreground; instead, such a study concentrates on the facts that lie behind all history. What, then, encourages people to make use of their freedom to commit violence, how do they cross the border, and what kind of world lies on the other side?

Imagination and transformation

One source of violence is the power of imagination. The imagination can always invent new forms of violence. It lifts human beings out of the sphere of their own experience, removes them from their environment and liberates them from established habit. It allows them to rise above themselves and become someone else. The imagination is not bound to experience and does not observe the imposition of restraints. There are no borders that mankind cannot imagine crossing. But imagined violence is free, it is safe to think about it, and so it invites the act. Once the temptation of crossing that border has entered the mind, it is often not long before the first step is taken. Perhaps the experiment is tentative at first, but that initial action clears the field for other ideas and other acts. There are no limits to the imagination: it devises new atrocities, tests new weapons, designs utopias, creates gods to justify any sacrifice. The power of the imagination usually does not even stop at killing, the final point of all violence. It thinks up new deadly torments, new ways of killing for a second time by desecrating the dead. That characteristically human quality, the imagination, ensures that the history of violence will go on. To abolish violence one would have to deprive mankind of its ingenuity.

So strong is the power of imagination that the idea of violence can become an obsession. Fed by ambition, vengefulness, bloodlust or greed for plunder, it forces itself into the foreground, occupying the conscious mind. Imagination shows the murderer the way he wants to go, brings out the inclinations he has harboured within him for so long, gives him the power to come to a decision. His eyes are fixed on the weapon. The handle of the dagger is turned towards his hand, begging to be grasped. The weapon encourages him, urges him on to do the deed; blood is already dripping from the blade. Sometimes the actual experience of atrocity is weaker than the horrors of the imagination. Fantasies haunt the dreamer, calling on him to act, fixing in his mind the pictures he has already painted for himself. They grow in strength, take firm root, and will not disappear until the deed is done.

As doom-laden as the human mind itself is the flexibility of its motivation. Violence can be linked to utterly contradictory attitudes, moods or feelings: submissiveness or a desire to wield arbitrary power, revulsion, pride or a sense of duty, a craving for recognition and a sense of honour, love of adventure or boredom, calculation, zeal or enthusiasm. The state of mind of the perpetrators of violence cannot be pinned down. Over and beyond man's basic animal nature, he is notable for his adaptable constitution. If he were solely driven by animal forces at least he would know what to expect. But because he is open to future developments anything is possible. That openness lends human beings the ability to transform themselves. A man may leave home in the morning, go to the office, work as usual, come home again – a day like any other. Then he changes his clothes, fetches guns and ammunition from the cellar, shoots his family, barricades himself into the attic and fires at any chance passer-by. Apparently overnight, neighbours can turn into deadly enemies, children into marksmen, village schoolteachers can run amok, software manufacturers may start abusing children, workers in a chocolate factory turn cannibal.

A man who transforms himself is no longer the man he was. He is not just different, he becomes someone else. He is liberated from himself. He relinquishes durable substance and stable identity. This transformation affects his whole person, his mind and body. Its most effective aid is the mask. Although the mask covers only the surface of the body its power goes deep. Masks are the medium of magical mutation.

Under his animal mask, the prehistoric hunter acquired the power and agility of the beasts he hoped to kill. He transformed himself into his prey; he came to resemble it. The act of killing was mimicked in a buffalo or gazelle dance that ensured good hunting. Killers of human beings used the same device of masquerade. Wearing lion or leopard-skins, they slit their victims' throats and clawed out the flesh. The animal skins lent them supernatural powers; masks transformed them into lion-hearted berserkers. The idol's bloodlust was transferred to the murderer, who broke all taboos beneath his mask. It was worn not for disguise but for transformation, for liberation from himself. At the moment of putting on the skin he himself became a beast of prey, but he lost all his potency if the mask was torn off again.

The archaic warrior setting out on the trail by night made use of another power: he gained commanding energy by wearing an ancestral mask. Suddenly he partook of the hidden, omnipresent power of the dead. He acquired the certainty of victory and immortality in the ranks of his warlike forebears. The spirits of the dead had survived all earthly battles and feuds, and now they would keep death away from their descendant too, preserving him from the blows, spears and arrows of the enemy. The mask froze the enemy's blood with fear and protected the warrior. It strengthened his courage in battle and helped him to cross the threshold. Beyond the border he was not the same man he had been before.

Ritual, orders, beacons

Rituals facilitate transgression. They are instances of transformation: of the shift from the secular to the sacred, from the status system to the community, from peace to war, from everyday life to the festival. The oldest forms of violence – hunting, sacrifice and war – were often prepared for or performed in rituals. Down the ages physical punishment, particularly the death penalty, has been strictly regulated, whether through mass executions in the arena or in the course of the auto-da-fé, the stoning of the scapegoat or ceremonial bloodshed in the marketplace. Feuds and duels of honour, gladiatorial combats and cockfights, tribal and gang warfare always exhibit ritual elements: the exchange of threatening gestures, mobilization of the fighting spirit, the first step over the starting line.

It is not the function of rites to elevate violence by giving it meaning. This currently fashionable cultural view of ritual is naive. The sacrificial customs of the Aztecs, the Carthaginians or the people of the kingdom of Dahomey in the nineteenth century were no more than mass slaughter, pious acts of bloodshed. Ritual unleashes violence, creating an exceptional and festive state of mind in a community where enthusiastic feeling has conquered terror. The power of killing overcomes the fear of death. Violence lends the ritual an aura of gravity and sublimity. The shock of the death-blow, the sight of bloodshed, the joys of the festive banquet – the sanctity of life itself is sensed in the experience of killing. Life is nourished by death.

Ritual violence is a way of creating community spirit. Sacrifice and murder as communal acts establish bonds of loyalty. Clans, guilds and alliances form as communities of sacrifice, swearing oaths of complicity on the sacrificial blood. The closer the link has to be, the more cruelty is lent to the ritual. As the community sets off to war or the hunt, it takes the individual out of himself in the stamping rhythm of the dance, or later as he marches in time. Elation seizes upon the collective entity. Everyone shares it. In binding individuals close together, ritual frees them from the fears and misgivings that they must otherwise deal with alone. Their relationship with themselves has merged into a social experience. Thus ritual as orderly turmoil paves the way for violence, death and sanctity.

Hierarchic social systems prefer another method of transgression: the giving of orders. An order demands instant obedience. It will tolerate no contradiction, and to doubt its legitimacy destroys its effectiveness. Consequently the giving of orders often entails very harsh penalties. Nonetheless, an order is not just compulsion; it also grants the welcome licence to strike the first blow. It is a mistake to believe that the majority of subordinates carry out orders only with reluctance. They have often been waiting inactive for some time before their orders finally free them from apathy and give rein to their desire for action. Soldiers who have been waiting in readiness for days impatiently await the order to attack. When that order comes, it focuses all their thoughts, feelings and energies on the battle; their fears and doubts suddenly disappear. Orders bring singleness of purpose, hence the sometimes suicidal readiness of soldiers to obey the signal and leap over breastwork defences. Orders push people over the border. Orders can send them out to kill, and also to certain death.

The order to commit an act of violence is more than a hostile arrow that one would like to pluck out and throw back. An order acts as an impulse that breaks the taboo. Once the border has been crossed, further orders merely confirm the licence already granted. A pointing finger is enough to mark out the next victim. A slogan sets a band of murderers on the move, a word from an informer opens the door of the nearest house. Quite often subordinates seize the power to give orders for themselves. So long as they get results it is left to the perpetrators of violence to choose their method. General directives grant licence: they tell subordinates not what to do but what they are *permitted* to do. They call for independence in the exercise of human liberty, and there is often no need to issue any further orders. Willing executioners always do more than they are told to do, carrying out orders that were never given.

Mobs follow beacons. Individuals band together in a

crowd – outside a prison, a palace or a football stadium, on the street corner where a police car is parked. They surround the vehicle, coming to within a few metres of it; it is as if a magical threshold separated them from it. The time is not yet ripe. But the more people join the mob the bolder it becomes. Its numbers in themselves stiffen its backbone. In such a throng, no one need fear the law. Suddenly a window smashes, a yell releases inhibitions, stones fly, then the mob surges forward, pulls the passengers out, overturns the car and sets it on fire. The barrier of prohibition is broken; the crowd has become a single massive entity. The formation of that mass entity cannot be blamed on a ringleader but arises from the crowd itself. The collective process runs its course independently of the reason or occasion for the riot. Fire or breaking glass act as beacons, liberating the crowd from inaction. Individuals merge with the mass entity that carries them over the threshold along with it.

If it seems desirable to make the other side take the first step, provocation comes into play. Provocation has served to foment wars as well as to start street fighting and duels. One side taunts the other until it loses self-control and hits back. Provocation lures the adversary over the border, thus publicly discrediting him. Or it entices him into a trap out of which he can break only by violence if he wants to retain his self-respect. The most effective provocation leaves little time for thought. It is so well aimed that it sets off immediate reactions. The provocation itself stops just short of the border, thus forcing the adversary to attack. It thereby shows him up and leaves him to take all the blame. Of course there are violent provocations as well, for instance the throwing of the first stone or a terrorist assassination, but they too always aim to make the other side overreact in a massive, disproportionate act of violence.

Habit and excess

What happens when the first step across the border has been taken? Sometimes matters go no further than the initial incursion. An exchange of shots, and the battle is over. But if a chain reaction is set off, then new modes of conduct, feelings and social phenomena develop. At least three courses of action may be distinguished.

Violence attains durability through force of habit and by being institutionalized. Mankind has the disturbing ability to adapt to almost anything, including its own violent activities. How are we to understand this? Habit is a one-way arrangement, set in motion almost automatically by recurring situations. No decision is necessary: the incentive to take violent action has shifted to the situation itself. The deed is done promptly and without reflection. Violence becomes routine, part of ordinary life, everyday work. The act becomes a regular action. After their initial transformation, its perpetrators have only to imitate themselves.

Day after day the slave-driver does his work; every afternoon the sniper takes up his position to fire at everything he can get in his sights. The more frequently violence is committed, the more of a habit it becomes. This pattern of behaviour becomes a personal characteristic. People who commit violent acts out of habit are to be found in torture chambers and concentration camps, at places of execution, in battle-hardened bands of experienced soldiers or in a warlord's closest retinue. War and terror are thus shored up by the habitual behaviour of their perpetrators. The violence goes on, and no one needs to assess every new situation. Habit releases the perpetrators from purpose and decision. Habitual violence is unmotivated violence. Questions of morality are superfluous. Violence is no longer an arbitrary act but has become a thing of flesh and blood. Habit spares the mind and the conscience. It is deaf and blind, and it has also lost any sense of fear. The murderer has supped his fill of horrors. Nothing can shock him any more, hence the notoriously clear conscience exhibited later by many mass murderers. If they are reproached, they respond only with surprised incredulity.

Individual habit-formation corresponds to the mechanism of collective discipline as we know it from the behaviour of firing squads, or the line formations of wars of manoeuvres as they were fought in the past. Discipline is a special kind of destructive force. The column is drilled to act like a single entity, firing a salvo at the moment when the order is given. The men's firing is coordinated to the fraction of a second. The platoon operates with the regularity of a social killing machine. As weapons are lowered and reloaded the next line steps forward and takes aim, thus ensuring constant fire. Everyone acts like his neighbour, and everyone relies implicitly on the fact that all the others will do the same. The troop realizes its unity in the act of killing. The collective unit manufactures violence itself, and since blood-guilt is shared by everyone no one actually feels it. In becoming one with the collective, violent body, the individual is free of his individuality.

Demonstrative violence aims to spread terror, instil respect and dispel tedium. There is a genuine social sense in this violence. The braver and more skilful the warrior, the brighter his aura shines. The crueller the execution the more magnificent does political majesty appear. Violence in this case is self-presentation and self-congratulation. In the process whoever outshines his fellows and offers the spectators an entertaining show wins particular renown. The spectators gloat over the torments of the victims, slapping their thighs as they relish the cruelty. Their laughter is uninhibited. It links them to those inflicting pain and to each other. *Schadenfreude* is known to be the cheapest form of human conviviality; laughing together creates a sense of community. So the spectators spur the murderers on to new horrors in mutual confirmation of the freedom of arbitrary licence, complete command of power over life and death.

Violent spectacles are directed at third parties, but excess has no social aim. The berserker is concerned entirely with himself. No social or individual relationship is at the centre of that phenomenon; his frenzy is violence for its own sake. What counts is the action, the experience, existence beyond the border. Habitual violence is regular and indifferent. Excess, on the other hand, is eruptive and expansive. The perpetrator feels euphoria, waxing enthusiastic over what he is doing. Every new idea, every further victim killed heightens his elation. Yet he is not 'beside himself', but expanding from within, extending himself, gaining the terrain of absolute liberty.

Excess is not self-presentation but an orgy of self-exaggeration, an act of liberation of the ego. Beyond the barrier anything is allowed. Awareness of morality is muted, indeed it is as if the frenzy did away with any awareness at all. Thoughts are consumed in the heat of sensation. And there is yet more: the perpetrator merges with the acts of violence themselves. The body falls into a mechanical rhythm. The clatter of the submachine gun is transferred to the sniper's nerves and muscles. He senselessly empties magazine after magazine until the victim is riddled with bullets. It is the same with a man thrashing a victim: he does not do it because he feels impelled to, but the rhythm of the blows takes over his arms as they thrash the victim on the ground until his wooden club is splintered. The stormy movement drives him further and further into a different frame of mind. He is all physicality in the intoxication of violence. He feels a sudden lightness, springing nimbly from place to place. The impetus of his violence carries him away.

This dance of violence gives the perpetrator a strange experience of inner unity. He acts entirely out of the core of his physical being, rid of the resistance of his body. The burdens of the self are lifted from him; he has escaped the compulsion to control himself. Excess frees a man not just from the observation of bans but from all the trials and tribulations of existence. He no longer has to relate to himself; beyond the barrier he is entirely one with himself and the world. Hence the desire to wade in blood. There is nothing to hold the murderer back, for he feels neither external nor internal resistance. He leaves himself behind. The old ego is extinguished, the need for individuation and the fear of death are suddenly cast off. Transformation has reached its ultimate point. The festival of violence is a leap into a utopian state which fulfils an ancient yearning: the dream of absolute power, of absolute freedom and wholeness, the dream of the return to paradise. But for the victims it is hell itself.

3
Actions

The craving to inflict pain calls for rooms screened from the outside world where the torturer can be alone with his victim. The perversions of the libertine thrive in secluded retreats devoted to dissipation. Torture, that cruel experiment with the body of another human being, is at home in the dungeons of autocratic authority, in torturers' huts and prison camps. Not so the manifestations of individual and collective crossing of the border. Excess seeks the public arena. It tears down all barriers, including the walls around the private sphere. Its stage is not the domestic home or the back yard but the street, the restaurant, the church, the marketplace, the open air.

The territory of excess is not the public arena of civilized conversation. The language of violence is shrill and piercing: the screams of the injured, the howl of the mob, the crackling of the fire. Excess is not a spectacle for a silent audience watching the show from a safe distance. Its violence reaches far and wide, seizing upon anyone in its orbit. It will not tolerate neutral witnesses; it knows only victims, fellow perpetrators and enemies. It does not aim to show or represent anything, it is pure action. A man running amok strikes down everything he meets. The crowd of football hooligans is intent on picking a fight.

The lynch mob aims to stir up its own indignation and destroy the cause of its fury. The murder squad combs the village and kills everyone it can lay hands on.

In the street, death is visible to everyone. Sometimes the dead are laid side by side in rows, as if to restore order, drawing up a neat balance sheet. But there are bloodstains left on the asphalt, rags of a shirt, a shoe, a broken pair of glasses. Passers-by keep returning to the scene. It is not grief that brings them back but a nagging perplexity as they think of the crime, a slow afterglow of horror at the sudden collapse of everyday normality. The state promises its subjects peace and security. It has always known how to disperse the mob, it has pursued and imprisoned criminals. No one can understand how the force of violence could break through the civil peace of everyday life again.

Running amok

He was ready to die, stated Charles Whitman in a note written on the evening of 30 July 1966, adding that after his death an autopsy should be carried out to see if he had some kind of mental disturbance. Then he stabbed his mother and his wife. Next morning he packed some sandwiches, lavatory paper, a transistor radio and a number of guns and pistols with the ammunition for them in a seaman's bag, and drove to the bell tower of the University of Austin, Texas. He shot the receptionist in the entrance hall and two students on the stairs. At the top of the stairs he stopped briefly, unpacked his bag and looked down at the campus. Then he began firing at anything that moved. Ninety minutes later thirty people were wounded and sixteen dead. At the autopsy a tumour was discovered in the twenty-four-year-old architectural student's brain. Whitman had been complaining of constant headaches ever since his parents divorced.

At midday on 28 April 1996 a Volkswagen Beetle pulled up outside a café in Port Arthur, a popular tourist resort in Tasmania. There was a surfboard fixed to the roof of the vehicle. The driver, a blond, athletic man of twenty, entered the café, took a semi-automatic rifle out of his tennis bag, and began firing. After each burst of fire he deliberately picked out a new victim. He then set fire to the building, took the driver of a car hostage and forced his way into a nearby boarding house. There he barricaded himself in, also holding hostage the proprietors, an elderly married couple. He fired at the policemen trying to negotiate with him and the helicopter that had come to fly the injured to hospital. Next morning the boarding house was in flames; he killed his hostages and walked out straight into the arms of the police. In all, thirty-five people lay dead and nineteen were wounded by his bloodthirsty actions at this historic spot – the remains of a penal colony can be seen in Port Arthur, for between 1833 and 1877 the British colonial power transported around 30,000 serious offenders to Tasmania. Thirty-five sentences of life imprisonment were passed on the mass murderer. Experts described him as responsible for his actions but with the IQ of a child of eleven.

Brain damage, insanity or delusions are the most frequent explanations for such incidents. The reasons why someone runs amok, according to police experts, ultimately lie in the unfathomable depths of the killer's mind. Such social circumstances as unemployment, loss of status, private differences of opinion, social exclusion or injustice tell us little, since cases of running amok are so rare that they cannot be explained by widely prevalent social conditions. Millions of people are socially disadvantaged, but it is rather rare for anyone to run amok. Most of those who do are so inconspicuously average that there is nothing whatsoever to suggest they might commit a spectacular act of violence. Murderers of this kind may be irascible or alternatively exceptionally friendly characters. Looking later for indications, symptoms or warnings of what might happen is usually no more than a helpless retrospective attempt to find something preceding the event that might make sense of it. Clearly, Western culture can ultimately understand murderous frenzy only as individual illness or a mental short-circuit.

The diversity of motivation also leaves us baffled. Losses on the stock exchange, professional failure, unrequited love, humiliation or a craving for recognition, despair or a desire for revenge, envy or ordinary everyday troubles can obviously induce such a state of fury that all inhibitions are abandoned. Often a cross word, scornful glance or mocking smile is enough to trigger the explosion. The man running amok is not troubled about the relative violence of his methods: the deed is always out of proportion to its occasion, reason or cause. On 20 December 1995, a young man drew a pistol in a New York shoe store because he thought the shoes too expensive and the salesgirl refused to haggle over them. This fit of petulance ended with five people dead.

But usually it takes time for the inconspicuous man in the street to be turned into a violent madman. Hatred for the world and himself matures slowly: hatred directed not against an individual but against the tyranny of his own existence. The metamorphosis is generally so gradual that few ever take it to its bloodstained conclusion. They carry their hatred with them to the grave before they ever reach the point of exploding. Many a man said to have led a peaceful life and died a quiet death has simply not completed his transformation in time for it to show.

A killing committed by a man running amok differs from other murders in its tempo and its element of excess. The violence instantly reaches its climax. Its aim is not to inflict pain or torture but to kill immediately. Like the assassin, a killer of this kind commits violence without any advance warning. People do not expect to see a man armed to the teeth force his way into a broker's office or a civil service building, a church, a school or a nursery, and mow down everyone inside. Who, in peacetime, would expect to be shot with a Kalashnikov at the supper table? The factor of chance and surprise gives the man who runs amok his deadly power. Resistance is almost impossible. The act breaks abruptly through the protective barrier of normality. Where people were going about their ordinary business just now, a single moment changes everything, leaving bleeding bodies, screams, incomprehension.

Such frenzy is so strange to modern observers that Westerners do not even have a word of their own for it. The term 'amok', as everyone knows, is borrowed from the Malay, and originally denoted a man who 'fought furiously in battle'. It comes from the vocabulary of war, not crime. The man running amok has an ancient tradition behind him. His predecessors' slogan was 'Death or victory'. Amok warriors in south India and Malaya belonged to a sworn elite and were trained to fling themselves into the enemy ranks with utter disregard for death. This method of fighting knew nothing of caution, circumspection or tactical calculation. It quite often resembled suicide, but few such commando troops have been able to cast whole armies into panic. Whether they acted out of loyalty to a prince or in religious zeal, fallen amok warriors were regarded as national heroes and the darlings of the gods. To sacrifice your life on top of a mound of enemies killed by your own hand has always been considered the highest honour for a fighting man – an idea shared by the Malay amok warrior with the rugged veterans and firebrands of historic battlefields, with the Greek heroes outside Troy and the bearskin-clad bodyguards of Viking chieftains, Odin's 'berserkers'.

To this day, hand-to-hand fighting is the preferred style of the anonymous figure who runs amok. War offers the rare chance to kill large numbers of other people; what civil society forbids is not only permitted but imperative in battle. Although the laws of war forbid random firing, self-defence may require men to fire at everything that moves during the conquest of a trench, a village or a street. Mowing down everyone who could still raise a hand to resist is by no means irrational in the heat of combat. The bayonet attack of European infantry cannot have been very different from the furious advance of Malay swordsmen; going on the rampage against the enemy is among the usual forms of violence in war. Commanders may wish to maintain discipline in the ranks, but murderous frenzy lends the necessary impetus to the attack. Not a few heroes decorated for 'bravery' have shown all the characteristics of a man running amok at the height of his frenzy: a craving to kill, presence of mind, contempt for death, the freedom of excess.

Running amok in war is the result of an escalating battle. The civilian who runs amok, on the other hand, vents his rage on defenceless victims until the weapon is struck from his hand. Amok warriors too were once concerned with ideas of death, faith and honour. To the honourable Malay fighting man, running amok was the equivalent of the duel to a European gentleman. Sometimes the bloodbath even assumed ritual features. In 1516 a Portuguese merchant travelling in Java noted, of a local custom: 'If they fall severely ill, many make a solemn vow to their god that, should they recover, they will die more honourably than by disease. As soon as they are better they take a dagger, go out into the street and kill anyone they meet, men, women and children. They rage like mad dogs, killing until they themselves are killed.' Clearly such frenzy was a disaster for the local population, but they were aware of the ever-present threat. Anyone could be affected, suddenly overcome by the murderous frenzy. In many villages 'amok catchers' were prepared for emergencies – long poles with forked ends and barbs to fend the madmen off. Not until the Dutch conquered the area were men who ran amok and survived tortured to death, to strip them of the aura of sacred power. At this point divinely inspired warriors mutated into street killers possessed by evil spirits.

The eradication of the code of honour robbed the amok warrior of his cultural significance. Killing now appears merely a pointless outbreak of rage. Admittedly its violence is often turned first on relatives, professional colleagues or business partners, but the phenomenon of running amok is distinguished by its indiscriminate nature from the deadly outcome of a drama within a relationship or family. The violence affects not only acquaintances but strangers who happen to be on the spot. The father who butchers his wife and children and then hangs himself in the attic has not run amok; the man who runs amok is driven out of his social circle and into the public arena. What may at first seem an act of vengeance soon shakes off personal connotations. The killer wants nothing at all of his victims. Once over the edge, he kills purely for the sake of killing.

In the early hours of 4 September 1913 Ernst Wagner, a village schoolteacher in Stuttgart-Degerloch, murdered his wife and four children by stabbing them in the throat, heart and lungs. He then pulled the bedclothes up over the faces of the corpses, washed himself, put the dagger away in a drawer and packed a travelling bag with three pistols and 500 rounds of ammunition. He went to Ludwigsburg by bicycle and railway train, strolled in the castle park there and drank a glass of mineral water in a café. He then visited his brother's family, changed his shirt and continued his journey. On the way he posted a couple of letters, ate a piece of yeast cake, and arrived in the village of Mühlhausen around eleven at night. He walked briskly through the village, stopping four times to fire indiscriminately at everyone he could see in the dark. He left nine dead and twelve wounded. The teacher also killed two cows before three brave men managed to overpower him. Wagner, later described as the psychiatric prototype of the paranoiac, accounted for the murder of his wife and children on the grounds that he felt 'sorry' for them; he explained his attack on the village, where he had taught twelve years earlier, as an act of revenge for malicious gossip about him. Why he shot the cows we do not know.

The teacher, who considered himself an unrecognized genius, had prepared this operation well in advance. He had bought his modern Mauser pistols years earlier, and practised shooting with them out in the woods on various occasions. He anticipated his serial murders in some autobiographical notes, but postponed the date for actually committing them several times. Wagner also had a notion that someone might make a film of his campaign of revenge against the village – rather in the manner of today's reality TV shows.

However suddenly the attack comes, many of those who run amok are not acting on the spur of the moment. The two adolescents who on 20 April 1999 carried out what amounted to the execution of twelve of their fellow high school students and a teacher in Littleton, Colorado, had been preparing their operation for a year. During the weeks before the attack they shot five videos in the basements of their parents' homes anticipating their personal Day of Judgement. But careful as his preparations may be, the amok killer's state of mind develops only during the act itself, after means and ends have been methodically thought out. The act completes the murderer's transformation. In the same way as war brings forth the warrior, the frenzy of his actions engenders the amok murderer.

The mental scenario usually follows a well-established pattern. The attack is often preceded by a phase of gloomy 'brooding', a period of self-initiation. The perpetrator withdraws from the world in silence, shuts himself up in a room, goes for a long walk in the country, sits under a tree, walks through a castle park lost in thought. Apathetic conduct on the part of any of our contemporaries may conceal this dangerous change to the world of his mind. Fantasies of destruction take hold of the murderer's mind, ideas that are now familiar and have long since lost their horrors. But this time the images will not go away; obsessive thoughts of revenge make their way into his brain, something like a smile may flicker across his face, and then uneasy feelings get the upper hand again, a throbbing excitement that seeks an outlet. Inhibitions gradually die down, the fear of death is superseded by a desire for suffering and destruction, for persecution and death itself.

Fantasies of violent acts are not the product of the modern mass media. Passionate imagination has always helped people to leap over the wall, but only the wild storm of physical action impels the perpetrator of such violence into that other state. He is swept away, free of the bonds of morality, free of shame and guilt. Unsuspected drives set his act in motion. What may appear to an outsider blind destructive frenzy, like that of a mad dog sinking its teeth into its prey, is in fact a state of existing entirely in the present. In the utmost excitement, the perpetrator's mind knows only the here and now, no past and no future, no memory and no expectation. With over-alert senses, he registers everything going on around him, every movement, every attempt at flight, every counter-attack. The berserker in action is not dazed, blind or deaf, but if anything the opposite. He is highly concentrated, his senses sharpened, every nerve stretched to breaking point. His hand and eye are one, joined in the same movement. When the barriers go down the ego seizes on the whole world to destroy it. Nothing can stop the murderer; triumphantly, he leaves himself behind. The old ego is extinguished, freed by the act from years of fear and gnawing hatred.

If he had been overcome by blind rage the man running amok could be overpowered quite easily. But he moves confidently, setting out his guns on window sills, depositing pipe bombs or throwing hand grenades, picking off his victims one by one. His presence of mind matches the transformation of his body. He utters rhythmic cries as he leaps from place to place in an ecstatic dance of death. As he fires or strikes out around him, the radius of his body expands, liberating superhuman strength, suddenly unleashing energies that he himself never even knew he possessed.

On 28 November 1999 a naked man armed with a golden samurai sword stormed into a church in the London suburb of Thornton Heath. The congregation was just saying the Lord's Prayer when the frenzied swordsman began attacking them. Panic broke out in the church. The sword caught one man in the face, cutting it open from his ear to his lower jaw. When he tried raising his hand to protect himself another blow severed his thumb and forefinger. The attack left eleven people injured, bleeding profusely from cuts and stab wounds. The fact that no one was killed was due to the courageous actions of several members of the congregation. Armed with music stands, candlesticks, chairs, a crucifix and an organ pipe they surrounded the amok swordsman and wrestled him to the ground. It took four strong men to hold him down.

Not all incidents in which men run amok end with their suicide. Many of the killers try to escape, and quite a number are killed by the forces of law and order. A man who has become entirely his true self on the other side of the border is not necessarily aware of his own reactions. He feels neither guilt nor the fear of death. It is hardly surprising that many such people prefer that state of freedom to normality. In their altered state, they see no way of return. Some fall into a deep sleep, others remained dazed for a long time once the excess of the senses has died down. If they are asked later why they did such things, they cannot say. Memory of their terrible deeds is muted. They have forgotten everything that existed beyond the border.

The mob

Two Belgian Hercules military aircraft were running a shuttle service to London Stansted Airport, carrying hundreds of handcuffed football fans arrested in Brussels and Charleroi during the weekend. Many of them had no papers, gave false addresses, and when questioned by the police claimed to have respectable careers. To the surprise of the press, the police and the politicians alike they identified themselves as members of the judiciary, solicitors, social workers, firemen, engineers or bankers. Later investigation showed that the Belgian police had arrested English football supporters indiscriminately. Hardly any of them belonged to the hard core of officially registered troublemakers. As usual, however, the incident led to much public breast-beating and expressions of indignation. The state once again declared war on hooligans, the right to freedom of movement was temporarily withdrawn, passports were confiscated and mobile phones tapped. Although thugs of this kind are perfectly harmless in political terms, the agitated guardians of the law generally react by repressing such rivals for the right to exercise violence in the public arena.

Hooligans are not an English speciality. During the European Football Championship in the year 2000 Italian and Turkish fans also attacked each other, and there were clashes between police and the home fans during victory celebrations in the city centres of The Hague and Brussels. Weeks earlier, in Copenhagen, Arsenal fans had struck up an alliance with Dutch and Danish contingents to attack Turkish hooligans. A foreign legion of German and Swedish fans joined this united front. In St Petersburg, hooligans supporting Moscow Dynamo shot an opponent with a flare pistol. Another victim was beaten to death.

Although hooligans by no means shrink from brutality, deaths are quite rare. Over the past few decades weekly riots at the match venues of the English and Italian leagues have been familiar disturbances of civil order. Ritual duels between the mobs take place, show-fights for fame and vengeance as fans seek out the experience of excessive violence. The course of events is strikingly similar to the tribal wars of earlier times, when no central power yet had a monopoly of physical force.

Skirmishing in the ancient world also took place before the eyes of young and old. The place and the time were agreed in advance. Warriors turned up in martial gear, but fought with weapons that did not do too much damage. The 'battle' was a combination of festival, picnic, drinking bout and a rather dangerous form of sport that sometimes cost a few lives. The young men flung insults at each other, made obscene gestures, and finally threw spears, egged on by the women, children and old people of their tribe. If a man was felled an emergency service would look after him, and he would display the scars proudly for years.

Today's street fighters throw stones, beer cans or fireworks instead of spears. Their uniformed adversaries set off smoke bombs and turn hoses or tear gas on them. In close combat the preferred weapons are truncheons, table legs, knuckledusters and heavy boots. There has been a certain amount of progress in the planning of skirmishes too. Messengers no longer have to be sent; the date is fixed over mobile phones or by email. Tirades of hatred can be found on the websites of prominent spokesmen. Spectators belonging to the tribes involved no longer have to participate directly. Reporters and camera crews have taken on their function, sometimes applying a little cash to freshen up the fighting spirit, and then transmitting instant pictures of the violence to the nation's living rooms.

The mob follows its own laws. Just before battle is joined the warriors set out in small bands to the scene of the fighting. News spreads like wildfire. The factions gather more closely together, drinking and waiting in suspense for the next development. Battle songs are heard at the sight of the first enemy, with jeers and threats, usually from those at the back. A magic barrier still separates the adversaries, but the atmosphere is growing more heated. The crowd knows all about the laws it is going to break. By now a great many, indeed a huge number of people have assembled. Suddenly an electric current runs through the crowd, there is loud shouting, chairs and bottles fly. All at once the barriers have come down.

Although every mob knows its own heroes, no ringleaders can be held responsible for the street fighting. The veterans with their mobile phones keep in the background during the operation. The mob is not a military unit prepared to obey orders; the impulse to fight comes from the crowd itself. Sometimes a well-targeted provocation or a rash move on the enemy's part leads to the discharge of collective energy. But an act of material damage opens the floodgates. The sound of shop windows or beer glasses breaking is the most usual trigger. In action, the uproar suddenly finds a sense of direction, coherence and unity. Individuals discover, in the mob, the frenzied joys of rising above the law with impunity.

It does not stop at broken glass. The aim of the battle is victory and triumph. Each participant wants to humiliate the arch-enemy and put him to flight, make him crawl in the dust of the street, his banner going up in flames. The violence of hooligans is not a matter of protest or a looting raid. In so far as it has any point at all, the point is revenge and retribution. The Moroccans who attacked the English fans in Brussels had been wanting to settle accounts with them since Marseilles in 1998. English fans had been nursing a grudge against the Turks since two Leeds fans were stabbed in Istanbul. Historically minded thugs might even have thought of Gallipoli in April 1915. But however chauvinistic the behaviour of the hooligans, in the last resort all that counts is physical excitement and the nervous exhilaration felt in the turmoil. Hand-to-hand fighting promises the intoxication of violence, the sensuous rage of the moment. The man wielding the cudgel wants to feel it striking bone, see blood streaming from noses, hear ribs cracking.

Once there was a code of conduct among fans stating that they would settle the 'third half' among themselves, leaving passers-by and the police out of it. But since the state has mobilized its forces the situation has become more acute. Two bands of adversaries have become three, and quite often the police themselves, once they are free to strike, are not proof against the attractions of violence. Recently the authorities in Eindhoven thought up another method, recollecting that there are other gates to paradise, and handed out marijuana to the pugnacious football fans, whereupon the warring factions dozed the evening away in peace and quiet. Transported to higher regions, their lust for battle had suddenly evaporated.

The pillory

Evening after evening at the same time, observing punctuality, the crowd marched through the streets of the housing estate. As soon as the horn hooted they set out armed with bags of crisps and cans of cola and beer. Even from a distance you could hear the children's laughter, the teenagers' shrill voices, the rhythm of the slogans accompanying the march. Local residents watched the procession from the safety of their windows. The crowd would stop outside a building, its shouting and laughter rose to an excited screech, and now and then came the jarring of window-glass and the sound of an incendiary device going off. Flames shot out of a car. Children not much more than four years old who had been playing hide-and-seek only moments before held up placards: 'Hang the paedophiles! Kill them!' Someone had painted a slogan in white on the entrance of a building. 'No perverts here.'

Paulsgrove, a rundown suburb of Portsmouth, was not the only part of the United Kingdom to see violent demonstrations in August 2000. For a few days the whole of British society seemed to be in the grip of hysteria. Anonymous threatening letters, lists of obscure criminals, suicides, the flight of respectable families from the advance of their neighbours were all part of the scenario of this communal terror. The lynch mobs were encouraged by the publication of descriptions of the 'wanted' in a tabloid newspaper. On the evening when it came out, an innocent man had to be given police protection in Manchester. A few days later, in Wembley, three men broke into the home of a suspected child abuser and beat him to death. The corpse had fifty-three fractures of the ribs.

Weeks later, in Namur in Belgium, the courts banned the publication of a list of child abusers. In Italy, the newspaper *Libero* began a naming-and-shaming campaign on the model of the English tabloid, which had published not only the names of paedophiles but those of punters who frequented the red-light district of Manchester. In spite of prompt criticism from the rest of the press and the police, pillory by the media obviously satisfies a need deeply rooted in society at all times and places. The point at issue is not so much the protection of children as the elimination of perverts, while anti-paedophile campaigners relish the emotions of fear and the pleasures of destruction. The media are merely calling on fantasies that are widespread anyway.

To be suspected of child abuse is an appalling stigma. The suspect is accused not of a single act but of a chronic flaw, an innate tendency to repeat his offence that can ultimately be prevented only by castration or death. Every paedophile is a potential child-murderer, a killer – so runs the popular equation. He is abhorrent, a sexual monster. He could be lying in wait for his prey on any street corner. He steals insidiously up to his victim, soils the child's body with his own, harms and destroys its spirit. Coward that he is, he seeks out the most helpless members of society, innocent, 'sexless' children. In so doing he undermines the normality of social intercourse. Every sign, every gesture, every smile is a temptation to the vices of the flesh. He offends against decency and morality, the sacred institution of the family and its offspring, and society in general. He must therefore be marked with a sign chalked on his clothing, he must be pilloried, cast out, exterminated. The public must be on its guard all round the clock, for the state and the police, inactive and only too tolerant of crime, cannot possibly keep their eye fixed on the monster lurking in the twilight.

The hysterical imagination does not confine itself to repeating the dark myths which have always grown up around the great offenders in the history of crime. The firebrands of the underclasses are by no means alone. Not a few social workers, nursery-school teachers, puritanical lawyers and supporters of a matriarchal society are possessed by the *idée fixe* that every close relationship between children and adults plumbs the depths of sexual abuse: every man is potentially violent, every father could be a child abuser. Often the media resort to tirades of hatred whenever a child's body is found somewhere – which in fact is quite a rare occurrence in criminal statistics. Populist rabble-rousers contribute their mite by fanning the flames of public anger to make political capital out of it.

It is in the nature of this phenomenon that the fantasy has little to do with reality. The small number of child murders bears no relation to the huge number of registered paedophiles. Child abusers are not shady, anonymous characters; most of them come from the child's immediate family or are close relatives. Incest is usually concealed or hushed up by the other family members. Consequently state supervision of paedophiles is far more effective than social vigilantism. Fear of persecution only drives the really dangerous serial abusers underground.

The excited crowd, however, does not distinguish between guilt and innocence. Suspicion is proof enough. The collective self-appointed judiciary does not want simply to convict and punish the offender, but to wax indignant, pass judgement, ban the criminal, wipe the monster off the face of the earth by social or physical death. Before turning to action the community uses the weapon of words. Far from being a harmless medium of communication, those words unite the community and concentrate its attention on the usual suspects. Every item of news, whether genuine, invented or a lie, is a titbit spread by malicious gossip, brought up again and again until everyone has had a chance to taste it. Denunciation and slander provide considerable pleasure. Taboo subjects can be discussed, first in whispers, then out loud, and at the same time the accusers can bask in the sense of their own righteousness. The gossip proves that they themselves are blameless. From time to time, however, it is almost as if they described the atrocity in such ghoulishly graphic terms only because they would all like to imagine themselves breaking taboos. Is not the temptation of forbidden fruit, the attraction of violation, the unthinkable nature of perversion the secret motive force behind suspicion and slander?

The vocabulary of horror so widely employed after the murder of a child is not to be trusted. The call for retribution has nothing to do with retribution itself. Its aim is to promote not justice but self-righteousness. The rhetoric of public denunciation is not satisfied with the principle of retaliation by returning like for like. It wants to see the offender punished two or three times over. The thug's hand should be amputated on the butcher's counter, the paedophile should have his penis and then his head cut off. The punishment demanded by public indignation must expose, dishonour and mutilate, cleansing the community.

The informer thinks he is only doing his civic duty in denouncing the criminal. The leaders of the lynch mob see themselves as the guardians of virtue in society. All involved feel that they are in the right, and it fills them with pride and satisfaction. Their unexpected taste of power liberates them from years of inferiority. All of a sudden they are rid of the poison of helplessness. As a result, the socially disadvantaged are often distinguished by particular brutality once the authorities give them their chance.

In the past there used to be a whipping post with a neck-ring outside town halls or churches. Malefactors were exposed to public mockery in the pillory for a couple of hours. The crowd pelted them with filth and excrement, a board was hung around the miscreant's neck naming his crime in words and images. And it did not stop there. Mutilation was added to the shame of the pillory: scourging, a particularly harsh whipping, branding on the forehead or back, and then banishment from the area.

Pillorying was an official punishment imposed by authority and carried out by the executioner and his henchmen. Not so the punitive village customs in which inebriated young men would assemble at night outside the homes of marginalized members of the community and create an uproar. Merry widows and adulterers, profiteers and fences, dilatory debtors and greedy creditors – local offenders against plebeian morality were the object of mockery, scorn and a beating. The guardians of morals set up their own pillories, until the authorities called a halt to the practice and reclaimed the monopoly of violence for themselves.

The modern lynch mob still employs the old rituals of public exposure. It indulges in the pleasures of pillorying and hunting other human beings, of communal execution. Its victims are interchangeable: witches, Jews, blacks, foreigners – and paedophiles. Different as these social categories may be, the stereotypes of persecution resemble each other down the ages. There are recurrent fantasies of defilement, sexual perversion and cannibalism. In the past witches were said to have roasted and eaten babies, and Jews were accused of the ritual slaughter of Christian infants whose blood they were supposed to have drunk as a sacrificial offering.

The phantasmagoria of terror drive the crowd to action. A few simple slogans will suffice, and no sooner have they been uttered than the mob assembles. Anyone can join, no one wants to be left out. The rumour of some abomination spreads like wildfire. The more people believe it, the more credible it seems. A house is surrounded, the mob comes closer and closer, jeering and laughing, flinging abuse and threats at those inside. Many carry other weapons too. Apparently there was a great deal of laughter during the nocturnal marches in Paulsgrove and elsewhere.

Masks and fire

On the morning of 27 January 1999 a mutilated body was found in a road near the small town of Newry in Northern Ireland. The corpse had suffered multiple stab wounds, its bones were broken and its face was unrecognizable. It took the police hours to identify the body. Eamon Collins must have known that his life was forfeit: a former terrorist, he had changed sides and turned Queen's evidence against his former comrades. He had written a book describing his experiences and confessing his crimes. Although officially pardoned by the IRA, he was henceforth regarded as a traitor. Neighbours cut him dead, local IRA leaders feared his knowledge, members of the radical splinter group the 'Real IRA' threatened retaliation because Collins had informed on them as the perpetrators of the Omagh massacre. His murder was only the end of a campaign. In April 1997 Collins had been knocked down by a car, and only just survived this assassination attempt. In September 1998 the house in Camlough where he had hoped to live safely with his family burned down. Graffiti on the wall of a building foretold his death in 1999.

On the night of 22 January 1999 an Australian Baptist missionary and his two young sons were burned alive in the village of Manoharpur in the Indian district of Orissa. Graham Staines, who for twenty-four years had devoted himself to caring for lepers, had defied warnings not to come to the annual assembly of Christians in the village. After the meeting he had settled down to sleep in his old jeep, as was his habit. Suddenly about a hundred extremist Hindus stormed into the village, yelling and blowing whistles. The mob immediately divided. Some of its members barred the doors of houses and stood guard, others threw stones at the jeep, breaking its windows and doors, a third group brought straw, poured petrol over the vehicle and set it alight. Villagers trying to come to the missionary's aid were chased away or struck down with wooden laths and machetes. The murderers stood round the fire for about ninety minutes and then disappeared into the darkness.

On 15 January 1999 tall figures, muffled up in clothing that disguised their identities, entered the village of Reçak in Kosovo and combed through the place, house by house. They wore blue or black uniforms, woollen masks over their faces, and leather gloves, and they were armed with radios and automatic weapons. They locked most of the women and children in the cellars and herded the men, both young and old and presumably including members of the KLA, to a nearby hill. The first of them were shot during the death march itself. After the Serbian police officers had left, the survivors found their relatives horribly mutilated. Many of the corpses had been beheaded, eight dead men lay in a grave with their arms outstretched, some of them shot in the neck. Twenty-three more bodies lay on the hill and there was blood everywhere. One old man's head had been torn off. The Reçak massacre, carried out by a special commando squad from the Ministry of the Interior on the orders of the highest authority and with the help of local Serbian civilians, cost forty-five human lives.

Incidents of this kind are known for their horrors and their political consequences. The murder of the prominent police informer threatened the peace process in Northern Ireland; the killing of the missionary intensified confrontations in the Indian coalition government and led to a ministerial resignation. Reçak induced the Western allies first to put more pressure on the Serbs and force them to the negotiating table, and ultimately the massacre served as the official grounds for military intervention in Kosovo.

Despite the rhetoric of indignation, these incidents are in no way isolated cases. In Ulster in 1998 there were 165 beatings by paramilitary secret gangs, 242 cases of violent intimidation, and seventy-two acts of punishment by kangaroo courts, usually involving the 'kneecapping' of victims by shooting them in the legs. Months of the arbitrary slaughter of Albanian civilians in Kosovo were part of the Serb strategy in a war of ethnic cleansing. In the weeks before the burning of the missionary, several acts of terrorism were carried out by radical Hindus who wrecked Christian churches and maltreated priests. These atrocities were not spontaneous acts of violence, but had all been planned or ordered in advance by higher authority.

Human cruelty does not exclude the possibility of rational planning, and it is wrong to think that it always arises from a sudden outbreak of ferocious passion. Vengeance and rage were certainly involved in the excesses in Newry and Reçak. However, cool calculation heightens the effect of even the strongest desire for retribution. The murderers of Collins, like all assassins, had observed their victim's habits beforehand. They knew that he used to walk his dogs early in the morning. The Hindus had also prepared for their attack, getting hold of information, vehicles and weapons. And the Serb commandos operated by the proven 'search and destroy' method, a military tactic requiring vigilance, cooperation and swift decision-making. It is this specifically human capacity for thought that makes acts of violence so effective. Rage alone merely liberates blind energy. Only combined with the human mind does it create the destructive power that breaks through the barrier against excess and seeks to destroy everything.

Although their political and cultural circumstances could hardly have been more different in nature, these murders had several features in common. They resembled an execution, an ostentatious ritual of destruction. The murderers were by no means satisfied with killing their victims. Their actions aimed at total elimination, the complete eradication of the dead. No sign of the identity or existence of the victims was to be left. The dead bodies were murdered a second time, mutilated, defiled, or consumed utterly by fire so that only charred remnants of flesh and bones remained.

The methods of murder by lynch mob and punishment killings are reminiscent of the most ancient forms of execution. Beating and disfigurement are among the traditional methods of inflicting shameful death. The victim is killed 'like a dog', thrashed by the murderers with wooden clubs and iron bars in an act of chastisement and humiliation expelling him from the human circle. Shooting in the legs or 'kneecapping', as practised in Northern Ireland, conveys the same meaning. It robs a man of his upright stance. He must crawl helplessly in the dust, 'like a worm'.

Violent execution takes this practice to extremes. Even when the victim already lies bleeding on the ground the murderers continue to strike, kicking him in the kidneys, the stomach, the face. The victim's screams turn to helpless moaning and whimpering. But each murderer gets as close as possible to the body to strike his own blows. He wants to feel them go home, see the skin breaking, hear the bones of the skull cracking. It is not true that human beings can kill each other only from a safe distance. Far from it: they seek close contact, striking the body until the bleeding flesh is visible and the internal organs show. Finally they stab it countless times as if endeavouring to penetrate the other's body completely, running it through with blades, riddling it with holes.

Iron bars and knives are not the only instruments suitable for mutilation. The modern automatic rifle, the long-distance weapon par excellence, can mutilate and disfigure a human body until it is almost unidentifiable. The technique of a shot in the neck derives, as we know, from the repertoire of the secret police. The killer puts his pistol directly to the victim's neck and fires. The Serb police officers did not stick to this rule of the torture chamber, but organized a bloodbath, killing the Albanian men by firing repeatedly at their heads. Many of them had been shot up to twenty times. The execution became a massacre. What began as a punitive killing developed into an act of excess.

The point of the masks covering the murderers' faces was not just to protect them from later prosecution and avoid political complications. Since time immemorial executioners, torturers and death squads have worn masks or hoods so that the victim cannot see who is torturing or killing him. The mask preserves anonymity and protects its wearer from the dying man's eyes and from his curse. But this disguise is more than a magical precaution. Death is already present in the mask. It allows no expression to show, no mimic movement in the executioner's face, not the slightest trace of feeling. Hence its spellbinding force. Even before the first blow is struck it has cast the victim into a paralysing state of deadly terror.

The mask is an instrument of the work of annihilation. Whatever the murderer's state of mind, whether he is angry, furious or cheerful, it lends him the moral indifference with which he habitually goes about his deadly business. He fulfils his task with calm concentration. Execution is not a battle, it is an anonymous action, but it involves close physical contact. The faceless executioner destroys the victim's face. At the same time, however, the mask opens up a new and unsuspected freedom. The executioner can do whatever occurs to him, in any way he likes, without being recognized. He is absolute lord of life and death, master of another person's body. By destroying the victim he realizes his entire destructive energy. He expands, he grows greater than he really is. The mask hides the childish grin of triumph on his face. As the massacre proceeds he takes pleasure in what he is doing and in himself. He enjoys the unbounded power of killing, the immeasurable strength of striking at the face of another person, a face with all the experience of a lifetime in it, destroying it for ever.

The militant Hindus employed another method, and we need not credit only the religious fanaticism of lynch mobs with the use of fire. The history of mankind has always liked piles of burning brushwood. Its way is lined with flaming pyres. Fire is the preferred weapon of the mob everywhere, whether it is used in the cause of revolution, repression or persecution. The ritual burning of heretics, witches and demons is part of our dark history, and not just in the West.

But the significance of fire extends far beyond rituals of cleansing and purification. Fire is the destructive force itself. Transported out of its usual state of mind, the lynch mob was no longer performing a ritual; it simply poured petrol over the jeep and set it on fire, an improvised action of ordinary brutality without any symbolism behind it. Yet the members of the mob relished their cruelty. They stood staring at the fire for over an hour, uttering war cries, whipping up their feelings. They hailed the festive bonfire with yells of triumph. Fire, a greedy force, all-exterminating, larger than life, is like a signal of victory. It shows very clearly that the border has been crossed. For a brief time human beings return to an earlier state, a state of original equality. There is fire in all their eyes at once, its inescapable compulsion uniting them all. It is among the strongest recurrent impulses of a human being to lay claim to fire, himself kindling the flames that unite him with the rest of humanity.

II

Terror and Persecution

4

The modern world and barbarism

The twentieth century began with the highest of hopes, and ended in many parts of the world in pain and despair. We have woken from the dream that reason will prevail. The world is as full of violence as ever. Countless human beings are still busy torturing and killing their fellows by every conceivable means. It is as if all our efforts had vanished without trace, defeated by the moral constitution of the species. The great story of the improvement of *Homo sapiens* and his behaviour was only a fiction, a myth. We no longer believe in progress. Ideas of peaceful utopias and ideals of mutual understanding have a curiously helpless and unworldly if comforting effect. To continue putting our faith in such traditional schemes we would need a short memory and a determination to ignore facts.

The epoch has been marked by an unprecedented unleashing of violence in the torture chambers of despotic regimes, totalitarian prison camps, execution pits, and the practice of genocide. Millions upon millions have fallen on the battlefields of technologically fought wars of annihilation, in bombed-out cities and the burnt villages and farms of colonial and civil wars. When thirty years of world war ended in 1945 and an interim balance sheet was drawn up, the nations briefly abjured violence. Yet it promptly continued on its way. The Soviet and Chinese camp systems spread, and a state of war became chronic in many parts of Asia, Africa and Latin America. Despite international condemnation, there were further instances of genocide. Millions of refugees had to leave their homes and sought asylum in neighbouring states or in the bastions of prosperity, where they quite often became the victims of renewed persecution. After the collapse of the Socialist dictatorships, liberal hopes for a world of global peace briefly revived again. But the new democracies lacked the political will and military means to stem violence, so in the end war, terror and expulsion returned to Central Europe. The hunting down and slaughtering of human beings, war and genocide are still on the agenda.

No one knows what name later generations will give to our age of mass murder. The history of the species strides on, unmoved, over the decline of civilizations and nations. Evil is usually erased from the memory swiftly, to leave the image of the world unimpaired. Those who lived at the time of the late witch-hunts could not have guessed that one day their descendants, glossing over the savagery, would call their period the Age of Reason. In the endless cycle of horror and exhaustion, followed by forgetting and the rearrangement of the facts, moments of light are rare, coming as seldom as those golden interim periods of peace. It would be foolish to expect a sudden change for the better at the beginning of a new millennium. There was a widespread belief in 1900 that global trade, democracy, reason and national autonomy had secured peace in Europe for ever. The educated middle classes were on the way to fraternization in a kind of international community. Fourteen years later they all went to war. It would run counter to all historical experience to believe that the worst, the 'unimaginable', could not happen again. It is therefore essential to dispel all deceptive idealistic images once and for all.

Civilization

The notion of civilization is still central to our image of the world today. Although the First World War inflicted some damage on that illusion, the idea obstinately persisted. When Europe entered upon a reasonably long period of peace after the catastrophes of the first half of the century, it regained its power of attraction. At the turn of the millennium it was once again fashionable to announce the dawn of a new epoch, an age of global unity and moral cosmopolitanism. It is certain that this episode in the history of ideas will pass away too. At the same time, however, a suspicion was felt that civilization, barbarism and the modern world might be interlinked in their own peculiar way. How far, then, do war and terrorism affect the idea of civilization?

Four arguments can be distinguished. First, we may think of the terrors of war and persecution as nothing but occasional lapses, temporary setbacks within an otherwise unbroken development working towards state monopoly of the means of violence, control of our primitive instincts and the taming of cruelty. Even taking the fragility and psychological cost of the civilizing process into account, this late version of the idea of progress can ultimately see Auschwitz only as the result of a peculiarly German ideology, mentality and state history. The mass murders there took place because the national conscience was still underdeveloped, the state unstable and civilization incomplete. Animal instincts were not yet tamed and controlled by the bonds of social interdependency. The principles of self-discipline and independence, and an ability to take the long view, were not yet firmly enough anchored in human nature, and since the perpetrators of violence lacked inner backbone they sought support in leaders outside themselves whose dictates they obeyed to the letter. But did not many of them go about the work of killing extremely conscientiously, while acting on their own initiative? And can their countless collaborators and accomplices who did not hold German passports also be seen as peculiarly German? Obviously civilization is not strong enough to stand firm against personality changes, against the mutation of a cultivated individual into a mass murderer.

Another hypothesis is the exact opposite of the first. It holds that the release of violence results not from the incomplete development of the modern world but from the overwhelming success of that development. Civilization itself is a condition which adequately explains its own collapse. It was bound to topple over into barbarism. Modern science was bound to invent the nuclear bomb. State bureaucracy was bound to be transformed into the practice of genocide as a public service, the authoritarian member of society was bound to become a mass murderer. Instrumental reason came into its own at Auschwitz and Hiroshima. The dubious nature of this theory is obvious. It ascribes inexorable linear force to civilization and reason, and cannot explain the other conditions that are enough to unleash collective violence, or why other societies with all the features of modern civilization have not also turned to genocide and mass terrorism.

A third position therefore suggests itself. According to this idea, modernity is a necessary but not a sufficient condition of terror. The Shoah is not a historical lapse or an accident but a genuine product of the modern world, a potential that was latent in it. Civilization exaggerates both our creative and our destructive tendencies. Without a state monopoly on violence the demands of everyday social life cannot be met, but without concentration of the means of violence, war cannot be empowered or massacre made a state institution. There can be no barbarism without the modern state's programme of law and order, without the moral indifference of rationality, without bureaucracy. At first sight there is something to be said for this thesis. It avoids historical determinism without excluding terrorism from its view of the world. Yet it remains unsatisfactory. Conditions that must necessarily be present are not causes. They tell us only how something could have happened, not why. The explanation remains incomplete. Does cold-blooded cruelty really require modern organization; was the moral deafness of the bureaucratic character really essential for mass murder to take place? What are the other necessary conditions for the modern terrors of war and persecution?

Finally, the last position states that there is no connection between civilization and barbarism because human behaviour has never evolved at all. Belief in civilization is a Eurocentric myth in which the modern world worships itself. Human emotions and drives have not changed with the change in social conditions. Personal compulsions are not of recent date but are a feature of every culture. Naked savages are not as wild as the theory of civilization claims, and the civilized are by no means as mild and full of the milk of human kindness as they would like to think. Violence and cruelty are among the invariables of cultural history. Every society must restrain them by imposing norms and controls. Successful as social and technical change may have been, it does not affect the moral equipment of the species. History alters much but by no means everything. Technology and good organization have simply multiplied the ever-present potentials. The intelligence of the modern age, its discipline and its rationality have not changed the human constitution, but they have immeasurably increased its faculty for destructive inventiveness. Even worse: the idea of civilization has itself served to justify violent excess. It was in the name of the nation, progress and civilization that European states sent off their gunboats and their legions to exterminate 'wild savages' in the forest wildernesses and savannahs of the South. The colonialists annihilated whole cultures and races with a sense of moral superiority and missionary duty.

The discussion of 'civilization and barbarism' serves a need for the interpretation of historical meaning. We cannot overlook the remnants of linear ideas of time and a teleological philosophy of history. Without them, it would be impossible to deplore a historical 'lapse' or the 'shortcomings' of our morality. The pattern of thought of the secular apocalypse also obeys this doctrine of finalism, remaining negatively fixed on the distorted image of an irreversible development. What did we expect of universal history: realization of the idea of freedom, moral learning processes, the resolution of all prejudices, collective cultural development? There is little analytical value in theories of history, civilization or society drawn up on the grand scale. Immune to detailed analysis, they are more suitable to sketching views of the world than providing a real understanding of events. Much is lost by abstraction in the lofty heights of global theory. Modern societies are shaped by the urbanization of the world, technological developments in labour and communications, and bureaucratic state government. But the idea of bureaucratic rationality does seem to have a certain significance in the analysis of terrorism. Can we use it to understand how terror is set off and how acts of violence are committed?

Bureaucracy

A bureaucracy is distinguished by a high degree of centralized power, the division of labour, formalization and standardization. Bureaucracies regulate labour processes and decision-making. Not only do they pre-programme action towards definite targets, they also ensure a certain potential for the replacement of the labour force. Bureaucracies need not make particularly high demands in recruiting their staff; they can be content to employ people with rather mediocre minds without any loss of efficiency.

The model of a rational bureaucracy, however, covers only a special case of social organization. Every bureaucracy is an organization, but not every organization is a bureaucracy. Labour programmes, the bureaucratic hierarchy and specialization vary independently of each other. The form of a particular organization depends on the environment in which it operates and on the disturbances and uncertainties in that environment. Bureaucracies work well only in relatively stable, manageable, predictable circumstances, but neither their internal nor their external functioning corresponds to the ideal of a rational bureaucracy. As a rule, official aims and plans are the ideas and myths of the elite, and do not impose binding ideologies and modes of conduct on all members of society. Organizational aims are subject to constant reinterpretation and adapted to the vicissitudes of time, quite often until they are unrecognizable. If a bureaucracy is to succeed, it must often ignore its stated aims and break the rules in order to avoid working as provided for by those rules. Informal groups who are officially not supposed to exist ensure motivation and collaboration. Orders are undermined, coalitions compete for power and influence. In short, neither the external nor the internal world of bureaucratic organizations matches the model of the perfectly regulated administration. The bureaucratic character doing his work strictly by the book or to rule would be the organization's downfall.

We cannot, therefore, apply the bureaucratic concept to processes of collective violence. Something that hardly ever works in civil society is even less likely to work in situations of armed conflict, persecution and mass murder. Certainly war between states calls for much better organization than the wars of the past fought by hordes, feudal armies or troops of mercenaries. But the logistics of war are not to be confused with the course of war itself. The battle cannot be planned ahead. The chaos of skirmishing is ruled by laws quite different from the planning games played by the general staff. War is a world of friction and coincidence, a 'true chameleon', as Clausewitz says, 'because it changes its nature slightly in every actual case'.

Terrorist persecution too has only a limited connection with bureaucracies. Terror is nourished by the arbitrary principle and by surprise and speed, in fact features that are the opposite of those that usually distinguish bureaucracies. The identification and selection of victims is admittedly a task for an administrative organization. But bureaucracies are not suitable for persecution on the spot, the police or military raid, expulsion, deportation and mass murder. Once slaughter has become a state institution, the execution of terrorism is usually the job of special units acting according to the tactics of a mobile taskforce, which may be a modern form of organization but is not a bureaucratic one. Although they kept daily records of their victims, the SS police battalions and operational commandos in Poland, Lithuania, Ukraine and White Russia were not bureaucratic units. If we look only at the office work of their terrorism and confine ourselves to the mountains of files they left, which are the main sources for historical research, we get only half the truth. State terrorism is executed not by deskbound zealots of the Adolf Eichmann stamp but by ordinary, average people who in civil life might not seem out of the common run. Many such people developed into much-feared murderers like Theodor Eicke and Josef Kramer, Gustav Sorge and Otto Moll, Maria Mandel and Hildegard Lächert, the 'Bloody Brygida' of Majdanek. These were not bureaucratic characters but ordinary men and women with murderously creative minds who could devise some new refinement of cruelty almost daily.

The annihilation of the European Jews was not 'administrative mass murder'; when we speak of 'bureaucratic' genocide we are thinking of Western Europe. But by far the majority of Jewish victims were not, like the Jews of the West, picked up separately, registered, dispossessed of their property, summoned in writing to assembly points and then deported hundreds of kilometres in journeys lasting many days, to be suffocated with exhaust fumes or hydrocyanic acid as soon as they arrived at the death camps. In many parts of Eastern Europe people were either summarily driven into ghettos or shot at once in the nearby forest. Those temporarily spared were worked to death, starved, beaten or shot. Anyone still left alive after that was transported to the death camps, but almost half of all Jewish victims were not killed in the gas chambers. The administration of the occupied areas had little in common with the bureaucracy of a modern centralized state. Deportations in Eastern Europe, unlike those in the West, were often carried out with brutal violence, and a considerable number of victims resisted, guessing that death awaited them at their journey's end.

That terrorist institution the concentration camp was not a truly bureaucratic structure either. The list of rules for inmates was such that it was virtually impossible to comply with them all. Over-regulation ensured calculated disorder, not order. Offences could be defined at will and disproportionately punished, whereas bureaucratic methods establish accountability and limit power. Concentration camp inmates, however, could expect the worst at any time. In this system of absolute power, even the lowest-ranking guards had complete licence to kill. The decentralization of power gave the guards a free hand; orders were carried out before they were even issued, the regulations of central command were simply ignored and violence was exercised with full autonomy. The organization of the SS was a polycratic system riddled with corruption, protectionism and rivalry. It demanded of its members not blind military obedience and bureaucratic observance of the letter of the law, but individual initiative, a talent for improvisation, obedience even in anticipation of the event, and the independent execution of violent acts. Despite the not inconsiderable amount of paperwork it produced, the concentration camp was no part of bureaucratic culture. In a bureaucratic office the staff generally work much as they are expected to work, whereas in concentration camps the guards beat, tortured and killed the inmates not because they were expected to, but because they could.

Sovereignty, community, nationhood

The roots of terrorism go deeper than the discourse of the modern age can understand. Violence is built into the basic forms of social life. Persecution draws a demarcation line between friend and foe, insiders and outsiders, natives and foreigners. Wherever people are marked out as troublemakers or intruders, criminals or traitors, it is only a small step to violence. Often the victims are not recognized as full members of society but classified as superfluous and dispensable. The exclusion and killing of outsiders is known even in societies with democratic constitutions, but under a tyranny anyone at all can find himself under suspicion. Even suspicion is not always necessary for people to disappear without trace.

There are three forms of society that carry the potential for persecution in them: sovereignty, the community and the nation. Sovereignty is intended to control violence and thus ensure the survival of society. Its legitimacy is based on its guarantee of order. But sovereignty itself depends on the violence of persecution. It protects life by threatening social or physical death, and its order is based not on belief in its legitimacy but on the fear of death. The sovereign's subjects recognize that his persecution must be feared. They are drawn to him because he lifts the burden of liberty from their shoulders and determines their station in life. They hope for protection, solicitude and justice from him, and the threat of death thus acquires binding authoritative power. Respect and the fear of death are very closely linked in the recognition of power.

The most important means of imposing sovereignty are norms and the law. Norms engender violence as well as restraining it. They admittedly create security by distinguishing the normal from the abnormal, but the measure itself defines the occasions against which it is directed. And whatever the basis of its principles, the law is a process of social control and persecution. Its personnel are recognized to have authority over life and death. The existence of this iron framework behind every society based on sovereignty may sometimes be forgotten during periods of the democratic rule of law, but to forget it is historically short-sighted and politically naive. Democracies do not last for ever either. Political life is not interested in compromise or consensus. Its foundation is power, the power to persecute and inflict pain which every individual subject may ultimately suffer. Once the system is set up, the interests of sovereignty shift from imposing peace at home to maintaining itself in power. Anyone attacking the regime – whether it is despotic or democratic – is committing high treason, which carries harsher penalties than acts of civil violence. Here the institutional maintenance of peace is part of a vicious circle: order is necessary to restrain violence, but conversely persecution and violence are necessary to preserve order.

This vicious circle exists on both the national and the international scale. Even the 'world state' for which many hope would have to maintain itself by a vast agency of repression. A global armistice would be impossible without a gigantic military and police apparatus. The 'world state' could contain small wars by means of massive intervention, or bring a few robber bands to justice, but nonetheless even global sovereignty, like any other force of law and order, would be subject to the logic of violence. Even worse, once set up the world state, that grand project in which all would be exactly the same, would tolerate no vacant areas. Like every empire, it would be founded on countless victims, with armies working in its service to secure its rule, and would abolish all borders across which anyone might flee to safe exile. Anyone wanting to leave the world state would have no refuge but the moon.

The other side of this coin is that even the model of the democratic sovereignty of the elite cannot guarantee global peace. An authoritarian world state would hold all the power of repression in its hands, while a league of democracies would be in no position to prevent social warfare. Public opinion in democracies is by no means always civilized and anxious to achieve a compromise; war between national armies and manhunts by the mob have always been particularly cruel kinds of violence. Democracies presuppose a population that can read and write, a middle class that pays taxes, an administration capable of functioning – and no civil war. If these prerequisites are not met, general elections often undermine social cohesion, intensify conflicts, and – as we have seen recently in many post-

Communist countries – make voters pledge their allegiance to xenophobic agitators. In such cases political parties serve as a disguise for parades of ethnic feeling. Self-determination in the name of the nation always goes hand in hand with the exclusion of minorities. The free exchange of ideas and goods leads to measures of defence and protectionism, since global competition often leads to local ruin. Finally, the democratic society is often unwilling to make the sacrifices necessary to achieve a balance between forces or join a federation of states. If death is no longer part of the social contract, the military power essential to impose and maintain peace at home and abroad will be lacking. The days of peace are numbered as long as democracies are not prepared to pay that price.

Another form of society is just as dangerous as sovereignty. The community defines its membership through exclusion. It separates those who feel they belong together from those who are cast out of society, or were never accepted into it in the first place. When a community is created, social circles are marked out. If you are on the inside, the community promises harmony, equality and fraternity, while it cuts itself off from the outside world by erecting protective walls and front lines. The establishment sets itself against outsiders; friends league together against foes and foreigners. People cannot band together without excluding others. Outside opposition creates and reinforces cohesion. It is the community that invents enemies and rivals. It needs the contrasting image of the outsider, and consequently tries to divide the world into two halves, excluding all who are 'different'. The people inside the community feel that they are good, even elect, civilized, noble and right-minded. Those outside it, however, are savages, barbarians, heathens, 'dirty', intruders, superfluous. They deserve contempt, and insiders may do almost anything to them, for the borders of morality are the borders of the community, and as a result those outside it are often not even regarded as human beings. The community thus opens the door to persecution. The laws of hospitality apply to strangers only until they unpack their bags.

In the society of the nation, both universal forms of order are historically united. Although the criteria for the concept of 'nation' are far from clear, in theory the nation combines the entities of the state, the community and its culture. Members of the national community must belong to its culture, speak the same language, share the same ideas, follow the same lifestyle. All members are expected to feel solidarity for their peers, defend the community against the outside world, or take its values out into the world at the risk of their lives. Even more: all members of the same culture, wherever they live, are to be united in a federation. The national culture is the foundation of the community and legitimizes the state, and the power of the state must protect the cultural community while exposing, observing or ejecting strangers. One culture, one state, one nation – such is the nationalist slogan.

Where there are no very forceful reasons to legitimize the nation, historical legends have sometimes been invented. They feature bold and virtuous popular heroes, scenes where the national blood was collectively shed, struggles against the rule of tyrannical princes or foreign conquerors. For preference such stories fall back on an archive of national symbols: cultural monuments, typical landscapes, folklore, costume, national dishes, national emblems. Yet this invention of a national entity is regularly accompanied by rapid memory loss. The idea of the nation carries weight only in so far as the true diversity of its origin, traditions and customs is forgotten. Once the nation is finally established in the image created of itself by society, the idiom of one social group becomes the obligatory national language. It now stands for homogeneity of culture, membership of the community and the unity of the state.

In Europe nationalism began by operating on an ideological paradox. Since it came into being in the name of freedom from rule by princes and foreign domination, it drew its emotional basis from nostalgia for the good old days of heroic warriors and peasants living close to the land. But the popular culture that it was supposed to evoke was only a useful self-deception disguising the imposition of a generally binding higher culture. Everyone must master the national language in order to guarantee communication and bureaucratic equality. Compensation for this endless anonymity came in the form of the illusion of the community and personal solidarity.

The making of a nation into a state and the setting up of an imaginary community inevitably entailed measures of exclusion. Nation states strive to extend their political borders to the borders of their culture, and to impose it at home. The violent measures employed under sovereignty become instruments of national community. Anyone who does not belong to the community, or deviates from its homogeneous culture, loses status and bears the stigma of the outsider. Anyone who shows disrespect for the sacred icons of the community or actually attacks them is regarded as an internal enemy and traitor. And as soon as economic or social crises undermine political and cultural stability, the pressure of persecution is brought to bear on strangers and outsiders. Just as those active in the service of the nation wage war abroad to stake out the borders of the community, they also ensure the order of sovereignty and the limits of national membership at home.

Human beings have always fought, persecuted and killed each other. In his capacity for hatred *Homo sapiens* is independent of the membership of any ethnic group, nation or social class. Agrarian societies already knew despotic forms of sovereignty and ethnic chauvinism, but the unholy alliance of state sovereignty, homogeneous culture and imaginary community under the national banner is of modern date. It is not very likely that the age of nationalism will come to a swift end. The more people are driven by hardship to the centres of wealth, the more dangerous is the sense of difference between natives and immigrants. As long as the state resists the social need to create a community, terrorism remains confined to isolated actions on the part of society. But once the state authorities set about actively imposing a homogeneous culture, declaring that the illusions of social community guide their policy, the dam keeping systematic persecution at bay is breached.

5

Auschwitz, Kolyma, Hiroshima

'We had no gas for gas chambers,' comments Alexander Solzhenitsyn on the mass murders during the building of the White Sea Canal. Tens of thousands perished there in the winter of 1931, and the camps were constantly repopulated. Over a million prisoners died after 1937 at Kolyma, a subdivision of the Gulag archipelago in north-eastern Siberia. They perished of hardship, overwork, starvation, cold, and mass shootings. No one was ever to return. Kolyma, an Arctic Auschwitz? For opponents of the Communist terrorist system, this comparison never meant counting up the crimes committed in their own land, let alone belittling them; it was drawn simply to clarify their historic significance.

Comparisons are an established way of trying to make sense of the nature of events. Only a comparison brings out common features, differences and contrasts. But it is unsuitable for political and moral exoneration. The crimes of others are not mitigating circumstances for crimes of one's own. What would we think of a man who committed murder during a robbery and tried to excuse himself on the grounds that other murderous robbers had done the same? Yet this erroneous moral conclusion is not unusual. It serves one party as a threadbare excuse, the other as a reason to wax indignant. Many see the comparison itself as an indication of moral corruption or political demagogy. But the apparent fear of winning approval from the wrong side serves only to reinforce our prejudices and immunize our own view of the world. To allow the alleged humanistic ideology of the Communist states as mitigating circumstances for the terror they exerted is a stance based solely on the system's own propaganda. To cite the mass murder of the Jews of Europe as unique before drawing any comparison contributes nothing to an understanding of the facts. A ban on comparisons means that we are not forced to learn from events, and so we remain under the spell of the past, blind to comparable problems in the present. But similar dangers require similar forms of the control of power, of resistance and of intervention.

Is there any point in mentioning Auschwitz, Kolyma and Hiroshima in the same breath? Although the first Soviet labour camps were founded fifteen years before the German concentration camps, no causal connection can be found, so we are left with a comparison between independent incidents and structures. But what about the epoch-making significance of the facts? Whose viewpoint is to be authoritative? The political influence of the nuclear bomb on international affairs is incomparably greater than the consequences of Auschwitz or Kolyma. The age in which mankind can wipe itself out at a single stroke began with Hiroshima. Genocide and terrorist persecution, on the other hand, are always regional. Their violence can be successfully denied, tolerated and quickly forgotten even in the immediate vicinity. Collective memory is obviously no criterion of the significance of a crime.

Does the number of victims make this comparison unique? Where does the threshold of values converting quantity into quality lie? The unleashing of violence is not a question of great numbers. If the population of a nation is only a few thousand, its annihilation is still genocide. But what about the millions and millions who died under the Maoist terror of the Great Leap Forward and the Cultural Revolution? What about genocide in Turkey under the Ottoman Empire, the intentional and deliberate starvation policy of the Soviet regime in Ukraine, the North Caucasus and Kazakhstan in 1932–33 which cost the lives of some six million people; what about the killing fields of Cambodia, the countless massacres in Indonesia, Nigeria, Rwanda, south-west Africa and the Amazon region? The list could be continued. But these places lie beyond the horizon of Westerners. We do not seem to perceive and empathize with mass murder in Asia or Africa in the same way as we do with a massacre of white European or American citizens. Indignation has local limits of attention; we distance ourselves from its cause by degrees, to the point where we ignore it. One can sometimes detect an attitude of Eurocentric superiority here. Such distant massacres, we are told, are only post-colonial civil wars or 'pre-modern', Stone Age tribal conflicts, not to be compared with crimes organized on an allegedly higher plane of civilization by methods involving the division of labour – as if the systematically planned massacre of 1.5 million Turkish and Kurdish Armenians, the murder of millions of Indian Muslims and Hindus during the partition of India, the mass murder of a million Cambodians or the extermination of most of the inhabitants of East Timor by the Indonesian army were only spontaneous raids carried out by savage hordes.

Crimes usually live on in the memory as the actions of others, so it is as well for us all to concern ourselves first and foremost with our own history. Only then can we draw comparisons without adjusting our ideas. At the same time, however, precise terminology and a typology of terror are required if comparisons are to be valid. We can immediately discount the idea of classifying types of terror by the circumstances or forms of society in which they occurred. Such a classification says something about historical conditions but not about the point requiring elucidation. Rejecting the comparison by suggesting that terrorism has, after all, occurred in many different societies is to confuse cause with effect. There is no general agreement on whether terror depends on a particular type of society, or a particular mentality or ideology. As a rule it has little to do with the context in which it arises. One of its laws is that it creates the conditions for its own continuance. To get a clear view of the facts, then, it is essential to distinguish between the social forms taken by terrorism itself.

Terrorism in war

A distinction has always been drawn between two different situations: the armed conflict of warring parties and the massacre of defenceless, unarmed civilians. Terms such as 'bloodbath' and 'butchery' have always been used for the slaughter of people who can put up no resistance worth the name. Even for the powerful, fighting is seldom without risk. Since violence is mutual, the strong can feel its force too. A massacre, on the other hand, is one-sided, asymmetrical violence. The victims have no chance to defend themselves. The idea is not to break their will or their resistance, but to wipe them off the face of the earth. This difference must be borne in mind if we are to describe the unleashing of violence in modern warfare more precisely.

Battles using war *matériel* are still fought in the context of anonymous, long-distance warfare, with hand-to-hand fighting now complemented by technology. War becomes both conflict and a job. Logistics and supplies assume greater significance as the number of fighting units decreases. Industrial mass production precedes military mass killing. However, that is not the same as total warfare. The propaganda of total war declares that all on the same side are comrades in arms. It aims to mobilize all resources and militarize the economy and society, while also justifying terrorist attacks on the enemy's unarmed hinterland. But the fact that many wartime activities resemble an ordinary job of work does not imply that the converse is true, and work done in the service of the war is a military engagement in itself. Workers in armaments factories and on the land are not actually fighting. The 'home front' is not really a front. An air raid that is met by anti-air raid fire is undoubtedly a conflict, but the slaughter of the defenceless population of an urban or rural area by conventional or nuclear carpet-bombing turns war into a massacre, or mass terrorism.

First, the battlefield is horizontally extended by the use of long-distance weapons, and if only one side has long-distance weapons at its command the inevitable result is a massacre. While the weaker side does not even get within fighting distance, the stronger side can hold the enemy at bay and shoot them down at will, like game. This situation was typical of many 'battles' in the colonial wars. While the conquerors had gunboats, artillery and long-range quick-firing weapons, the colonized people were often armed only with knives, spears or muskets. One-sided long-distance killing made war a kind of deadly sport. For the conquerors it was more like shooting game than fighting, for the conquered it was a massacre.

In the past the butchery of defenceless opponents was not unusual in 'ordinary' wars fought on land either. Historically, war waged within clearly defined limits is an exception. Even in the medieval feuds of the nobility, war never resembled the duels of the chivalric tournament. It was not far from the soldier to the berserker or marauder. Campaigns of conquest, like the founding of new states, frequently begin with a massacre intended to strike terror into all adversaries. In partisan, civil and revolutionary wars the difference between the battle area and its civilian environment is eliminated anyway. But there are often massacres in wars between states too, both on the battlefield and in conquered villages and towns: the slaughter of defenceless soldiers, women, children and the old. If no prisoners are to be taken a massacre is unavoidable. Finally, victory at the end of a war is often accompanied by acts of vengeance, robbery, rape and murder. Lust, loot and retaliation are, after all, among the most ancient driving forces of warfare. Nonetheless, such triumphalist celebrations of violence, disguised as they may be by military uniforms, have nothing to do with acts of war in itself.

The extension of the battlefield vertically to include war in the air has enlarged the scope of the massacre in ways that could never have been imagined before. Typical of technologized wartime terrorism are strategic bombing, rocket attacks and the constant artillery fire that batters besieged cities. In such warfare the number of civilian victims regularly exceeds the number of actual combatants killed. Terror is intended to break the enemy's morale and force the survivors to surrender. Whether this calculation is appropriate to the purpose or, as the usual phrase goes, 'a military necessity', makes no difference to its evaluation. Mass terrorism is mass terrorism whether it succeeds or not. Like any form of terrorism, however, it has a particular dynamic. If resistance continues then the terror must be stepped up, so that the violence of warfare clearly comes close to being violence intended to exterminate the enemy.

However, selective terrorism in war should be distinguished from a war of total annihilation. In principle, the violence of war is limited. Its aim is surrender, not extermination. The concept of war is an armed conflict of power with a view to the destruction of a military, ruling or class structure, not the annihilation of everyone within those structures. Wars of annihilation, on the other hand, take the fighting to its ultimate conclusion and are waged mercilessly by all available means. Anyone who surrenders is killed. Violence becomes an end in itself. It frees itself of political ends and becomes violence for its own sake. This unleashing of cruelty is part of the dynamic of a war of annihilation from the start. As soon as the battle is over the massacre begins. The victor is not content with the surrender of survivors: he wants them all dead. The carnage is only the logical sequel to victory. A war of annihilation is therefore, of its very nature, an antisocial phenomenon *sui generis*. Its concern is not with power and domination, assimilation or exploitation, conversion or capitulation, but with the occupation of territories now empty of other human beings. Wherever land-hungry settlers appear in the wake of the fighting men, the native population is threatened with total destruction.

Terrorist persecution

Very different forms of violence arise from social and political persecution. Here the situation is always asymmetrical. Power is not evenly distributed. Persecution is not a matter of military engagements and conflicts, but is one-sided. The victims can do little about it, even if they are merely stigmatized. The persecutors' power of definition is all but absolute. The labels they give their victims serve very different criteria: social or political, religious or ideological, national, ethnic or racist. And since these criteria can be substituted for each other or combined, the circle of potential victims may be enlarged at will.

The scale of action ranges from the spontaneous atrocities perpetrated by a mob to pogroms, police or military raids – the *razzia* – and finally to the founding of camps and other institutions intended for killing. Just as a victorious war of annihilation ends with the death of all opponents, persecution aims to kill all the persecuted. However, persecution and warfare are still independent of each other. The fact that they may share a time and place does not make them identical. Admittedly, the approach of war drives people from their homes, which is often a declared aim of the conflict. The persecution of large social groups, however, whether they are social classes, ethnic peoples or religious communities, can also take place in peacetime. The area must be under the persecutor's control if terror is to be fully felt. There must be no more fighting for the terrain itself. The fact that acts of terrorism are often carried out by uniformed units is not the criterion of an armed conflict. It is true that the perpetrators are only too ready to camouflage their activities by using a military vocabulary, but persecution, camps, death squads and death factories have nothing to do with war. Mauthausen and Babi Yar, Auschwitz and Treblinka were not war crimes.

Concepts like victory, defeat and surrender have no meaning in the context of social persecution. Its purpose is expulsion and annihilation. Its victims are not to be conquered and forced to obey, but to be removed from society altogether. The targets of terrorist persecution are not so much enemies as strangers and outsiders. These victims may often be described as enemies: enemies of the state, of society, of the people. But this is a wholly misleading redefinition. Enmity is always mutual; each side regards the other as its adversary. The persecuted are seen as enemies only by their persecutors. In fact they are no danger to anyone. Usually they do not even have the weapons necessary for self-defence.

Persecution draws nourishment from the idea of social homogeneity. Deviations are to be erased, society must be converted to a state of permanent conformity. Even more: the laws of terrorism demand the suppression of all differences, thus calling for the anthropological transformation of the species. The unpredictability inherent in every social relationship is to be eradicated once and for all. Since human conduct can always differ from our expectations, since human beings can change at any time, and can even still exercise their freedom under coercion, terror will not end until every human life has been extinguished. Terrorism in the name of order must not simply perpetuate terrors but do away with all differences and deviations. Consequently it will turn against its own executioners sooner or later. Taken to its logical conclusion, this implosion of terrorism means the destruction of the whole of society.

The unleashing of modern violence in war is the result of the organization and technological transformation of armed power struggles. Persecution requires organization. A manhunt by a mob still comes within the context of spontaneous competition for the trophies of violence. But raids of the *razzia* type call for a certain amount of preparation, coordination, and division of labour. Means of transport and agreed timetables are necessary for deportation over long distances. Areas to be starved out cannot be blockaded without constant surveillance. Mass murder by mobile commando squads cannot be contemplated without the delegation of power and a routine of killing. Many genocides are carried out by methods of flexible, improvised organization, but they should not be confused with spontaneous pogroms.

Just as a war of annihilation leaves vacant territory behind, terrorist expulsion aims at the 'clearance' of an area. The victims are hunted out of the country by means of harassment, encroachment, attack, or systematic 'cleansing'. The process begins with a climate of ostracism, followed by the imposition of prohibitions of every kind in daily life, the official stigmatizing of the victims, the theft of their property, and finally an overt incursion leaving fear and terror behind it. If the persecutors want to cut short this long process of escalation, they resort to violent means at once. Buildings are set on fire, property confiscated or destroyed, cultural institutions are plundered, desecrated and blown up, spokesmen are publicly assassinated, there are deliberate acts of gang rape, arbitrary arrests create an atmosphere of constant fear, people disappear into camps, torture chambers or mass graves until finally any inhabitants still left flee the area. Even when this kind of terrorism is practised by uniformed army or militia units, it is not war. 'Ethnic cleansing' is one of the methods of terrorist persecution.

The central institution of violence in modern persecution is the concentration camp. Its purpose is not so much to imprison political opponents as to transform and destroy those regarded as superfluous. Situated in the middle of society, part of a complex structure of political and economic institutions, the camp is a little microcosm on the borders of the social world, a universe of unparalleled destructive power. The inmates are registered, shown their quarters, and usually set to work. Almost entirely isolated from the outside world, they are subjected to a terrorist regime that rules all aspects of ordinary human relations with the world. Space and time, social feeling and identity are so badly abused that any ability to take independent action is destroyed. Human beings have no legal rights and are forced into a life of the utmost misery. Anyone too exhausted to go on working is picked out and killed. Almost anything is possible in this laboratory of absolute power. Human beings are tortured and killed in every imaginable way, through overwork and starvation, misery and epidemic sickness, humiliation and the murder of the spirit, horrible cruelty or poison.

The concentration camp is the experimental laboratory of terrorist persecution; the death factory is its extermination centre. Death factories such as those built at Treblinka and Birkenau were institutions where large numbers of people could be destroyed without trace. The concept of a 'camp' is misleading here. There were no prisoners to form a camp society. The few people granted a brief reprieve had to keep the murderous work going. Everyone else was killed on arrival. As in any other factory there were technical complexes, overseers, foremen and trained assistants, the division of labour, shift working, a balance sheet of profits and expenses. Events were organized on the conveyor belt principle and imitated the guidelines of rational industrial procedures: continuity, time-saving, accountability. However, there were three essential ways in which the camps differed from an industrial plant: most of the workers, members of the Jewish 'special commandos', were killed and replaced by others at regular intervals. The 'raw materials' of the work were human bodies – and the 'end product' was bales of their hair, gold from their teeth, and ashes.

Mass annihilation did not just set out to kill. A whole group of the population was to be blotted out of memory. There was to be no sign of the dead. Nothing was to be left to remind anyone of them, no tomb or monument. They were to disappear from the face of the earth as if they had never existed. In its most radical form, terrorist persecution does not even tolerate mortal remains but endeavours to cancel itself out, following the principle of absolute disappearance. Even death was to be obliterated.

Differences

To equate Hiroshima with places of such institutionalized terrorist persecution as Auschwitz and Kolyma obviously does not do justice to the facts. The first use of the nuclear bomb had nothing to do with persecution. Hiroshima was an act of terrorism in war, designed less to bring about the surrender of Japan than to demonstrate superiority over all future adversaries in war, more particularly the USSR. Furthermore, the USA wanted to prevent Soviet troops from disputing the occupation of Japan with them. Clearly, the bomb was dropped more to impress the Allies than to intimidate the enemy. Nor can Hiroshima be seen as a campaign of total destruction. The extermination of the Japanese population was not the USA's strategic aim. Hiroshima marks the technological climax of selective terrorism in war. The nuclear bomb was preceded by strategic bombing of the urban centres of Japan in a campaign which had killed about a million people within a few weeks. The aims of technological slaughter in war had already been more than met. What happened at Hiroshima may symbolize the global self-destruction of mankind, but look closely and it has another meaning. It stands for nuclear terrorism against an opponent with no nuclear weapons of its own. This situation became more relevant than ever after the end of the Cold War.

'Auschwitz' and 'Kolyma' are names that stand for terrorist persecution by the state. Unlike the Kolyma complex of camps, however, Auschwitz was both concentration camp and death factory. There were no parallels on the Gulag Archipelago to the industrialized scale of mass murder in the gas chambers of

Treblinka, Sobibór and Birkenau. Mass killings were carried out by means of death marches, shootings, deliberate deprivation and starvation. But the Kolyma phenomenon does correspond to Auschwitz and its subsidiary camps in that a healthy man became a wreck after six weeks at the most in the Kolyma gold mines, while a Jewish prisoner's average expectation of life at the synthetic rubber works in Monowitz was about four months, or about a month in the coal mines attached to the camp. The camp system of the Gulag Archipelago can therefore be appropriately compared with the Nazi concentration camp system.

The two terrorist systems are not dissimilar in the logistics of their deportations either. For purposes of 'ethnic cleansing', the Bolshevik secret police transported whole ethnic groups to the east between November 1943 and May 1944. These deportations were centrally planned in every detail. Hundreds of thousands of Kalmuks, Tartars, Chechens, Ingush and Balkars were loaded into cattle trucks and taken thousands of kilometres to Siberia. Mortality was extremely high. About 120,000 soldiers were detailed to guard them, although the war was then at its height. There is no missing the parallels in the structures of camp organization, the terrorist order, the conduct of the guards, and killing by overwork and violence. The ironic maxim *Arbeit macht frei*, 'Work Makes One Free', stood above the entrance of many German camps; the equivalent over the entrances of the Kolyma camps was: 'Work is Honour and Heroism'. Workuta, Karaganda and Kolyma far outdo German camp complexes like Buchenwald, Mauthausen and Majdanek in the number of their victims and the extent and duration of their existence.

The comparison of instances of genocide moves on a different plane of analysis. 'Genocide' denotes not a form of terrorism but a group of victims and the end result. Both civil wars and wars of annihilation, as organized forms of terrorist persecution, can lead to genocide. In the process ethnic persecution is frequently overlaid by political or social motives. The methods of genocide are many and various. The annihilation of European Jews by the Germans and their accomplices was carried out through a variety of forms of terrorism. The Jews were deported, crowded into ghettos and forced to live and starve there, debilitated by work or killed outright. In the concentration camps, Jews were the pariahs and were under the strongest pressure to be exterminated. In the occupied regions of Eastern Europe, they were hunted down by mobile death squads, summarily murdered or herded into the trains. In the death factories of Operation Reinhard and at Birkenau, victims were either shot on arrival or tricked into gas chambers where they were poisoned and then burned.

Some of these forms of terror are found in other instances of genocide: deportation to poverty-stricken regions, blockades to starve the population out by cutting whole tracts of country off from supplies, concentration camps or similar institutions, summary police or military raids based on lists of suspects, inspections or denunciations, murder by being worked to death, mass executions or death marches. The Shoah was not the only case of genocide in the twentieth century. But mass murder in death factories built especially for that purpose was a German invention.

6

Time and terror

The Museum of Modern Art in New York contains a lithograph of 1915 by George Grosz. It bears the title *Das Attentat* – 'The Assassination'. On the left-hand side, the exploding, bulbous cloud of a bomb can be seen. Its pressure wave distorts the facades of the buildings and flings dislocated human bodies through the air. The figures furthest from the detonation have scattered in panic. Their faces are twisted into grimaces, their hands curled into claws. The bomb has gone off in the middle of a city, plunging the world into chaos.

Grosz, who had volunteered to fight in November 1914, was demobilized after six months as unfit for service, and he returned to Berlin. The picture transposes the experience of trench warfare into a city environment. An assassination resembles the explosion of a grenade or flying bomb. Violence erupts suddenly and without any warning, as if it fell from heaven. It is all over before anyone can take it in. At the moment of the detonation human beings are overwhelmed. They have no chance to defend themselves, run for cover, escape. The bomb gives them no time to react. While experienced front-line soldiers might guess the trajectory of a grenade from the sounds it makes as it comes over, an assassination catches civilians entirely unprepared. A deafening bang – and people who were there a moment ago have vanished without trace.

An explosion takes instant effect. The detonation of a bomb is not a process, not a state of affairs, but an event. It neither continues nor intensifies. It just happens. The bomb suddenly crashes through the continuity of time, exploding past and future. Where the violent event breaks in, it destroys time. Everything is simultaneous, and since the temporal structure of the turmoil, the sense of what came before and after, has been annihilated, panic reigns after the explosion.

Time is a weapon of a peculiar kind. There is slow violence that takes its time about prolonging human torments and human pain. It is set in motion step by step, it is perpetuated, cut short, intensified once again, interrupted once more, until the final stage is reached. In stark contrast is the violence of the sudden attack, the assassination that kills the victim on the spot. The many temporal variants of terrorism range between these two poles: acceleration and deceleration, interruption and intensification.

Time is not violence itself. Time neither heals nor wounds. Rather, it is a structure within which human beings act and suffer. Time creates sequences, divides them into phases, states of existence, periods of duration. It intensifies when several incidents occur within a limited space of time; it accelerates when events follow one another at increasing speed and everything happens in swift succession. And it perpetuates itself when events are regularly repeated. Time can point a certain way, take a linear or cyclical course; time can stand still when a certain state of affairs persists and nothing new happens. Although it is only a formal concept, time is not an external attribute or a chance appendage of terrorism. Time directly influences its intensity and its operation.

The suffering inflicted by violence has its own time scheme, applying to the physical sensations and rhythm of pain as well as the victim's thoughts, feelings and perceptions. Time experienced in terror also denotes a human being's internal time. The event bursts through the temporal structure of the conscious mind and the relationship of memory, consciousness and expectation, retention and perception. Furthermore, specific temporal structures exhibit the feelings and sensations that accompany violence: the compression of time at moments of panic, the lengthy duration of despair, the accelerated fear felt in flight, the enduring sense of gnawing hatred, the pulsating excitement of the fever of the chase and the fury of battle, the joy of triumph, and finally the return of trauma in memory and nightmares.

Assassination

The quick strike is the swiftest form of violence. Its purpose is direct destruction, immediate annihilation. The assassin aims not to injure but to kill instantly. The violence immediately reaches its climax in the death of another human being. Assassination is violence without forewarning. The victim may live in an atmosphere of threat and try to protect himself with bodyguards, informers, bullet-proof glass, but the quick strike can still take him by surprise. He knows neither the time nor the assassin, and goes blindly to his doom. For the initiative is entirely the assassin's. He alone knows when and where he will strike. He knows all about his victim, his habits and his movements, his weaknesses and preferences. He has armed himself by gathering information, with weapons, through planning. Once all the preparations have been made and the right moment comes, he strikes. The most immediately notable feature of assassination is this asymmetry of information, plans and weapons, the contrast between passivity and initiative, defencelessness and action.

An assassination gains in effect by happening so suddenly. It abruptly breaks through the continuity of normal time. Lengthy as the work of planning has been, the violence itself is an act, not an activity. A single moment alters everything. Where people were going about their usual business only a moment ago, everything is suddenly in ruins: shattered glass, limbs ripped off, the smell of burning. The assassination does not initially cause fear or alarm, it arouses horror. The sudden nature of the event is heightened even more by the entirely unfamiliar, unknown aspect of the devastation. Before it happened, no one had any inkling of the nature and extent of the violence to come, no one had formed any idea of it. Now, suddenly, the world is out of joint. Confidence in the continued existence of the usual order is shattered. Before the storm of panic breaks loose there is a brief interim moment when everything is frozen rigid, a moment lasting longer than the second of terror felt during an accident. Some people are so paralysed by shock that their bodies, although apparently uninjured, can scarcely move.

The sudden nature of the effect is a unique phenomenon, not to be confused with the here and now, that borderline outpost linking past and future whose constant forward progress ensures the continuity of time. What has been ends in the here and now; what is to come begins in it. The sudden event, on the other hand, does not fit into the progress of time but destroys it. The here and now exists in time; that sudden moment lies outside it. For that reason it is not an object of intentional observation, not something on which knowledge or perception can fix. The instant that strikes like lightning has no identity, is not something definite that can be distinguished from all else. It abolishes all distance and differentiation. The event merges with the experience of the event. At the moment of the event itself, it has no meaning; only in retrospect can we see and understand what has happened.

The destructive force of assassination has long been put to human service. It is a form of surprise by violence that occurs through history. Regicides and terrorists are not alone in practising assassination; they are joined by the killer commandos of cartels and syndicates, guerrillas and secret agents, death squads and military combat troops operating in the enemy hinterland. Their aims, motives and justifications are as interchangeable as their social, political and historical circumstances are different. The swift strike is intended to wear the enemy down through terror and undermine his logistical basis. It is employed for purposes of spectacular punishment or revenge, the intentional provocation of repression by the state, or to destroy pockets of resistance, defend the ruling power or bring down its representatives. Assassination is not the prerogative of resistance movements. The propaganda value of the act intended to be a spark lighting the tinder of revolution is only one historical variant on the theme. Massacres too are organized in the name of honour, of the old order or the new, of faith or of fate. They number prominent people among their victims as well as the anonymous, conspirators as well as hated tyrants. The distinction between the political and criminal elements is not always clear. Political murder is still murder, but sometimes the banners of terrorism proclaim the highest values: the nation and the fatherland, God and justice, liberty and progress. Such cultural fantasies open the gates wide to terrorism, for the higher aims are set, the more victims may be sacrificed.

From the technical viewpoint, the destructive force of

assassination has been greatly increased by advances in armaments development. Until dynamite was invented, assassins usually had to make do with poison, daggers or pistols. These weapons, suitable for use at close quarters, were risky, since the assassin had to approach his victim directly. Modern time-bombs with delayed fuses and remote control systems, limpet mines, photoelectric beams, poison gas, guns with telescopic sights and rocket-launchers have turned assassination into a long-distance killing method. The killer plants his explosive in a letter or a parcel bomb, under a car or in a ventilation shaft, and leaves the scene of the crime. He can now wait safely in hiding. The bomb usually strikes down not only his chosen victim but innocent parties who happen to be close to the explosion too. It operates indiscriminately and like lightning. It has turned assassination into a massacre.

Modern acts of terrorism often evoke public reactions. Violence is sensational, a gesture that commands publicity and is intended to spread fear. It aims to signal a resolute and unpredictable striking force. The danger of terrorism seems omnipresent. No one knows where or whom it will strike next. The more indiscriminate the violence and the greater the slaughter, the deeper go the fear and confusion. Everyday life is overshadowed by uneasiness and apprehension for the immediate future. Which aircraft, which underground railway station, which department store is still safe? Public admission of responsibility by the perpetrators reinforces fears. How invulnerable they must feel if they can even reveal their underground identity! What they glorify as a symbolic act means imponderable risk to the man in the street. This side effect is by no means unintentional, for in the last resort the aim of such terrorism is not the death of an individual but collective fear, showing the terrorist how influential he is. The assassination serves to confirm the assassin's self-confidence. He imagines himself the representative of some real or fictional opposition. By striking fear into large numbers of other people he shakes off his own sense of impotence. The fear they feel is his victory – hence the hand raised in the victory sign that he turns to the camera after his arrest.

Yet there is rational calculation behind the act of assassination, an assessment of the forces involved. The assassin wants to avoid conflict. He seeks to disappear before the other side can strike back. The idea of the temporal weapon of the sudden strike is to compensate for his lack of fighting strength and avoid losses of his own. That is why he is often accused of cowardice and underhand conduct. At the same time, surprise is frequently the only weapon available to the weaker side if it is to emerge from passive submission and defy a superior force. Only the suicide squad does not work out its chances of getting away unscathed; the suicide bomber is assassin and martyr combined, uniting in his person the two most radical forms of resistance. In killing his victims he sacrifices himself. For this, he is honoured and celebrated by his like-minded friends. They see him as a hero because he pitted himself against a superior power, gambling on the highest stake a human being can offer, his own life.

The surprise attack often calls for extensive preparation, and if it is a collective operation it requires organization and the division of labour. Weapons have to be acquired and explosives prepared, safe houses must be found, the victim's environment must be studied and a plan worked out. The more conscientious the preparation, the smaller the risk. But even in assassinations problems may arise, making the plan impracticable and forcing the plotters to improvise. The assassin is by no means safe from being taken by surprise himself. The victim's car may unexpectedly take another route, the scene of the planned attack may be better guarded than was expected, checkpoints may put obstacles in the way of access, the field of fire may be obscured, the bomb may fail to go off. Such incidents require presence of mind in the assassin, courage and even daring. Does he give up, does he wait, or does he accept the higher risk involved? Life and death now depend on moments, on seconds and centimetres. Assassins therefore sometimes make alternative plans, adopting double tactics. Several weapons are used instead of just one, a second location is prepared, more troops stand ready in reserve. The less clear the context of the assassination, the more resources must go into it, and the more does the group of assassins resemble a general staff centralized army unit.

Conspirators operate under cover of anonymity and secrecy, which keeps them alert but at the same time endangers them. Indecision and treachery are threats to the group. On the one hand, their secret binds all its members to the group; on the other, anyone can destroy it if tempted by the Judas price of immunity from punishment. The group anticipates this danger. It keeps the attitude and mindset of individuals under surveillance, revealing knowledge in such a way that no one person knows too much. Sometimes the assassins recognize each other only by pre-agreed signals at the scene of the assassination. Internal and external conspiracy are necessary so that the group can publicly claim responsibility. Conversely, however, the secrecy itself is a temptation to violence. Only the deed reveals the hidden power to kill, showing onlookers and fellow members that the group really does exist. To the group of assassins operating in secrecy death, horror and fear are confirmation of their own value. The effects outside and inside the group are thus directly linked. The assassination strengthens the group itself. If it stays together, it will either transform this episode in its existence into a legend, a political myth, or it will soon strike again.

The *razzia*

First you hear the motorbikes and trucks approaching, then the squeal of brakes, the sound of nailed boots on the road as men jump out of their vehicles. Orders are shouted, dogs bark, rifle butts batter a door, there is shouting, the door crashes open, knocking into the mirror above the chest of drawers in the entrance hall, there are men in helmets everywhere, in the corridor, in the rooms, chairs are upturned, one man hits the duvet in the bedroom with his rifle, a man in civilian clothing wants to see papers, has a list of names, asks questions, shakes his head, and then everything happens even faster. The soldiers herd people out of the building, allowing them to take nothing with them, not even a jacket. Out in the street there are uniforms, black cars, the beams of headlights. As soon as the truck is full it drives away.

The *razzia* is a sudden onslaught. The district is encircled within a few minutes, and there is no escape. The raid begins by establishing a border hermetically sealing the area off from its environment. Roads are closed, guards posted, patrols check the spaces in between. All this happens very fast indeed. Before the inhabitants can react, their exit routes are blocked and they are cut off from outside help. The erection of this barrier means that everything is already decided. The authorities carrying out the raid can act freely, the people inside are caught in a trap. Robbed of their freedom of movement, they are delivered up to any incursion.

Once the place has been encircled the manhunt begins. The

pursuers go through the quarter, taking it over completely. They storm through the streets, force their way into buildings, search all the rooms, the cellars, the attics. No one is to escape them. Civilian prerogatives and areas of privacy are instantly swept aside. Every corner is searched, and the pursuers appear as outsize figures, not because of their number but because they take brutal possession of a place that had seemed invulnerable. They ignore all private values, demolishing everything that stands in their way and sometimes wantonly destroying anything dear to its owners. People are seized and their identities checked either thoroughly or cursorily – if the operation aims to make summary arrests then a quick count of heads will do. The instant obliteration of all privacy swiftly cows the victims. The illusion of personal invulnerability which lies at the heart of civilian relationships is suddenly destroyed. Resistance is useless. Many simply give in and let themselves be taken away with apparent composure; only a few venture to protest or strike out. They all guess that they can trust in nothing now.

Even before there are any physical injuries, power is very evidently present as the authorities make incursions and occupy the area. Power is suddenly there, occupying the physical space, the senses, the emotions. The *razzia* is always carried out to the sound of loud shouting and yelling, orders, insults, curses, the mocking laughter of the superior force. The noise pierces the local inhabitants to the marrow, casting them into a state of helpless fear. For the transition from an attack on the eardrums to physical violence is only a brief phase. Bodies are searched for weapons or valuables, anyone who resists is beaten or restrained, people are seized by their arms or shoulders and driven from their homes, defenceless, with blows from rifle butts.

Part of the dynamic of the *razzia* in action is the way that violence follows the breaking down of boundaries. It opens all doors to the persecutors, who acquire greater freedom for themselves by depriving the victims of theirs. They occupy other people's space, take possession of it, fill it with their power. The slighter the resistance, the greater their sense of potency. Once the legal rights of individuals are abrogated the threshold of inhibition has been crossed in any case. But the *razzia* itself tends to break through rules and conventions. Every new act of violence, every further arrest gives the perpetrators a sense that they can do as they like unhindered. This freedom is stimulating in itself, spurring them on to arbitrary action. Quite often a *razzia* degenerates into an orgy of beating, if not an actual bloodbath. It generates a surplus of violence that often has little to do with the official reason for the raid. Some of the perpetrators fill their own pockets, tearing watches or jewellery from their victims. There are rapes, pain is wantonly inflicted for its own sake and the pleasures of the freedom to exercise violence.

The *razzia* is an operation carried out by the forces of law and order: the police or the army. Its initial aim is not to destroy but to search, investigate, and make arrests. The raiders embark on either a purposeful search for hiding places and suspects or an indiscriminate one for outsiders, potential hostages or political undesirables. In the first case the *razzia* is a limited operation carried out by the social authorities, in the second an act of summary terror, an organized form of collective persecution. Forces of occupation are particularly likely to employ the method. The *razzia* is directed against real or suspected opponents of the regime, against separate groups or against the local population in general. Its purpose is to retaliate, to 'cleanse', to instil systematic insecurity or make periodic demonstrations of the power of the occupying regime. In its most radical version, however, it aims to destroy everyone on the proscribed list of a programme of annihilation. The violence begins with the *razzia* and ends in the torture chambers of the local military or police base, in camps, or perhaps immediately in a backyard, a nearby wood, a gravel pit. The intention here is not to demonstrate superior power or instil fear and obedience into a subject people, but to wipe them out entirely.

The *razzia* is a process in which power is seized swiftly, but while an assassination is instant, breaking into time, the *razzia* takes longer. The assassination lasts seconds, the *razzia* hours if not days. However much of a hurry the persecutors may be in, searching, checking and arresting their victims takes time. There is work involved in the *razzia*: the work of persecution. Block after block of buildings must be checked, street after street. The persecutors go about their work busily but without haste. Aware of their superiority, they act with an air of calm routine. After the swift encirclement the operation proceeds step by step. There are changes of tempo, delays, repeated searches of the same place when a new clue turns up. Consultations and interrogations slow the pace down, and there are pauses to interrupt the job of making arrests.

The persecutors are not living in the same time scheme as those they have arrested. The former are doing routine work, the latter feeling the force of a violent attack. While the persecutors move in the consciousness of their power, the latter are abruptly torn from their everyday security. Even before the commando squad forces its way into their homes they hear the danger approaching. They wait behind drawn curtains or closed blinds for their own turn to come. Incursions and arrests are made at top speed, the people arrested are herded out of doors, and then a new period of waiting begins at the assembly point. The change in the rhythm of time is itself a technique for inducing insecurity. Before the victims are taken away, they await their fate delivered up to the whims and harassment of their guards, torn between despair and hope, between disbelief, apprehension and fear.

The duration and speed of the *razzia* varies, depending on how easily the area can be searched, the number of its inhabitants and the extent of the task. The more summary the command the more intensive is the search, and the sooner it is all over. If the place is to be emptied there is no need to check individuals. Everyone the authorities can lay hands on is taken in. If only a predetermined number is to be arrested each patrol brings as many as it can muster to the assembly point, and once the quota has been met the *razzia* is called off. If the operation aims to find certain individuals, however, and if there are many potential hiding places in the area, then all of them must be thoroughly searched, information must be collected, informers induced to cooperate or confessions extorted. All this delays the course of events and increases the need for coordination and supervision. Arbitrary action, on the other hand, saves time, and violence is a labour-saving device.

There are several reasons why the *razzia* degenerates into physical violence: the destruction of symbolic distances between individuals, the pleasures of arbitrary action, the effectiveness of the work of persecution, and the decentralization of power. Admittedly the raid has been planned in advance, the area divided into sections, the patrols, guards and troops engaged in the manhunt have been allotted their tasks, the timing of the operation has been fixed and the target group identified. But even if the raid is centrally controlled there is considerable scope for freedom of action by those on the spot. General orders relate only to the result, not to the operation itself. There is no supervision of what goes on in individual buildings and rooms. The turmoil of changing situations forces the raiders to be flexible and improvise. The typical features of the *razzia* are not bureaucratic planning but arbitrary, rapid adaptation to circumstances. The raiders act like independent bullies linked by camaraderie rather than hierarchy, and consequently the *razzia* endangers the discipline of the unit. But the fewer the orders which must be borne in mind and the greater the licence for violence, the more successful is the operation as a whole. Violence does not delay the action but accelerates it. Even excessive violence, which can sometimes hamper the course of events, does not cancel out the calculations involved in the work of persecution. It intensifies the commitment of the perpetrators and leaves any survivors in a docile state that paralyses action. It relieves the monotony of the raiders' job and at the same time obeys the temporal law of terrorism: the sudden and unpredictable nature of the attack.

The death march

The death march is a slow form of collective annihilation. The victims are entirely in the hands of their guards and overseers. They are driven from place to place without enough food, clothing or shelter, and often towards no precise destination. In its purest form, the death march is aimless movement. The idea is not for the victims to arrive anywhere but for them to march themselves to death. Sometimes the march ends in a distant wilderness, a swamp, a wasteland of boulders or snow where any survivors are abandoned or killed in a final massacre. But even where there is a planned destination to which victims are transported in cattle trucks or barges, there is no particular need to make the journey quickly. The trains or convoys can wait for days on end en route, while the people crammed into them are given no food or water. Most of the deportees have no idea where they are going anyway.

They are travelling or marching into the unknown. And since the transport lasts days or weeks, time loses all sense of direction. The journey is not from one place to another, and as there is no meaningful arrival in sight time becomes pure duration, interrupted only by outbreaks of panic or moments of random violence.

The death march is one of the vaguest forms of collective violence. It can, of course, be seen in its social and political context. It is a modern technique of deportation and mass annihilation. State and society are to be transformed into a homogeneous community from which all strangers and enemies have been removed. The victims may include ethnic or religious minorities, prisoners of war, outsiders, political opponents, or simply all those deemed superfluous by the regime. To give the operation the appearance of legitimacy, a place where the victims are to work is sometimes announced as their destination. But the march or the transport complies with no functional economic conditions; ultimately it does not matter whether the survivors are still capable of work, or indeed whether any of them at all will reach their destination alive. But why are they not killed at once instead of being transported hundreds if not thousands of kilometres in order to perish on the way? The organs of state terrorism have never been squeamish about using swift techniques of mass murder, so why go to so much trouble when the march is to end in debilitation, exhaustion and death? It is as if the death march were violence running on automatic pilot, beyond the rationale of purpose and compulsion, even beyond the rationale of power and killing.

The death march is a combination of direct and indirect destruction. The phenomena of gradual debilitation are familiar: exhaustion, enfeeblement, demoralization, the destruction of mental and physical vital power. Debilitation is induced by hunger and thirst, the climate, sickness, beating and guns, and finally time itself.

The transport begins with a loading operation. Prisoners are herded into trucks amidst shouting and blows from the butts of guns. The idea is that they are not to be in full possession of their faculties or even capable of envisaging flight. Resistance is immediately broken with the utmost brutality. Although the guards are in the minority, the deportees have no chance to defend themselves. The guards are familiar with the course of events, and their weapons are a deadly threat. The tempo and the atmosphere of haste break the prisoner's will. His mind is on his family, their possessions, a place in the truck where he will be safe from the dogs, the cudgels and the shots.

Once the trucks are crammed full the doors are bolted or nailed up. The gap in the side of the truck is covered with iron bars or barbed wire. People stand wedged together in the dim light, one person's elbow pressed into another's ribs or belly. If anyone is to have both feet on the floor of the truck then his neighbour must raise one leg. Knees soon begin to ache, and people can be heard gasping for breath all around. The way to the toilet bucket in the corner is barred by the sheer mass of bodies, so many prisoners relieve themselves on the spot. There is a danger of suffocating to death in the stinking, cramped space. The prisoners have to endure like this for days on end, tormented by terror and the fear of death. The journey seems endless, all sense of time is lost in the half-light, and desperate weariness takes over the prisoners' bodies. Since no water is distributed they become dehydrated, and their throats and tongues swell. If several happen to collapse at once, dragging others down as they fall, there is panic in the truck and the fallen prisoners are trampled to death. On hot summer days the roof of the truck heats up, and many people collapse in the muggy atmosphere. In cold winter months, bodies freeze to each other and then, if the train reaches its destination, a frozen mass of human bodies standing upright must be broken apart to find any survivors.

Transport by water operates on the same principle of the annihilation of a mass of people forced together. The prisoners either stand close to each other or lie stacked like sardines in alternate rows with their heads or their feet to the wall. Light falls into the hold of the barge only through a narrow ventilation shaft. The bucket of excrement has to be heaved up a steep stairway. Prisoners urinate in glass jars passed from hand to hand. There is nothing to eat but what the stronger prisoners leave from the sparse provisions: mouldy bread, perhaps some salt fish. Drinking water is always in short supply. The hold is swarming with lice, and it is forbidden to go on deck. It can take days or weeks to die in this darkness. The prisoners are left to their own devices, as they are in the bolted cattle trucks; the guards have only to keep an eye on the way up to the deck, and a burst of gunfire will prevent anyone from putting his head out for a breath of air. This way of reducing the prisoners to wretchedness works without any need for the guards to lift a finger. They torture and kill by neglect and deliberate indifference.

In marches on foot the escort is always in view. Guards hover round the column, going up and down it, driving it on with shouts. The speed of the march is an instrument of violence. The faster the pace, the more quickly exhaustion sets in. Even the slightest acceleration costs vital energy. As long as the prisoners' will to resist and sense of solidarity are not yet broken they will try to slow down. But they soon lose this struggle to control the tempo. Anyone falling back to the end of the column, or loitering a few metres behind, is in deadly danger.

The guards will attack the exhausted prisoner, raining blows down on him with their cudgels. A prisoner who loses contact with the column completely has forfeited his life. A guard will stop, the column marches on, no one turns round, a minute later comes the stutter of gunfire and soon afterwards the guard rejoins the column, on his own.

The guards will also kill as an anticipatory measure, to keep the march going at their chosen tempo. They will gradually pick out prisoners whose strength is already beginning to fail from the centre of the column. A brief stumble, a few dragging footsteps, anything of that nature attracting attention marks an individual out for death. He is picked out, stands by the road-side, the others march past, listening for the moment when they will hear shots behind their backs. You are temporarily safe only at the head of the column, so a good many try to get as far forward as possible. In this way the marching column drives itself on. One man will seek to overtake another in order, briefly, to escape death, but by leaving his companion behind he delivers him up to his certain downfall. Together, the prisoners face a deadly dilemma. To escape execution they must exert all their remaining strength, but the more effort they make the sooner it will be over. One by one they lag behind and are shot by the guards.

However, this mortal rivalry does not last long. No one can possibly keep the original tempo going permanently. In any case, speed is only deadly harassment, for the prisoners' strength and will to survive decrease with every kilometre. Apathy spreads through the marching column. Any hope of being spared is gone. The guards can strike at any time. They will beat a man who falls out to relieve the call of nature and stays squatting too long. Nor do they pick only on the exhausted. Anyone can be selected, and often the next victim is chosen at random.

Desperation grows. The prisoners drag themselves along in silence. The bonds of friendship break, and so does the emergency alliance between two people that can keep them going for a while in circumstances of great danger. Now it is every man for himself, and never mind the rest. People forget each other; they lose the power of speech. Every individual is now fighting against himself and his own body. Backs bend, muscles stiffen, the legs still work automatically but then the feet fail. When the march pauses the prisoners lie curled up on the ground and do not move. Many will never rise to their feet again; they have given up.

The march is a form of torture by instalments. The struggle against the body is hopeless. The guards hasten its destruction by violence and by urging the prisoners on. To the last they watch closely as human beings gradually become tottering skeletons, trying in vain to rise, dwindling and dying. They register this mortal struggle with indifference, perhaps with malice, enjoying their own power and sense of triumph. Many marksmen take the chance to practise their skills. Some of the guards enjoy burying an exhausted prisoner alive. The death march is a welcome opportunity for the pleasures of excess, collective torture. Its point is not so much death as the prolongation of suffering, a slow, agonizing way of death. But cruelty needs time in which to develop and intensify. If all the victims were killed at once it would have no chance to develop. No executioner could gloat over the torment of the victims and experiment with any torments he likes. The length and slow duration of the death march, however, give him plenty of time to satisfy the pleasures of torture.

Those particularly skilled in the practice of atrocities, men and women alike, tend to come from the middle ranks of civilian society. A regime of violence never has any problem in finding willing accomplices and executioners. The transformation of ordinary people into mass murderers requires little time and effort, for they learn violence from the exercise of violence itself. The perpetrator wins freedom by claiming it for himself, crossing the border opened up by the orders he has been given. Once granted licence, he can do as he likes. In transit he is removed from the control of his masters. Headquarters is a long way off. Nonetheless, he acts quite naturally as headquarters would wish, not out of blind physical obedience but because violence itself creates the tendencies that it satisfies. The community of violence has its own charms. Arbitrary terror reigns here, rather than ideology and a sense of hierarchy. The solidarity of these accomplices rests not on the principle of helping and sharing but on the shared experience of torturing and killing. It is violence that binds them together, and they free each other from the burden of morality. For the perpetrator, the death march is a rare and exceptional state of absolute freedom.

The time in which terror occurs exhibits several forms. There is the sudden moment that breaks the continuity of linear time. There is the surprise of the assassination and the steady rapidity of the *razzia*. And there is the long, slow duration of torture, the endlessness of atrocity. But while each form of violence has its own form of time, determining its basic structure, the violence itself takes place *in* time. Situations change, and with them their temporal modes. This sometimes happens abruptly. Time changes as violence occurs. The sudden explosion is followed by a moment of horror and then by the long emotional storm of panic. In the *razzia* the area to be searched is first encircled and cut off swiftly, and only then gradually occupied, so that the speed of its seizure gives way to periods of anxious waiting. Deportation begins with the rapid loading of human beings. Once they are shut into trucks or barges the aimlessly long journey begins. The death march sets off in haste until the movement gradually falters, but it is interrupted by the violent tortures inflicted by the guards.

The time of terror is not common to all concerned. What appears to the observer a single form of time is in fact radical antagonism. The social asymmetry of violence is matched by the asymmetry of time. The time occupied by the act is quite different from the time in which it is suffered. The assassin prepares his operation thoroughly, waiting patiently for the moment to come, then strikes with lightning speed and disappears. The victims, on the other hand, are overwhelmed in an instant. Any survivors will take a long time to grasp what has happened. The authorities carrying out a raid hastily encircle the area and then do their work of persecution at a steady pace. The people caught up in the raid, however, are taken unawares and must wait in fear and uncertainty. The guards of the transports relieve the tedium with all kinds of tortures, but their prisoners exist in a lengthy present of anxiety, apathy and death. Terrorism shatters the social aspect of time. The time of terror is antagonistic time. The gulf between the perpetrators and the victims of violence could hardly be deeper, yet the time taken to commit the act and the time taken to endure it condition each other, not in a socially reciprocal sense but as mechanical causality. Sudden violence provokes horror and panic, an assassination engenders anxiety and helplessness. The angry shouting and long duration of a transport drive its victims step by step into a state of agony and timelessness.

Violence destroys any sense of community between its victims. An assassination sends them scattering in panic. Uncertainty and desperation at the assembly point cast them all on their own resources. Violence dissociates and atomizes human beings, forcing them back on their naked physicality. Pain, fear, panic and despair are forms of internal violence that destroy all sense of relationship to the world or distance from it. The destruction of the sense of time is a central effect of acute violence. Its result is complete desubjectivization. The experience of terror is absolutely present, compressing time into a here and now without any horizon, making it a moment outside time. The victims are in no condition to understand what has happened in the light of the past or the future, and thus stand back from it. They can no longer relate to the situation, and so they cannot relate it to themselves or other people. Even before death, terror casts human beings into a time outside the world of society.

III
War

7
Societies of war

The *Daily Mirror* of 5 January 1915 printed a remarkable photograph. It shows British and German soldiers posing for a snapshot. They stand there muffled up in coats and scarves, hands in their pockets. Some still have their uniform belts and cartridge pouches strapped on; one, cigarette in the corner of his mouth, is holding a small rag doll out to the camera. They are unknown soldiers. Their faces all look alike, and only the wearing of a cap or spiked helmet shows which army a man belongs to. The picture was taken during the few days of fraternization in Flanders in the first winter of the war. At Christmas the soldiers met in no-man's-land or visited each other in the trenches. Candles were lit on the defences, sausages and chocolate were thrown over the wire entanglements instead of hand grenades. The men sang carols, did conjuring tricks, exchanged tobacco and military badges. In this barter the Germans showed a particular liking for British marmalade and canned beef, which was not as fatty as the German equivalent. A Scottish rifle battalion managed to trade a couple of its guns for two barrels of German beer. Legends proliferated around this unofficial armistice. There is said to have been a football match, and in one sector a snowball fight took place, although rather a strain was placed on the sporting spirit when a German soldier hid a stone in a snowball and hit a Tommy in the eye with it. After vociferous protests, the culprit apologized.

By definition, fraternizing in wartime is an exception. War is first and foremost a matter of collective killing and being killed. Yet this episode was repeated a year later, if on a smaller scale. In 1916 the Russians were still arranging ceasefires on the Eastern Front at Easter and Christmas. On the 'inactive' sectors of the Western Front in the Vosges mountains, the Belgian mining district and the Argonne area, a state of war coexisted with a ceasefire for months on end. This tacit agreement was contravened only by zealous officers trying to keep their sectors 'active' by deploying units of shock troops or firing mortars by night. Experienced soldiers always prefer periods of inactivity in which the 'live and let live' principle prevails. At Petersburg during the American Civil War, in the Crimea, even at Stalingrad such local agreements were known from time to time. Admittedly, episodes of ceasefire and harmless verbal skirmishing never kept the soldiers from attacking each other hours or days later. Interludes of social exchange by no means cancel out the hostility that governs war.

By the time of the Christmas ceasefire of 1914, losses were already immense: in the first five months of the war the Germans had over 800,000 casualties, including 240 dead; the French had around 300,000 dead and 600,000 wounded or missing; most of the 160,000 professional soldiers of the British Expeditionary Force had been killed. Austria-Hungary had lost 1.2 million soldiers by the end of the year; the Russian army, which had numbered 3.5 million men when it was mobilized in July, was reduced to two million. The shape of the 'primal catastrophe' of the twentieth century was already emerging, although the bloodbaths of Verdun, Arras and Passchendaele were still to come. The twentieth century has been called, for good reasons, the century of the camps, but it could equally well be called the century of war. Mass killing in the violence of warfare marks the epoch just as much as the death of millions through persecution and terrorism. The thirty years of world war in the first half of the century cost the lives of some fifty-five million human beings. It is estimated that another forty million people were victims of warfare in the second half of the century.

In view of this mass slaughter it seems pointless to speak of 'societies of war'. Now that the world has been demythologized, the concept of society is reserved for the living alone. But are there not imaginary societies that exist only in the mind and yet guide human conduct? Nations, communities and institutions are imaginary structures without material substance, yet they have a tangible, real effect. Is not the society of war the great number of dead, disabled, and those who have disappeared without trace? Half of the casualties who fell in the First World War could not be given a funeral. Their bodies were never found or were beyond identification. Shells had torn them to shreds, and they lay buried in the ruins of dugouts, or decomposed in ravaged ground. Monuments to unknown soldiers were the last recognition the living could give to the silent company of the dead. And is not the purpose of war to keep adding to that invisible company? With every day of warfare the mountain of corpses grows higher. As long as a state of war exists the living are anxious to increase the number of their dead enemies. Whatever is claimed to be the purpose of war, the ultimate foundation of enmity lies in the antagonism between the dead and the living. The principle of annihilation is not a modern invention but the principle of war itself. Everyone wants to be a survivor, and consequently to kill as many of the enemy as possible.

Yet the destruction of people and objects is a social process. War gives rise to its own particular forms of society, socialization and social exclusion. Societies of war are marked by pain, misery and death, and are not to be confused with those militarized societies that arm themselves for the next engagement and accord high status to their warriors. Nor have they anything to do with a civilian and national society that has just sent its troops into the field. Societies of war, rather, are those social forms of which war itself consists. They are antagonistic double collectives. The parties are hostile to each other: the combatants on the battlefield, besiegers and besieged, pursuers and fugitives, the occupiers and the occupied. In war, adversaries do not simply confront each other; such figures of speech merely gloss over the situation. Instead, direct mutual hostility permeates all other social forms: power structures as well as the structures of the family, work or the community. Consequently societies of war are dedicated to their own downfall. Death is not the means to a political or economic end, but the purpose of war itself. The most intense desires and fantasies concentrate on the destruction of the enemy. To think of war means to think of society in the aspect of its potential destruction, its point of nullity, the death of society itself.

Military engagement and sieges

War involves more than fighting and death. There are pauses in wartime in which the violence is stilled, there are oases of peace and security, regions where everyday life seems to go on unchanged. Not every war affects the entire population; not every war is total war. Even if the civilian hinterland is regularly bombed, ordinary life still goes on between the air raids. The principle of normality is so indestructible that it withstands the most adverse conditions. No sooner do the sirens sound than the local inhabitants make for the nearest shelter, without haste, without panic, night after night, week after week, month after month – until the hour when the firestorm comes. If the war has reached stalemate then the firing line is strictly segregated from the civilian world. In spite of its extremely heavy losses, therefore, the First World War was curiously limited. In the west, the line of defence ran from the Swiss border to Nieuwpoort in Belgium, but it consisted of a zone of devastation only about ten kilometres wide made up of trenches, muddy pools, heaps of rubble and tree-stumps. Outside the range of the heavy artillery, the landscape remained almost untouched. While hundreds of thousands died in the combat zone itself, the wartime economy of shops, cafés and brothels flourished in the hinterland. Survivors retreated to their tents, encampments and barrack huts to return to the front line after a short period of recovery. The base behind the lines served to multiply the forces of destruction. If the local population was not too heavily burdened by requisitions, it continued with ordinary civilian life and took advantage of its new customers.

The society that most clearly determines the image of war, however, is the society of battle. Its territory is the battlefield. Here enemies encounter one another directly, whether they are state armies, mercenaries, militia or other armed groups. We may justifiably ask where the boundaries of this zone of violence are drawn today, now that front lines disintegrate, long-distance weapons can cross hundreds of kilometres, and area bombing moves the zone of destruction into the middle of civilian society. As everyone knows, the entire globe can now be transformed into a battlefield within a few minutes.

Nonetheless, local battles and skirmishes still take place on land, at sea and in the air. The society of the military engagement differs from all other societies of war in its extreme drama. The front-line trench is a territory different from the civilian air-raid shelter, the tank or helicopter crew is a social group different from the family sheltering in the cellar, the tactical corporate body of warfare is not like a civilian corporation. In the society of battle, death is ever-present. It can snuff out hundreds of human lives within a second. Many battles have decided the fates of entire nations and turned the course of world history in a new direction, but most such battles are episodes recognizing only one victor: death. Whatever the strategic importance of the battle may be, its purpose is always to prepare the field for death. The engagement itself is a social event whose main aim is to decimate the living. The god of war rules undisputed here, that great money-changer who takes human lives and gives back urns of ashes.

But what actually happens in the confusion of battle? The noise is deafening. Shouts and the thunder of the guns batter the eardrums; acrid smoke, jets of earth flung up from the ground and clouds of vapour darken vision. It is hard to make out where the shots are coming from. Though the troops may have marched to the battlefield in good order, everything changes once they come into the firing line. Order, discipline and hierarchy collapse. Connections break, your nearest neighbours are struck down, many men are suddenly left to shift for themselves. The social order shatters; primal groups are torn apart. Under the pressure of such turmoil, the social molecules will split into their elements. Emotions overwhelm the newcomer to warfare: rage and horror as the first men fall, disgust at the sight of charred or mutilated bodies, despair, then excitement and enthusiasm at a successful breakthrough, until hours later an internal apathy sets in, that leaden exhaustion with which all old soldiers are only too familiar.

Emotional and social attitudes change repeatedly during the fighting. Between attack and defence, cohesion and dissociation, the battle gradually dies down. Many encounters admittedly have no decisive outcome, but a victory always means social transformation. It is not just the loss of territory, morale and the physical ability to resist, the loss of men and guns, but a process of social disintegration that strikes the final blow. The enemy is defeated as soon as the members of the tactical body flee in different directions. It becomes impossible for them to come to an agreement and concentrate their forces. Leaders find no one willing to follow them, orders are ignored, survivors make for the wide open spaces, and even attempts to retreat in good order are useless. The extent to which discipline disintegrates among the defeated is in proportion to the triumph of the victors, whose battle order splits into separate mobs taking up the pursuit in the certain knowledge of success, bent solely on death and loot. This social change is feared in state armies, since it threatens discipline and undermines the authority of the officers. Once the danger is over, the tension that had brought the social body together is relaxed. The solidarity, readiness to render aid and comradeship of companions in arms gives way to the community of fellow looters, and rivalry between looters and corpse-robbers.

A siege follows a much less dramatic course. The besieged society is largely cut off from the resources necessary for survival. It consists mainly of civilians, with fighting units offering resistance only on the outposts. Sieges are admittedly less common in the modern history of warfare than in earlier periods, but we may think of Sebastopol and Vicksburg, Liège in 1914, Kabul in 1929 and Madrid in 1936, Tobruk, the 900 days of the siege of Leningrad, Gorazde and Sarajevo. The recent war in Bosnia was notable not only for the terrorism of 'ethnic cleansing', but for the besieging of the larger cities in the area.

Encircled by enemies, the besieged find that all ways of escape are barred. Firing is unpredictable, delivered by howitzers, mortars, or snipers who get graduated bonuses for their quota of hits. Sometimes the gunfire is accurate, sometimes random. The besiegers do not anticipate house-to-house fighting, which would cost them many losses. They want to spread fear and terror rather than to conquer the city. In the Middle Ages, the heyday of siegecraft, it was not uncommon for human excrement or parts of diseased corpses to be catapulted into besieged towns, to contaminate drinking water or spread the plague. Every inhabitant of a place under siege must expect to be struck down anywhere and at any time. The idea of terrorism is to wear the besieged down and finally force them to capitulate. Fear soon has all parts of society in its grip. A state of emergency is the new normality; no one can guess in advance where and when shells will strike. Crossing the street can be deadly dangerous. People scurry along close to the walls of buildings, racing across intersections when the dry crack of a missile is heard. Where are the snipers, where can they be safe, where is the firing line? A curiously superstitious feeling spreads. Anyone about to move from one place to another thinks he knows that a shell will strike the place he is about to leave very soon, perhaps next minute.

However, the oldest weapon in siegecraft is not gunfire but starvation. If no relief arrives, a besieged society is delivered up to want. Hardship dominates everyday life. The infrastructure gradually fails: electricity, buses and trams, the water supply, the sewage system. There are no warm rooms, no electric light, no street lighting, no drinking water, no street cleaning. At first the inhabitants use carts or sledges to transport firewood and take away the dead. Despite the danger, long queues form outside shops. Rumours send people to any stores said to have bread or sugar for sale. Muted agitation spreads among the crowd. Those who arrive early hope they still have a chance, and their fury and disappointment are all the greater when the shop proves to be empty. But the longer the famine goes on, the quieter the streets become. People withdraw into cellars, bunkers and wrecked buildings. Apathy falls over the ruined quarter. The city seems paralysed. Most of the people seen in the street are emaciated and seem irascible and touchy. They move slowly and uncertainly; a number of them have swollen knees. Many faces are dark and bloated, others are a pallid green hue, their eyes wide and lifeless. The sole subject of conversation is food: gluten cakes, the flesh of cats, dogs and rats. The dead lie in doorways. People are often too weak to go any distance. Families send their strongest members out to buy or 'organize' food. As long as one in a family can still walk, the others, who can no longer leave their beds, remain alive. But once the last of them is immobilized the end has come for the whole family.

Although hardship affects everyone, a besieged society is not an egalitarian one. All are not equal in the face of starvation. Thieves and looters are at work, organized gangs run the black market and plunder homes. Neighbours are killed for the sake of any bread or ration cards they may have. There are glaring contrasts in a society under siege, contrasts between life and death. Society is destroyed by impoverishment, dissociation, apathy and the struggle for survival, every man's hand against his neighbour. A process of progressive disintegration sets in, a piecemeal division of social life which will ultimately affect even the core structures of the family.

Often the besiegers on the other side of the walls are not much better off. They have to stay outside the fortifications week after week, they are exposed to direct fire on the glacis, within the encircling ring itself they are threatened by sorties of the besieged and attacks from relief troops coming up. Their own attacks fail in the face of superior defensive power. The casualty rate is high. They are running their heads against a wall of fire, iron and concrete. Bastions and bunkers, hidden fox-holes and communications trenches, mines and camouflaged artillery positions make it almost impossible for them to capture the ring of fortifications. In self-defence, the attackers have to dig themselves in too, working their way gradually closer to the encircling barrier. Siege warfare means first and foremost entrenchment, the digging out of a network of trenches and galleries. Next to starvation and the cannon, the spade is the third most important weapon in siegecraft. Over the centuries, and right up to the trench warfare of the Western Front, the drudgery of constructing defensive positions was part of the daily duty of the European soldiery.

The work of warfare is tedious, laborious and wearing. Whether they are mercenaries or regular soldiers, the besiegers must be fed and supplied. Sieges halt the army's advance and tie up troops urgently needed for the offensive. The further the fortress lies from the centres of its own supplies, the more its inner coherence is endangered. Military discipline can do little to halt the virus of self-disintegration endemic to besieging armies. Death, wounds, epidemics, emaciation, isolation and desertion reduce the fighting forces. The land around is soon plundered, the prospect of loot dwindles, relieving forces do not arrive, supplies fail to reach their destination and disappear somewhere in a camp on the way, rations are reduced, sickness spreads – scurvy; cholera and other infections. The temporary field hospitals are poorly equipped. Patients lie on planks or on the ground where their comrades have laid them down. There are hardly any medicaments, and a shortage of the simplest instruments. The dead lie next to the living, side by side. While the existing infrastructure falls apart in the besieged city, the attackers in the camp outside cannot get hold of even the most essential supplies. Day after day the troops decrease in number, and the dying are taken from the first-aid station to the nearest base on carts, packhorses and mules.

Flight and occupation

A siege forces people to stay where they are; theirs is a stationary society. In flight, however, everyone is on the move. The society of flight changes position with every hour. People are fleeing from the firing zone, the advancing front, air raids, pursuers. A wave of flight can also be set off by terrorist expulsion. From the pursuers' point of view, forcing their victims to flee is an economical method of expelling them; they no longer have to chase every individual fugitive over the border themselves. Unlike deportees, who are under the surveillance of a superior power, fugitives are left to their own devices. Deportees are entirely in the hands of their persecutors, fugitives are not. They may still be attacked by the military, but such attacks can only speed their flight so long as they are not caught.

Flight en masse has its own laws of motion. It is not always easy to make out which way the fugitives are going or where. Fugitives often have no idea where to turn, but simply know they must get away from the danger as fast as possible. Fear of death drives them into mountains, forests, impassable country that promises a deceptive security. The emotional instinct behind flight is matched by the numbers involved. The more people join the company, the greater the danger seems. Even those who have held out longest will finally pack a few essentials when the last of their neighbours leaves. For a while this mass movement has an egalitarian effect. Danger threatens not just individuals but the whole company, and can strike anyone down. Fear spreads to many of the fugitives, and the presence of others gives hope. Someone who falls is helped up, someone whose strength threatens to fail is supported by the others. The movement of so many creates a sense of solidarity beyond individual self-preservation.

But this cohesion does not last. Readiness to help fails as distress increases. The bonds of the village community, close relations and the family hold for longest, but then, inexorably, the law of the stronger prevails. In a brutal act of selection, the society of flight discards anyone who can no longer keep up. Those who fall behind are left to fend for themselves, those who sink to the ground lie there, those standing in the way of other fugitives are pushed aside. The slow are overtaken, the exhausted left behind – one regretful, pitying glance may be cast, and then the column marching on feels only indifference for its lost companions. It passes places of terror: smouldering ruins, the mutilated bodies of horses, a cart shot to pieces, searched baggage scattered around, the groaning of an injured man. The survivors drag themselves on, their pace perceptibly slower now. The sight of these terrors has the insidious effect of destroying hope. In the end it is more or less every man for himself in flight. The fugitive stares straight ahead, not even glancing to one side again.

Flight is successful if the fugitives end up somewhere that offers protection from enemy attacks. They are given temporary accommodation, makeshift huts are knocked together, tents quickly put up. But help is not always waiting on the other side of the barrier. Quite often the fugitives are driven back, straight into the mouths of their pursuers' guns. Or the exhausted people are allowed to rest for a while before being shut up in a camp and left to themselves. Survivors will look for relatives among the thousands of others there, or join the group of young men getting hold of shoes and provisions in return for various services rendered. The society of flight turns into a refugee camp, a social interim measure that often becomes a permanent institution, the source of new kinds of inequality, power and vengefulness. At first the foreign refugees hardly come into contact with the local people at all, but form a social group on the outskirts of society. Plans for going back home to drive the enemy out of the occupied territory begin to be drawn up in the camp.

Those who stay behind in their native land after defeat must come to terms with the foreign conquerors and their occupying regime. Town and country alike are taken over by the enemy, the official fighting forces have surrendered and been disarmed, imprisoned or killed. Now the survivors must submit to the victors. Yet occupation does not begin only after the official surrender or signing of an armistice. Even as the victors are advancing, an occupied society comes into being behind the lines. In the unauthorized warfare of marauders there is no distinction anyway between war and peace, between a combat area and civilian society. The people of the country itself are sucking it dry, going on raiding expeditions, terrorizing their fellow inhabitants. The borders between the occupied zone and an operational area, between irregular and regulated occupation are blurred when no front line can be made out any more, and the map resembles a patchwork of small districts with a different warlord laying claim to each.

The aims of the occupying power are often contradictory.

The measures they take appear unpredictable and arbitrary to the indigenous people. Several groups compete for new authority in the power vacuum. The soldiers who have just escaped the firing line with their lives are chiefly intent on sexual conquests, jewels, money and food. The civilians who follow them are more interested in the exploitation of the country's mineral wealth and labour force. State representatives officially annex the area, set up a new administration and try to found a new order. Intellectuals of the occupying power are intent on cultural hegemony, and its thugs comb the area carrying out death sentences on the spot. A ceasefire does not mean that the violence is over. If a campaign is conducted as a war of annihilation, the end of the fighting means the beginning of terrorist persecution, the hunting down of slaves and the 'superfluous', the elimination of members of the occupied society. The 1937 massacre in Nanking, in which over 100,000 people are thought to have died, began only after the Japanese had conquered the city. The annihilation of the Polish intelligentsia and the genocide of the Jews followed the defeat of Poland and the occupation of Europe by the German Wehrmacht.

Occupation is an illegitimate form of power. The old institutions are done away with: abolished, replaced, or converted into auxiliary organizations. The new regime relies on its bayonets at first, while there is still no agreement or consensus of opinion. Hostility cannot be removed overnight. The defeated have not yet accepted their fate, are looking for scapegoats in their own ranks and refusing to cooperate. But sooner or later this illegitimate power must become a government. The regime can employ many proven means of shoring itself up – not just threats and arbitrary violence, but also draconian punishments, reprieves and privileges for loyal collaborators, the exclusion and arrest of the recalcitrant, the setting up of camps, the founding of intermediary organizations and administrations, re-education, brainwashing and political propaganda. Admittedly the occupying power gets long-term obedience only when the defeated adopt at least an ambivalent stance somewhere between anxiety and collaboration, between seeing where their advantage lies and resignation to their fate. This attitude on the part of the conquered is expressed in a broad spectrum of conduct, ranging from withdrawal into private life, through opportunistic adaptation and humble collaboration, to passive or active resistance to the occupying power.

The occupying power itself reshapes society and the distribution of wealth. A black economy run by both local and foreign war profiteers often develops. Those who have good contacts with the occupying power can get hold of coveted goods, concessions, passes and means of transport to supply the black market. Considerable profits are made in this kind of trade, although only the occupiers and their accomplices have the large sums of money necessary to pay high prices. At first, management is the business of professionals in the occupying forces or private profiteers in their employment, while the workers are often forcibly recruited or hired for very low wages. Production is intended to supply the victorious power rather than the society of the conquered; loot, after all, has been a prominent war aim since time immemorial, and the labour force may be regarded as loot, along with reparation payments and the removal of everything not actually screwed down. In the new system of exploitation and redistribution, rapid rise and fall is the accepted rule. All property is confiscated, one elite takes the place of another, new proprietors are appointed by decree.

However, the occupying power cannot rely solely on its own personnel for ever. It needs indigenous assistants, interpreters and informers, police and civil servants, foremen and company directors. But reliable forces are hard to come by, since at first few are willing to throw in their lot with the victorious power. Only when they can no longer decline the advantages on offer do the local population take service with the foreigners, for they must fear being despised and ignored by their own compatriots, even being harassed or lynched in some vengeful nocturnal operation. The collaborator is a genuine product of the occupied society. The dilemma of the conquered is concentrated in him. He moves in a no-man's-land between privilege and betrayal, old loyalties and new adaptations. His social existence is extremely precarious. If the occupying forces reject him he will be delivered up to the mercies of his fellow countrymen, and if the occupiers are driven out again he will be the target of popular fury. If he is to survive he must either leave with the occupiers or change his identity and keep quiet about his reprehensible activities for years to come. Even if the victors stay in the country permanently, the fact that he made common cause with them at an early stage will always be held against him. Sooner or later, admittedly, people always fall in with the dictates of those in power. They follow the person they must fear, partake of his ideas and value the ordered society he guarantees. But conformism is always a question of timing. The early collaborator is never forgiven for going straight over to the enemy. An aura of duplicity clings to him, of treachery to the fatherland. He allied himself to the enemy even while the war was still in progress and all hope was not yet gone, just to get some contemptible advantage. He was observed in the company of enemies when most people were still avoiding such contacts, he was seen doing mysterious deals, conveying information, distributing loot. In the end the collaborator fares no better than any other traitor. His patrons no longer need him, and his countrymen hate him for the misdeeds they dared not do themselves.

Occupation, finally, also changes the system of the distribution of information. Public discussion withdraws into the background. News and rumours are circulated in doorways and backyards, not in the marketplace. The permitted media are censored anyway, and report nothing about the war except what the occupying regime likes. Subliminal fear runs through occupied society, fear of the next *razzia*, the unknown informers in the neighbourhood, in the block of flats, in the family. Those who have good reason to fear persecution stay in hiding. Suspicion contaminates social relations, and in the end power affects human relationships too. The persecuted can live only by covering up their identity – by telling the lies usual in times of war.

The societies of war are social forms *sui generis*, a fact that is frequently overlooked, since people like to cling to the illusion that economic and democratic developments can guarantee peace. It has always been historically short-sighted to link the concept of society to the modern nation state and its internal policies of pacification. But peace and war are the hard facts of history, involving the life, survival and suffering of human beings rather than matters of significance, symbolism and culture. War is organized destruction and killing, and it also brings infinite misery on the battlefield, in flight, and in besieged and occupied zones. The society of war is defined by deadly enmity. Thousands, hundreds of thousands, millions lose their health or their lives in war. The violence of war eradicates whole groups, collectives, peoples. The number of dead is so great that many are left to rot where they lie, which is why the period after a war begins with the burial of the dead, for whom fraternity is most readily felt. Those Christmases in Flanders were not spent solely in exchanging presents and staging sporting events: here and there British and German soldiers joined together to bury the dead in the no-man's-land between the trenches, while clergymen read the Song of Lamentation, first in English and then in German.

8

The violence of war

Shoulder to shoulder, the young soldiers dragged themselves through no-man's-land. Bayonets fixed, packs weighing half a hundredweight on their backs, they leaned slightly forward as they marched on, in defiance of the onslaught of heavy firing. Immediately after they left the shelter of the trench, their certainty of victory had changed to numb indifference. They trudged forwards unmoved, without any cover, unable to see where they were going. The nearby stuttering of the guns was almost more than the ear could take in. Their ranks thinned out at every step as comrades fell to left and right, mown down by bursts of machine-gun fire. Wounded men crawled into the craters, wrapped themselves in their blankets and died. The German defenders watched this show of brave and pointless sacrifice in amazement. Many of them must have been so nauseated by the bloodbath that they held their fire, allowing the more lightly wounded men to crawl back to their positions.

The first hour of the Battle of the Somme is a primal scene of modern warfare. Of the 100,000 British who set out into no-man's-land on that day in 1916, 20,000 never returned, and 40,000 were brought back wounded. Whole battalions disappeared without trace in the shambles. The losses were the highest in British war history. The Germans suffered only one tenth of British casualties that day: 6,000 men dead, missing and wounded. After several weeks, however, the losses were level again. The Somme campaign cost the Germans around 650,000 dead and wounded, while the estimated losses of the British were around 420,000 men and of the French 194,000 men.

Not for nothing is the First World War known in Europe to this day as the 'Great War'. Out of the armies involved, every major battle killed numbers amounting to the population of a large city. At Verdun, around 420,000 soldiers had been killed and 800,000 wounded by the end of the war. At Gallipoli the Allies lost 265,000 men, including many Australians. The victorious Turks did not even take the trouble to count their dead. The eleventh and penultimate round of engagements in the Isonzo valley cost the Italians 100,000 men. At the end of the war Germany mourned two million dead, France and Russia 1.7 million each, the Austro-Hungarian Empire 1.5 million and the British Empire around a million.

No violence is as devastating as the violence of war. It leaves behind millions of dead, mutilated and disfigured. War has been one of the most popular activities ever known in the history of *Homo sapiens.* Obviously the human species likes war. Many will flock to the sound of the trumpets, whether out of a spirit of adventure or an urge for freedom, a thirst for blood, inordinate ambition or a sense of duty. Mass slaughter in war cannot be blamed on a few military commanders, any more than the evils of a dictatorship can all be blamed on the tyrant alone. Just as terrorism finds willing accomplices, city dwellers and countrymen alike readily answer the summons to war. Without the eagerness of its soldiers, an army would be only an empty shell; without their cooperation discipline could not be maintained; without a passion for killing, and without the courage of men ready to sacrifice their own lives, no war would last much longer than a few days. But wartime is the only occasion when soldiers are required to survive by killing with their own hands every day.

From the high standpoint of politics, war is only a strategic means of imposing the politicians' own will on the enemy. Once set in motion, however, war rapidly liberates itself from political or ideological ends. It creates the conditions for its own continuation. Even when the situation has long been hopeless and losses are greater than anyone estimated, wars are sometimes fought to the very last. Violence becomes an end in itself, generating the will to kill of its own accord. War creates the warrior and the society from which he comes. If we leave aside all explanations and interpretations, one simple fact emerges: war is waged for the sake of war.

But where does the dogged fighting spirit come from, the steadfast tenacity, the suicidal readiness for sacrifice? The First World War is a striking example of the way a war follows its own course even when scarcely any of the participants really know why or for what they are fighting. The men could hardly expect to take valuable loot, prisoners were worth nothing, the combatants were fighting neither for a religion nor for their native lands, nor even to protect their own families. Honour, a word much bandied about at first, soon sank in the mud. No infantryman in the front line could for very long have believed the platitudes about saving culture or civilization, democracy, the nation, the Emperor or the Tsar. So why did the soldiers leave the shelter of the trenches, to drag themselves over no-man's-land before the mouths of the enemy guns? Was it the coercion of the policy of slaughter, was it fatalism, self-denial, loyalty, courage, blind confidence, high spirits? Although the jubilation of the first weeks, which mainly affected young men of the middle classes in big cities, soon died down at the front, the survivors still held out. And the newcomers recruited to fill the gaps in the regiments clambered over the defensive earthworks as sure of victory as their predecessors.

It is a rationalist error to conclude that morale will necessarily be lowered as the number of casualties rises. The calculation of profit and loss may occupy the minds of the bookkeepers on the general staff, but war is always a huge waste of energy, life, knowledge and the spirit of sacrifice. The greater the suffering and destruction, the firmer is the will to fight. There is a sense that none of the many dead should have fallen in vain, and since the countless sacrifices must not have been made for nothing the living must fight on. Every new death validates the sacrifice of those who fell before. And every victim who has just fallen shows that the ultimate reason for war is death itself.

The spirit of sacrifice is bolstered by solidarity between comrades, but most of all by the quality, or rather the incapacity, that human beings have always required for their follies: pure ignorance. The recruits thrown into the firing line had not the faintest idea what awaited them. They stormed their way straight to their death. More new recruits would replace them in the next offensive, marching equally unsuspectingly into the milling turmoil of bloodshed. Veterans who had already come through several battles gambled on surviving the next attack too. Survival nourishes the illusion of immortality, which resists even the most direct challenge. Old soldiers firmly believe that they will never die. Matters approached mutiny, revolution, and flight en masse only when there was a widespread sense among the men that it was 'their turn next'. Once your own death is not just accidental but highly probable the spirit of sacrifice turns to panic. The armies disengaged when the number of dead was roughly the same as the number of soldiers still fighting at the front.

The disaster of the First World War destroys the illusion of war as a duel between equals, a military engagement joined for the sake of victory and honour. The idea of a contest has always lured men to arms. This deadly serious game with its uncertain outcome casts a spell over the fighting man. He seeks danger because it promises him an awareness of life that is absent from everyday existence, a sense of freedom and adventure, the kick to be got from fighting, the intoxication of battle in which he forgets himself: all these are experiences in the sport of war which seem to lift the burden of everyday reality.

However, the reality of the Great War had little to do with any such contest. Within seconds, the sportsmanship of British officers who entered no-man's-land carrying only a little baton proved to be deadly folly. At first the French still thought they could go to war clad in brass helmets, bright red trousers, breastplates or, in the case of the Armée d'Afrique, sky-blue uniforms. The shiny cooking pans they carried on their pyramidal packs made an excellent target in sunlight. At the first Battle of Ypres, German volunteers discovered that patriotic enthusiasm was useless in the face of rapid fire. The 'massacre of the children at Langemarck' which later provided material for heroic tales of patriotic songs under fire was mere tactical idiocy. The Germans in this encounter, who included students and secondary schoolboys with no military experience, moved forward in close formation and were mown down wholesale by the guns of professional British soldiers.

It is misleading to see the concept of violence in war as comparable to single combat. War is not a duel between collective entities. What may look from outside like a contest between nations, states or bands of mercenaries often strikes those on the spot as a situation in which they are completely ineffectual. Most soldiers on the modern battlefield have to stand and be shot at without ever seeing the enemy face to face, and battlefields were never just the terrain of collective contest, they were also scenes of slaughter. The model of the *agon*, the sporting contest of classical times, has a threefold structure. Competitors aim to win a trophy which is bestowed on the victor by a third party. War, however, knows no umpire. The trophy of war is your enemy's head. The dogfight in the air between fighter pilots may still resemble a personal duel of honour between 'knights of the air', the duel of fire between two enemy batteries is still reminiscent of single combat, if at long-distance range, but a constant barrage from a distance of several kilometres away is a one-sided attack on defenceless infantry. Similarly, an assault by a broad front line that is mown down from a few machine-gun positions has nothing to do with traditional battle but leads straight to a massacre.

War is the organized exercise of collective violence between large social groups, whether they are regular national armies, hordes, bands, militia, irregulars or civil defence units. Violence is practised by both sides, not just occasionally but with a certain regularity. Nonetheless, a considerable number of one-sided situations arise in the course of a war. For it is the aim of war to weaken the enemy, sap his will and destroy him. Even if the fighting forces are relatively evenly balanced at first, both parties are intent on getting the upper hand and winning the victory. They aim to turn a battle involving many casualties into a massacre which will force the other side to surrender, and do it as soon as possible.

The concept of violence in war, therefore, embraces a large number of different operations which cannot be reduced to each others' terms. The violence of war can be mutual, like all forms of direct battle. But it can also be unilateral, as in long-distance bombardment, massacres or devastation. Direct attacks, assassinations or lengthy sieges, military engagements and battles, 'the 'cleansing' of positions and pursuits, bombing by land or air, rape and pillage – all these are manifestations of the violence of war.

An attack on the senses

From a distance it looks like a firework display: sparkling stars, red pencils of rays, trees made of lights, grey plumes of smoke rising from the ground and slowly dispersing, little clouds of white, yellow or black in the sky, grey-green or coppery red mushrooms of smoke, globes of black dust. Every kind of artillery fire has its own shape and colour. The dense, yellowish-green cotton-wool tangle comes from a chlorine gas grenade.

Where the shots come down the noise is ear-splitting: a thunderstorm of dull explosions, with screeching and whistling, a constant bawling and howling, the chirping of flying detonators, the sharp hiss of fragments, exploding shrapnel, the sound of mines flying over. Aerial torpedoes bury themselves in the ground. When they explode the walls of the dugouts shake. Noise assails the eardrums on all sides, as if the missiles were cruising out of control in their trajectories. The untrained ear cannot pick out the origin and cause of individual hits. The ground booms and shakes underfoot, fountains of soil shoot up, the pressure wave flings human bodies against the trench wall, the lungs cannot get enough air. An exploding grenade overwhelms all the senses at once. At the moment of detonation there is a crashing in the ears, lightning strikes the eyes, gunpowder gases penetrate the nose. The soldier must use his presence of mind to fling himself in the mud, his mouth full of filth. Will the next shot land further forward or further back, further to the right or to the left?

The positions are under a barrage of constant fire for days on end. The wave of firing returns again and again, its endless ebb and flow shattering the nerves. Shortly before the attack the noise rises to a bellowing that turns to a wild roar outside the range of human hearing. Men crouch in the shelter of bunkers, galleries or dugouts as if in a trap. There are several metres of earth and layers of tree-trunks or slabs of concrete over their heads. At every hit the ground trembles and soil trickles down from the ceiling. What is it like to suffocate in earth, your body immobilized by the weight so that you cannot move your arms or legs, with pressure on your ribcage, every breath sucking dirt into your mouth and nostrils, feeling an instinctive wish to retch, the heat of mortal fear? A clod of earth comes loose from the wall and falls to the ground with a thud. The men have withdrawn from the annihilating power of the missiles into underground fortresses, where they wait for the next hit. The air smells of saltpetre, sweat and chlorine. A direct hit could make the shelter fall in and bury the whole group alive. A detonation blows out the candles, there is screaming, torchlight passes over the distorted faces, the hunted, popping, glazed eyes. One man sits rigid in a corner, alternately clenching and opening his fists; his teeth can be heard chattering. He suddenly jumps up, trying to get outside. When three comrades haul him back he strikes out, panic lending him furious power, and when they let go of him he knocks his head rhythmically against the prop holding up the roof, as if to numb his brain so that he need not hear or feel any more.

Such an assault disproves many assumptions about the activity of the human senses. It is true that the soldiers soon learned to recognize the trajectory of different kinds of missiles by the sound they made. Anyone who had been through this baptism by fire quickly developed a good ear for danger and knew how the grenades would fall and how to protect himself. With time, men acquired an animal physical feeling for the terrain, for movement behind cover, for passing dangerous firebreaks and keeping close to the ground. But they had to learn these lessons in surroundings where any mistake had fatal consequences.

Nonetheless, the overwhelming of the senses in war is an event *sui generis.* It forces a man into complete passivity. Even before he suffers any physical injury he is subjected to an attack on his organs that no protective filter can withstand. You cannot close your ears. The vulnerability of the body becomes a trial. Events break through all anti-irritant measures, directly penetrating the nerves and the brain. There is no escape. The assault destroys your ability to distance yourself from the situation, often preventing you from applying your usual patterns of perception at all. Extreme pressure on the senses shrinks awareness, extinguishing the horizon. War occupies the senses, takes over human limbs, disrupting perception and motor control. The shattering sounds outside quiver through your body, as if your skin were getting progressively thinner and would tear when the roaring within you explodes.

The men's own trenches and dugouts were familiar terrain, even under fire. As troglodytes, they knew the distances inside them, the bends, corridors, barriers, islands of resistance, foxholes. Even when the barrage levelled defences and trenches and disintegrated the front line, the cratered landscape was still your own area. It was different when you were attacking in no man's land, with no cover from the barrage of enemy bombardment blocking your way ahead. You could fling yourself into a crater to escape bullets but not grenades. Once you had climbed out of the trench on an assault ladder, if you were not instantly mown down you suddenly found yourself in the open, exposed to fire. You stood there unprotected, staggering through the mud from crater to crater. Rain and decay had made these craters into sticky latrines, and now many men noticed the sweetish stench for the first time. They sank in mud to their ankles, one of them getting stuck now and then, sinking deeper and deeper until he disappeared from sight.

Suddenly the barrage would open. Clouds of smoke obscured vision, soldiers tried to cling to one another, craters opened up, hot iron hissed into the water, a hail of splinters swept past the men's heads, clods of earth rained down, a sharp sensation pierced the temples, shrapnel burned brightly, there was a red and yellow wall of flame, a droning in the ears, eyes streamed, it was boiling hot, fire belched from the mouth of a machine gun. Nothing could be made out in front of the wall of smoke, soil, iron and flame from which the bullets and grenades were coming. The attackers had to get through this deadly wall if they were ever to get near the enemy positions.

The organism reacts to the overloading of the senses by anaesthetizing itself. The anxious tension of waiting for the attack turns to a dull, hypnotic condition. As soon as the last protective shield in front of death is broken down, the senses and the mind freeze. Consciousness shrinks to a single idea: on, forward! Almost mechanically the attackers trudged on. For minutes on end they did not know where they were or what they were actually doing. It was not the cheerful indifference of a man who has finished with everything that made the attackers go on, or a nervous feverishness in the face of danger. In the utmost need, blind reflexes guide your movement, and this personality change turning men into physical machines was some protection against panic attacks. But it exposed the body to deadly fire. The guiding function of the eye was switched off, and so was the body's control over its motor impulses. Only in front of the enemy trenches did this state of mind swing round once again to the fury of trench warfare.

The assault

Only a handful of men reach the wire entanglement in front of the enemy trenches. It is still intact in many places. They try to get around it, or wait in a crater for reinforcements. They are already within throwing distance of the breastwork. But even fewer arrive with the second and third wave of attackers. The enemy's defensive fire has torn great holes in their line. When the whistle gives the signal to retreat the survivors stumble back, exhausted. Many lose their sense of direction and run along the breadth of no man's land. Severely wounded men lie where they have dropped, huddled in craters. Many mass assaults ended in failure like this.

The reason for such recurrent catastrophes was not just the grim resistance of the defenders, who always had the advantage in the siege warfare of the Western Front, despite poison gas, tanks and accurate firing. The defenders knew the labyrinthine tangle of their own trench system and kept in touch with their artillery, whereas the attackers regularly lost contact with their own batteries. And defeat or victory was decided not only by the inequality of industrial capacity in the warring states but also by a tactical dilemma. Battles were fought to firing plans made in advance, so that you could protect your own infantry with artillery fire. The rigid time scheme allowed no last-minute changes, and there were no channels of communication for quick reaction to difficulties and unforeseen events. The fixed plan of battle thus led straight to disaster, since a measure intended to protect the fighting forces in fact increased losses.

Only hours later did the divisional staff know what had happened to the individual regiments. The staff officers at command headquarters could unleash chaos but not control its course.

Industrialization of the violence of war in the form of the 'battle of *matériel*' is generally regarded as the most important innovation of the First World War. Repeating rifles, machine guns and barrel recoil artillery hugely increased the firing rate, and turned killing into a regular, mechanized activity. This might seem to bear out the widespread notion that there is hardly any direct combat in modern warfare. It is true that the duel of old fought with sword or bayonet belongs in the age of the guns, tanks and mortars of the past. Yet to this day the old observation, based on much experience, that a terrain will be taken only when the conqueror actually sets foot on it is still true. Stalingrad was a battle between infantry troops, an unrelenting conflict fought street by street, building by building, floor by floor. Dien Bien Phu, Ia Drang, Goose Green and Grozny were all fought out on the ground. Even if the range of the weapons thrown and fired in battle has been extended, and enemies only rarely clash in person, face to face, the old laws of direct violence are still in force. To this day man-to-man fighting is the climax of a skirmish, even if the enemy is anonymous and invisible behind cover or armour-plating. It is enough to know that he is there and represents mortal danger.

After days of constant barrage, and the impotence of existence in no-man's-land, an attack on the enemy trenches would suddenly liberate unsuspected fury. Many men had fallen, many of the survivors were exhausted. But now it was the attackers' turn. Trench warfare was the decisive and most dangerous element in attack. Grenades and machine-gun fire tended to strike indiscriminately and at random. In direct confrontation, however, the individual was clearly visible as a target, so that everything depended on making use of this moment of crisis and clearing the enemy terrain as quickly as possible.

The taking of the trench is like an assault. The attackers storm the passages with sharpened spades, carbines and hand grenades. Everything happens very fast. As the men run past, gas bombs and concentrated dynamite charges fly into the dugouts. The attackers slide over slippery boards, stumble over weapons, pieces of tent and cooking utensils that have been cast aside. A foot treads, reluctantly, on the soft, yielding bodies of the dead. A circle of dead enemies lies at the entrance to a dugout. In view of the deadly uncertainty of the situation, senses are sharpened to the utmost. The mind is fully concentrated. Perception is entirely directed at the acute danger, the moment of the next leap forward, evasion, throwing or firing.

The labyrinth of parallels and covered passages was far from easy to survey. To limit the effect of gunfire, the passages and battle trenches were laid out in zigzag lines, so that the enemies could get very close behind the lateral shoulder defences, but without seeing each other. Despite the very short distance, duelling with hand grenades was completely anonymous. The grenades to be thrown were handed forward from man to man until they reached the leader of the troop. The advantage went to whichever side could look up from below, since only against the paler background of the sky did the iron globes stand out sharply enough for their targets to avoid them in time. If a man raised his head above the cover of a trench he risked being shot, and those who just stared at the mud wall did not notice the grenades being silently rolled along the covering overhead. Only energetic attack could resolve the deadlock and get the hesitant assault going again. Particularly reckless or brave men chose to go up above the covering of the trench. The more cautious dodged round its zigzag course immediately after throwing a hand grenade, so as to be in place directly after the explosion.

The body's reactions must be automatic if a man is to be fully on the alert. The mechanical response to an assault is drilled into the soldier's flesh and blood. Since the body acts as if of itself, the eye and ear are free to scent danger. Smoking out the galleries, throwing and jumping aside were actions carried out almost of themselves, but with the utmost concentration. That storm of movement transformed the attacker again. He now existed entirely in action, in a kind of mechanical excess of violence. Consequently he knew no morality or mercy, but fired at everything that moved. Prisoners were taken only after the assault, if at all. No conventions are observed in the heat of battle. Surrender and the taking of prisoners call for voluntary intervention in the automatic course of the action, a change in the situation and in the soldier's state of mind.

The assault inspires the attackers. They overcome resistance and give themselves free scope. The fury of destruction rises with the number of the dead and the extent of the terrain taken. But the moment of victory is a very dangerous one. In that instant of survival, relief and triumph the attacker is required to transform himself immediately into a defender. At the very climax of the action he must look round, make out the direction of the counter-attack, repair the covers of his trenches and establish good firing positions. The victors must reorganize themselves, and they also hear of comrades and friends killed or wounded. The reality of battle returns, drowning the euphoria of survival in renewed fear of death.

Wounds

During the attack, scarcely anyone would have noticed how the ranks were thinning out. Comrades were falling but the assault went on, leaving dead and wounded behind. As long as the battle lasted, no one knew who was still alive. War marches relentlessly over its victims, for casualties are of no military value anyway. Only the fit are any use in warfare, which is why, over the centuries, so little attention has been paid to the wounded. It is an old law of warfare to let fallen men lie. Only since the numbers involved have decreased and the prospect of aid has become indispensable to the fighting man's morale have modern armies invested in medical care. Yet even today it can take hours to die on the battlefield. Although first aid and the transport of the wounded are incomparably better organized than in the past, even now soldiers die at the scene of the military engagement and no one pays any attention to them. It was the same with many of the wounded in the First World War, men who took refuge in grenade craters only to die alone there in agony, amidst the mud and blood.

The dead were everywhere in trench warfare. Clouds of flies settled on the corpses, huge rats nourished on human flesh populated the trenches. The stench of decomposition lay over the front. Pieces of tent fabric covered severed body parts in the mud of the trench walls. There were parts of maggot-ridden corpses in the sandbags of the breastwork defences, accidentally added to the sand by labour units building the entrenchments. Grenade explosions churned the soil and kept bringing up severed legs, skulls and bits of bones. The advance across no man's land was lined with remains of the dead from earlier attacks, and a man who jumped into the cover of a fresh crater might land next to a torso that had just been ploughed up. Dozens of mouldering corpses could lie hidden in a very small space underground and be brought back to the light of day by a direct hit. Last month's dead still lay in front of the defenders' own positions, their eye sockets empty, their brownish-black skulls laid back, their legs curiously distorted.

Monotonous as the desolation of everyday life in the trenches was, war is unusually inventive in devising ways of death. Death in modern warfare is not like death on the battlefields of history. Wounds made by slashing, stabbing weapons were different from the injuries inflicted by mines, poison gas or rifle grenades. In earlier wars more people died of epidemic disease, starvation and privations than as a result of direct violence; it was only with the increased technological potential of destructive force that weapons became deadlier than the depredations of nature. Even during the American Civil War the number who died of disease and hardship was twice the number of those who fell in battle. Once again the First World War marks a historic watershed: most of its losses were through deliberate killing by the human hand.

Explosives caused terrible wounds. Shrapnel was sharp as razor blades, soon lost velocity but kept together as it whirled through the air and could thus make several deep wounds at once. Grenade splinters were irregularly formed and could rip off whole limbs, cut faces to shreds or behead a man. If parts of clothing or other foreign bodies were forced into bleeding tissue, infection was inevitable. The blast alone could cause embolisms by putting too much pressure on the body, or might tear apart the lungs or coeliac artery so that the victim died of internal bleeding invisible on the surface. A direct hit could obliterate a man without trace in the fraction of a second, his body torn so violently apart by the explosion that nothing was left of him. The cries for help of men mutilated by mines were particularly distressing for their comrades. Shoes, clothes and flesh were torn from an injured man's bones, and there was nothing his friends could do. The extreme heat of the detonations caused severe burns, first on the lips, mouth and jaws, then on the hands and arms, finally on all limbs and the parts of the body singed through the man's burning clothes.

Bullets caused wounds of a different kind. When a projectile enters the flesh at high velocity it sends a kind of shock wave through the muscular tissue and organs within fractions of a second. A hollow space forms in the body, a relative vacuum that sucks in bacteria and dirty fibres from the victim's clothing. The skin around the wound is usually polluted. As soon as the injury is inflicted the muscle fibres begin dying off, increasing the danger of infection yet further. In the best-case scenario, the cone-shaped bullet passes cleanly through the body, but if it meets bone it will ricochet. Splinters of bone, acting like secondary shots, destroy more tissue. If the brain, heart or a major artery suffers a direct hit, death is instant. Shot wounds in the lungs or stomach, on the other hand, often lead to a long death agony. Wounds in the lower body cause internal bleeding and inflammation of the peritoneum unless the victim is treated at once. Stomach wounds can always be recognized by the painful distortion of the victim's body. If the lungs are hit a suction wound is created, and unless the entry and exit holes are sealed at once the victim will take more air into the chest cavity with every breath, thus leaving the lungs less room to expand. Panic-stricken at the prospect of suffocating to death, he begins to pant, making matters even worse. With his breath coming so short, he cannot calm down enough to hold his wounds together with his own hands.

The wounded die of rapid blood loss, shock and infection. When the missile strikes the victim feels a dull, often painless blow in his body. His legs bend, his muscles cramp, and then comes the first wave of pain, an animal cry when the injured man sees his wound, and his legs begin to shake and thud on the ground. He tries to grasp at the place from which blood is pouring, he feels dizzy, there is a rapid drumming in his ears, his throat constricts, sweat breaks out on his grey skin. His panic brings on more and more waves of pain until he suddenly collapses, unconscious.

The destructive power of war does not stop short at killing the human body, it also dismantles and disfigures it. The bereaved were often assured that the dead man had not suffered for long and his face was unharmed. Obviously it is comforting to think that a man killed in war looks like a dead civilian – falling asleep gently, features peaceful, with at most a tiny hole in the region of the heart. None of that was true. Most victims were mutilated: noses torn off, jaws shot away, the skull crushed to show the pale mass of the brain seeping out. The human body could be hit anywhere: in the stomach or the spine, the kidneys, the pelvis, the throat. Wounded men who survived the war populated post-war society with cripples. Many had lost both legs, others had an arm amputated. Marks on the body under its clothing were invisible, but many faces were disfigured by the scars of burns, holes in the flesh, corroded foreheads, empty eye sockets. For a while the stigmata of the violence of war were a common sight in the streets. Then they gradually disappeared, until a new generation set about acquainting itself with the violence of warfare again.

9

Unauthorized warfare

We have come to the end of these long historical narratives of world war, and now there are only two short stories in circulation. One is entitled 'Globalization' and describes the way in which the financial centres of the world are converging, while pictures and news race through the air and the Sony and Coca-Cola culture takes over the human mind. The other story tells a tale of chaos and anarchy, wars of attrition, drought and malaria, starvation and overpopulation. The first story is acted out in London, Tokyo, Singapore and Budapest; the second in Grozny, Vukovar, Freetown, Jolo. Until recently there was little connection between the two. The security of the rich lands of the north hardly seemed threatened by the decline of the peripheral countries. Strategic interest in these poverty-stricken regions had evaporated with the end of the Cold War. All the talk of the 'global village' and the 'unity of international society' merely concealed the rift running through the globe itself. Today, however, violence has established new links between the hemispheres. In the global terrorist war New York and Kabul, Washington, Islamabad and Kandahar are within close range of each other. Activists from the periphery threaten the inhabitants of the Old World, the bombers of the greatest power in the world drive the inhabitants of Afghan cities from their dwellings, while their search commandos comb through the mountainous desert.

For a decade diplomats, experts and trade representatives flew round the globe, spending the night in luxury hotels and believing that the whole world spoke English and had nothing to do but exchange news, goods or ideals. They saw everything in the global perspective, that is to say looking down from above. If they had ever left their well-shielded hotel rooms they would soon have come up against the limits of civil order. Nothing has changed there. War is endemic in many regions where hardship and cruelty reign instead of law and the state. Men with a reckless look lounge on street corners: renegade soldiers down on their luck, militiamen, mercenaries, adolescents. These champions of unauthorized warfare are not intent on gaining power in the state, moving the boundaries of the nation or defending a political or ethnic identity. Unauthorized war is waged for its own sake, and nourishes those who wage it. War is their life and their life is war. Peace would deprive them of the foundation of their existence.

Such warriors are not very particular about selecting their methods. Some forms of violence derive from partisan or anti-guerrilla conflict, others from warring cultures and religions, terrorist persecution or the traditions of gang warfare. Unauthorized warfare recognizes neither the rules of military intelligence nor the norms of military honour and discipline. You look in vain for any central command. Everyone wages this war on his own initiative. Violence has been privatized. Such war is reminiscent of the time before the birth of the modern state, yet it determines the present and future of many parts of the world. After the wars of revolutionaries, nations and technicians, war waged by marauders and commandos now dominates the globe.

This war is of slight but steady intensity, instigated by groups whom representatives of Western states regard as terrorists, guerrillas, bandits or robbers. They follow charismatic leaders, are motivated by a desire to take plunder, and sometimes also by religious fanaticism or a masculine craving for adventure. Their 'battles' are fought not in the open field but in woods and villages, in squares, at roadblocks, in embassy forecourts, in the tunnels of underground railways or the trade centre of a great metropolis. Attacks, assassinations, street fighting, vandalism and massacres are the features of this small-scale warfare without front lines. The distinction between war and peace, soldiers and civilians, war and crime is no longer valid. The army of the state government, which strives for a monopoly of violence, can do little against street fighters, guerrillas operating in the forests and suicide pilots. Soldiers have always hated police work, and heavy weapons are no use for taking mountain caves or skirmishing on street corners. Regular fighting forces who bring their technical superiority to bear on an inferior opponent will sooner or later feel a loss of morale. Men firing from tanks or established machine-gun posts on boys throwing stones, or shooting an adolescent who has aimed his catapult at the occupying forces, lose first their sense of justice, then belief in their mission, then their self-respect, and finally belief in the war.

The return of the marauder

> 'I always wanted to kill legally, that's the feeling I was always after. I know I can survive if I be just like what I'm fighting. No pity, no emotions. No love in war. Total pitilessness. I'll kill without any sympathy for my enemies, even if they are women. I want that feeling, it's better than any drug.'

This statement by a British mercenary fighting on the Croatian side against the Serbs is brutally frank. He went to war not for an idea, a nation or even money, but to experience pure violence. He was not the only one to follow the siren call of war. Hundreds of foreigners fought in the civil war in the former Yugoslavia for starvation wages. Many belonged to the standard corps of professional mercenaries and had previously served in West Africa, Surinam, Sri Lanka, Afghanistan or the Sudan, others came from regular armies, the French Foreign Legion or the East German People's Army. Most, however, were civilians whose life at home had become too boring and who hoped to get a kick out of war.

These foreign mercenaries differed only slightly from their indigenous fighting comrades. They all wore the international uniform of marauders: camouflage gear, cartridge belt, sunglasses, woolly hat or headband. The same raffish image was cultivated by the militia who only recently had been living next door to their deadly enemies. No sooner had they crossed the dividing line than they turned into dreaded arsonists and murderers. They destroyed their neighbours' houses, drove them away from the region or shot them down, raped the women and mutilated the dead beyond recognition.

Western observers have ascribed the 'outbreak' of collective violence in the former Yugoslavia to the decline of the centralized state and the polarization of elites, to old ideas of the enemy, ethnic opposites, or nationalism flaring up. But this is to confuse cause with effect. The marauder is not much concerned with propaganda, ideology or old traditions. He is not fighting for a faith, he needs neither an ideological pretext nor political conviction. He shows which side he is on by getting an enemy in his sights, and creates his enemy by attacking him. The practice of violence helps him to acquire a new identity. For violence breaks old links and draws a line that cannot be crossed between former school friends or work colleagues. It clarifies social relationships and crushes personal doubts. No language speaks more clearly than the language of violence. Of itself, it creates the facts to justify it.

The selection of victims shows how little any political aims matter to the marauder. He does not even spare civilians belonging to his own national group. While the partisan operates under the protection of the people whom he seeks to bind to his own ideals, the marauder recognizes only his own band of comrades. He is as brutal to the followers of other warlords as to the civilians who stand in his way. Marauders slaughter the peasants and townsfolk whom they claim to be liberating; they blow up hospitals and butcher their inmates whether or not they are their own countrymen. Their aim is to eliminate all the defenceless: the women and children, the old, the sick and the disabled. Marauders are not trying to free a region from foreign rule. They want to decide who can live on their territory at all. As they see it, anyone without a knife, machete or machine pistol is fit for nothing but slaughter.

Bands of fighting men are found all over the globe: in Guatemala and Colombia, Somalia and Sierra Leone, in Zaire and Rwanda, in Tadjikhistan, Burma and New Guinea. The marauder is the dominant figure in a world war waged not between nation states but by local warlords, drugs barons, leagues of clans or private militias. Although regular forces may be involved at first, the dividing line between the military and bands of murderers blurs in the course of war. The hierarchy disintegrates, discipline breaks down, the company becomes a mob, the soldier a marauder. He no longer draws his pay from the state treasury but takes it straight from the land. Highwaymen lie in wait on the roads, extorting protection money, helping themselves to goods sent into the country by international aid organizations. The marauder lives and nourishes himself by war. He likes its arbitrary nature, and he has time on his side. He is not interested in peace. As a result modern wars often last for years, if not decades.

Armed gangs avoid seeking a decisive, violent battle. They are as little concerned with the strategic calculations of the military as with the conventions of modern warfare. They take no prisoners, unless to extort a ransom, and they draw no distinction between combatants and civilians. In so far as they actually fight at all they prefer the methods of irregulars: skirmishing, ambushes, raids, minefields. Their violent activities are not to be confused with the regular or even the irregular soldier's art of warfare. The partisan wears the mask of a revolutionary. He plays a waiting game, on the defensive, attacking the transport lines of a superior foreign power, spreading unrest and panic, then disappearing again at once. The soldiers of massive state armies generally operate under orders in self-contained units that concentrate their power. Since they are highly equipped technologically, they need a cumbersome supply system. Their advance is expensive, the huge assembly of fighting forces must be coordinated, rehearsed and constantly supervised. In spite of the accelerating speed of modern transport, state armies move like dinosaurs. Partisans resemble chameleons, but marauders fasten on their prey like bloodsucking leeches. One hesitates to describe them as warriors at all, for a warrior worth the name is constantly fighting himself as well as the enemy, fighting anxiety, fear and pain. The marauder, however, is unacquainted with courage and daring. He seeks the experience of killing without risk. His trade resembles the trade of the butcher and knacker.

He does not lack for historical predecessors. They are not the skirmishers of the American War of Independence, the Spanish rebels against foreign domination by the forces of Napoleon, or the *guerrilleros* of the twentieth century who drove the satraps of the colonial powers from their countries in the name of national liberation. Nor do the new marauders have anything in common with the irregulars of the Second World War. Their ancestry goes much further back, to the epoch before the modern nation state with its standing army. In the Thirty Years' War, bands of lansquenets and mercenaries roamed Central Europe burning and pillaging, robbing the local population. Having no particular religious allegiances, they changed sides whenever a new lord promised better plunder. During the Hundred Years' War, countless gangs of disreputable characters laid rural France waste. Some of them of noble descent, some of humble origin, these soldiers of fortune acted entirely on their own account. Not for nothing were they called *écorcheurs* – extortionists.

Modern war bands include a number of adolescents and children in their ranks. Since the weak are worth nothing anyway, warlords will recruit twelve- or even eight-year-olds. It is estimated that there are at least 300,000 'child soldiers' in the world. 'Recruiting officers' get them from orphanages, schools or straight from the football field. Village elders supply an agreed number of children as payment of tribute. Many young people volunteer freely because the gun ensures them their daily food. They are used as beasts of burden, couriers, guards and spies, or pumped full of drugs or alcohol and sent to cross minefields as living mine detectors. They may be forced to watch the execution of their families, then taken to the neighbouring village and allowed to satisfy their desire for revenge.

There is usually little attempt to give these young auxiliaries any military training. They do not need to learn techniques of self-defence, since marauders regard their bands of children merely as cheap cannon fodder. At most they are handed a semi-automatic weapon and allowed to practise loading and firing for a couple of days. In the rain forests of Sri Lanka, the Tamil Tigers took to sending young girls into the firing line as what might be called one-way warriors. At the end of January 1998 a troop of teenage girls who had been locked up in a jungle hideout for months before were sent out, armed with a few Belgian machine guns, to break through the defending line of the government troops. The army struck back with howitzers, mortars and helicopters. Of the ninety girl soldiers, only one survived.

Any of the adolescents who survive their protectors' mistreatment and a looting expedition rise rapidly to the rank of 'sergeant' or 'lieutenant'. The change from victim to killer shows in their appearance. Expressionless eyes hide behind the mirror lenses of sunglasses, they wear looted top-brand trainers, baseball caps, parachutists' red berets or old steel helmets. Over their shirts dangles a tin eagle, a chain of Coca-Cola cans or a plastic death's head. Bazookas, Kalashnikovs or carbines with bayonets are slung over their shoulders. Their movements are studiedly casual, cool. For the benefit of foreign TV news cameras they mimic the muscle-bound killers of American movies, calling their leaders Superman, Mosquito or John Rambo. When they are bored they fire a few volleys into the grass of the steppes, turn their guns aimlessly on a hut, or try out an anti-tank rocket launcher on a parked car. The idea of saving ammunition, which is drilled into every soldier at an early stage of training, is entirely foreign to them. These young people are already well on the way to becoming fully fledged marauders. The initiation rite of the war band calls not for tests of their courage against equal opponents, but for a martial outfit and bloodthirsty treatment of the defenceless.

Gang terrorism in war is a unique form of violence. The marauder roams the country, terrorizing the population, seeking the physical cruelty that gives him a sense of his absolute power to kill. The technology of his weapons is primitive; a submachine gun can be assembled with a couple of manoeuvres. He prefers weapons that perceptibly heighten his sense of power: knives and machetes that slice through muscle and sinew, rapid-firing guns, grenades that liberate phallic energies as they explode.

The presence of marauders cannot be overlooked. They lie in wait at street corners, lounge about in the village square, zoom around on looted motorbikes, patrol a restricted area standing upright on the platform of a rusty truck, as if riding in triumphal procession. They set up a base in a place where they feel safe and turn it into a fortress. From this base they survey the terrain and spread an atmosphere of constant insecurity. Even in a conquered country there is no peace, only an incessant state of deadly danger. There is no room here for industrious labour, since no one can be sure of reaping his harvest. The economic ruin of the region is inevitable.

The favourite location of marauders is the barricade. Treetrunks lie across the paved road, there is a corrugated iron hut, a great deal of garbage, a few burning car tyres, a smell of paraffin. The guards are armed to the teeth; bathed in sweat, eyes wild, they storm a truck, drag out the driver and his mate and press the points of their machetes into their backs. It is a test of willpower and the control of human instincts. Anyone who tries to flee or attack has forfeited his life at once. Another favourite activity at the barricade is to pour paraffin over passers-by and burn them alive. Only a man who keeps perfectly still, withstands the threat and shows no vulnerability has a chance. Many of these highway robbers are under the influence of drugs, and suffer from the heat and boredom of the barricade. For a driver to insist that his documents and permits are in order merely provokes scornful laughter. The guards want to see him produce money, diamonds, food or medicaments from his vehicle. The barrier is a focal point of violence, serving to control mobility and finance the war. This is where aid convoys are robbed or forced to pay tolls, this is where the possessions of local passers-by are confiscated, hostages are taken and ransoms extorted. The barricade rules the political economy of unauthorized warfare.

Warlords need the aid of these assassins to extend their conquered territory. Their stronghold also serves as a refuge and base for secret commandos. Beyond those spectacular assassinations in capital cities which bring world powers on the scene, we have the ordinary terrorism of small-scale warfare, attacks on the surrounding countryside, on a police station, an enemy convoy, a mission, a group of tourists, a trader or a village that owes tribute.

Assassinations on foreign terrain call for different conduct. Preparations can be elaborate. The attack must be planned, the location spied out, weapons and explosives brought in, the commando troop must reach the scene of the action unobserved. Unlike highway robbers, bombers must not be discovered too early. Camouflage and a lightning strike are therefore of prime importance. Assassins often take considerable risks. They will not achieve their aim without discipline and daring, even a readiness for self-sacrifice.

Nonetheless, what these bands do should not be confused with the familiar propaganda of activists. Their aim is not to raise the banner of resistance or leave a sacred mark in blood. It is a European prejudice to see religious or political fanaticism behind every violent act, as if experienced killers needed any other conviction in order to arrange a massacre. The modern terrorist and the marauder share an exaggeratedly militant attitude and a sense of contempt for all civilians. The more who die in the attack, the greater is the public panic aroused and the higher the assassin's reputation among his own kind. The bomb is meant to destroy or expel local inhabitants and leave the region free for conquest.

In matters of technique, terrorists have long been considered conservative. Their tools have been the bomb and the gun. Today explosives and guns are handier and better than before, and easier to transport, and assassins, however anti-Western their idea of the enemy may be, are increasingly likely to use the achievements of modern technology: electronic devices, photomechanics, photoelectric beams, rocket launchers, plastic explosives, aircraft, viral and bacterial weapons. They get their assembly instructions and recipes from the Internet.

Countless nuclear warheads are stored in the arsenals of the great powers. Aircraft and ships are equipped with long-range rockets; satellites survey every stretch of land. There are tens of thousands of armoured vehicles in military barracks, and special troops wait for the next alarm at a number of bases: handpicked elite soldiers who speak several languages and are trained to operate fast. Their success rate, however, is only moderate. They are useful for a surprise attack, freeing hostages, or evacuating threatened embassies. But a strike force can do little about the small wars devastating many parts of the world and costing millions of human lives. The history of warfare after 1945 has been a tale of disaster for the regular armed forces of the developed countries. When marauding bands wage war there is no front line, no battlefield, not even an identifiable main enemy to be conquered in strategic operations. Massive interventions by third parties can enforce a temporary cease-fire or set up a protectorate, but many losses will be entailed and the structure will instantly collapse as soon as the foreign troops leave.

The illusions of diplomacy match this military impotence. Negotiations need to be between reliable parties who will observe the terms of treaties and can be impressed by threats. The idea of the reconciliation of interests presupposes clear political aims and centralized power groups whose representatives speak with one voice. There can be no such thing in the world of the marauders, and in guerrilla warfare the commandment of strict neutrality to which negotiators and aid organizations have always been bound means that without intending to they are rendering aid to the murderous, pillaging bands. Speaking to everyone involved means official recognition for mass murderers, but if no tribute is paid to the local warlord it is hardly possible to deliver aid to a hospital or food depot. It is not surprising that, in view of this military and conceptual dilemma, the world powers sooner or later withdraw from areas which bring no economic profit and are strategically worthless, and leave the war to get on with itself.

Where marauders, murderous thugs and bombers make the countryside unsafe, the laws of massacre, raids and annihilation reign supreme. Such wars are long and cruel. They will go on until the societies in which they are fought have been destroyed. And they will always attract new legionaries and oppressors for whom violence is the only conceivable way of life.

The massacre

30 December 1997: many of the bearded men who attacked three villages in Western Algeria on the first night of Ramadan wore the baggy trousers and jackets of Afghan national costume. Their leaders kept in touch with each other by radio, sometimes using code names. The bloodbath went on all night. Next morning corpses with their throats slit, their heads cut off or their breasts amputated lay about the streets. Many of the bodies had been hacked to pieces, and the battered corpses of babies lay by the walls of the buildings. Eighty dead people were found in two houses. In all, 412 villagers of the Relizane region fell victim to the massacre.

22 December 1997: the refugees in Chenalho, a village in the Mexican province of Chiapa, were just celebrating Mass in a makeshift church when the trucks drove up. The men in the trucks immediately surrounded the refugee camp and began firing into the crowd. Some made for the refugees with bush knives and butchered women and children. Those who hid in the nearby caves were rounded up later and killed on the spot. The massacre went on for five hours. At the end of it forty-five refugees were dead and thirty-four injured. The bloodbath had been planned in advance at a meeting; the mayor of Chenalho himself had given the men of the murder squad the weapons.

13 July 1995: the Serb guards in the Bratunac warehouse not far from Srebrenica were particularly hostile to the younger Muslims who had been well known locally before the war. One by one they took the men outside the gate, made them run the gauntlet and clubbed them with crowbars. One guard specialized in striking the prisoners in the back with an axe, another cut their throats with a knife. By evening only 296 of the 400 or so men who had been locked in the stuffy hall the day before were still alive. That night they were taken in buses to a gymnasium and made to wait there for several hours. A narrow road led from the school yard to the place of execution. When the prisoners arrived there they saw hundreds of dead Muslims laid in rows on the ground. Five soldiers were waiting beside the corpses while a bulldozer dug a mass grave.

There are horrors that seem to go beyond what is historically familiar. They give rise to apprehension, abhorrence, perhaps a sense of bafflement. Although the imagination can range wide, these horrors elude immediate understanding. Massacres are certainly not rare. Countless such incidents are recorded in the black book of history, but we generally keep that book closed and prefer to forget. However, different as the circumstances may be, massacres are strikingly like each other. The bloodbath is a universal form of excessive violence. Mass murderers of every kind have made use of it, those whose terrorist methods are to expel their victims as well as the militia and marauders of unlicensed warfare.

Beyond the border, neither the calculation of utility nor the economy of killing counts for anything. Once the scene of battle has been barricaded off – it may be a residential quarter, a village, a building – the butchers can take their time. They want to relish the slaughter. Nothing would be easier than to kill the victims out of hand, but the pleasure of that destruction would be short-lived. So the murderers often change the tempo. They stroll round the area picking out individuals at random, arbitrarily, relishing the mortal fear of those waiting their turn. They bask in their own immunity, stalk about, take a break for a cigarette or a bite to eat, fill their pockets if there is anything to loot, seize the next victims, drive them on ahead, seize them again and kill them. The criterion of their cruelty is not its efficacy but the pleasure they take in it. The murderers need not economize on their destructive methods, for the point of this excess is not victory or terrorism but the act itself, the festival of blood.

Murderers quite often seek the proximity of their victims. It is a pious error to suppose that a natural inhibition prevents people from attacking those who are close to them, and to recommend intensive one-to-one meetings between criminals and their victims as therapy. Every fratricide, every murder in the close or extended family circle proves the opposite. No war is more cruel than civil war, no hatred goes deeper than hatred between relations and acquaintances. The closer the connection between groups, the more unrelenting their hostility. Since their everyday life has so much in common, violence, that passion of proximity, knows no bounds. Unauthorized warfare offers an excellent opportunity to settle all vengeful private accounts. In Algeria survivors of massacres often recognized former neighbours, friends, sometimes even their own relations among the murderers. In the 'ethnic cleansings' in former Yugoslavia, many who killed and looted displayed particular cruelty towards neighbours or professional colleagues from the same home town. In Rwanda the organizers of the Tutsi genocide ordered their militia to kill not with automatic weapons but with machetes, thereby also making use of the passion of slaughter to establish solidarity among the murderers. Proximity rather than anonymity incites people to their worst deeds. Far from raising the threshold of inhibition against violence, it heightens the neighbourly spirit of cruelty.

Every group of the perpetrators of violence uses the weapons that are familiar to it and ready to hand. Military units use explosives, automatic weapons, knives and gun butts. The militia in Mexico liked the machete too, the Serbian and Algerian slaughterers favoured hatchets, axes, sawn-off shotguns, iron bars, daggers and butcher's knives. These are the tools of bloody hand-to-hand fighting. The aim of the massacre is not to eliminate victims without trace but to mutilate the body. The victims are slaughtered like cattle, their bodies hacked to resemble pieces of meat, their sexual organs cut away. In so far as there is any religious feeling behind the practice of massacre it is not some 'fundamentalist' idea of God, but reversion to the bloody and archaic ritual of human sacrifice, a sacrifice made by the murderous group to its idol, which is itself.

What circumstances favour the unleashing of collective cruelty? The murderers do not need fanatical convictions, nor do they necessarily have long criminal careers behind them. Such assumptions ignore the fact that the threshold of inhibition is really very low. The perpetrator of excess becomes what he is in the situation itself. The practice of cruelty engenders a desire for further cruelty, until at last it becomes the reason for it. At first, however, mere opportunity is enough to make the killers do anything that they *can* do with impunity. They have nothing to fear from third parties in any case. In Chenalho the police stood by and watched, and the state authorities and civil service, although they issued warnings, let the murderers have their way. In Algeria many massacres took place near army posts, but the military did not raise the alarm or intervene. The suspicion that special military units had committed several of these crimes themselves so as to give public legitimacy to the repression of Islamists was by no means unfounded. Nor was any resistance to be expected from those terrified neighbours who were not on the proscribed list. Passive spectators encourage murderers, whether out of cowardice, impotence, tolerant complicity, political calculation, or indifference disguised as cultural relativism.

The cruelty is promoted by the group's cohesion. Massacres are always collective excesses of violence. The murderers egg each other on. Proudly, they show off their trophies. Should a novice hesitate he is urged on by the others: an encouraging slap on the back, a playful nudge in the ribs, a mission he can't refuse. A man who does not want to be mocked or accused of treachery has to join in the slaughter, the shooting, the laughter. Violence is regarded as evidence of belonging.

The bloodbath creates a new social community. Whether the killers belong to an army, a militia, or a robber band, their cohesion is confirmed beyond the border. The solidarity of the slaughterers rests on the common experience of torturing and killing. A murderer is not to exist in isolation. Excess realizes one of the oldest forms of communal human feeling: killing in company. Its beacon is fire. On the night of 4 January 1998, a commando troop attacked the mountain village of Had Chekala. After the killers, as usual, had struck down many of the inhabitants with knives and axes they set the village on fire. More than a hundred human beings were burned inside the houses, many of them alive.

The weapon of desecration

Palestinian street fighters demolished the walls of the tomb with picks, sledgehammers and their bare hands. They waved their banners on the white dome of Joseph's tomb, fired volleys of shots into the air and praised their God. Sympathizers combed the burning ruins for remains. They broke the charred Star of David away from the entrance of the tomb and carried it around as a trophy. Then they shredded the scriptures, scattered the pages on the ground and trampled on them. A Palestinian dentist managed to save a sacred book by Rabbi Isaak Luria, a sixteenth-century mystic, from the furious mob.

In recent years the tomb, a place of pilgrimage for radical settlers, had been made into a fortified enclave in the middle of hostile territory because there were so many attacks. At the beginning of the new *intifada* an Israeli NCO bled to death in the mausoleum, where he lay for five hours under fire. For fear of snipers the reinforcements who had arrived dared not try to save the wounded man. Days later the Israeli army vacated the area and left it to the rebels. When the tomb had been raided its white dome was painted green, the colour of Islam.

The violation of holy places is among the most effective weapons of street warfare. Rachel's tomb became a focal point for skirmishing in Bethlehem; in Jericho the mob set fire to an ancient synagogue. Since the war of symbolism recognizes no boundaries, the effects were felt abroad and very far afield. There were more than eight attacks on Jewish institutions at the time. The revolt had begun after an attack that was far more than an act of political provocation. In the eyes of Muslims, the advance of their deadly enemy Ariel Sharon on the Haram al-Sharif was no more or less than desecration of their sanctuary. It was immediately defended with bottles, chairs and stones.

The destruction of memorials, the burning of flags and straw dummies, the smearing of tombstones and religious monuments with filth, forced entry into sacrosanct precincts – these acts of desecration strike at the enemy's very core. The destruction of the enemy's emblem is meant to extinguish his history. Whether such acts are a sign of victory, protest or terrorism, their point is their emotional and not their material value. They do not leave an empty space behind; they aim to disfigure and defile what is sacred to their opponents. Since the desecration can be recognized only by what it leaves behind, destruction must never be complete. Ruins of the synagogue must be left, the dome of the tomb, the torso of the statue. There is no desecration unless something of what was once sacred is left. Only then does the violation achieve its aim, exhibiting what it destroys.

Violation is a cheap weapon, and particularly suitable as an offensive on the part of subject people. No explosives or machinery are required to demolish an aura. A plastic bag full of paint, a cigarette lighter, a chisel will do the job. While the opposing side is armed with tanks, helicopters and VDUs, the pioneers of symbolic destruction work with the most primitive of methods. They do not even need a particularly high degree of courage or daring to attack sublime values. All they need is public reaction: the jubilant shouts of spectators, the glee of sympathizers, and indignation expressed by the international media on behalf of the desecrated icon.

Although technologically primitive, desecration is extremely effective. It does not stop at material damage. Instead, it reverses the meaning that attaches to sacred objects. Something laden with significance – the significance of the origin of a tradition, a faith, a nation – is trodden underfoot. The sublime is brought low, perfection of form is ruined, what was whole is hacked to pieces, purity is pelted with filth. That which cannot be touched without being polluted is holy. What is holy demands respect and a proper distance. Ritual prescriptions regulate the transition from the secular to the sacred, and the liturgy tells worshippers how to conduct themselves in the presence of the numinous. Any who ignore all this are committing sacrilege, offending against the highest values of a culture or a religion.

Desecration is a magical act. Shabby and profane as the act may appear, it rests on an imaginative idea that has survived all secularization: the idea of the physical presence of the sacred. What is usually invisible suddenly becomes visible in the holy object. That was why conquerors used to put out the eyes of the statues of their enemies' gods. The god itself is present in its image, the sacred place is imbued by the spirit to which human beings pray, the words of the gods are recorded for ever in sacred books. Temple and altar, idols and fetishes, statues and relics are part of the power that they denote. The tombstone is far more than a memorial and a reminder. The cemetery, a necropolis, holds more than the bones of earlier generations; it is the dwelling of the ancestors who are placated by the honour paid to them and by gifts of food and flowers. The desecrators of a cemetery do not just besmirch the reputation of the dead: by disturbing the ancestral peace they are arousing evil spirits to new life.

The desecration of such objects creates small victories when a major triumph is still far away. The mob becomes even more rabid once it has laid hands on a living human body. The lynchings in Ramallah showed all the characteristics of a second murder, the mutilation and violation of the dead. The murderers killed two Israeli soldiers in the police station at Ramallah and slit their bodies open. They threw one of the men head first through the window for the delectation of the crowd. The mob kicked the lifeless body and struck it with iron bars. Finally the corpse was dragged through the dust of the street to the nearest road junction. After this bloodthirsty celebration, young people danced around the bloodstains where the body of the Israeli had been torn apart, calling to one another, as if in the refrain of a song: 'Here we gouged his eyes out, here we tore his legs off, here we struck him in the face.'

Kosovo: the double war

At first it was only the arrogance of power. Politicians and the military alike thought a few bombs would be enough to make the tyrant sign a document of surrender. However, the air raids went on for weeks, doing considerable damage, but the military balance sheet showed little in the way of profit.

Illusions are the engines that propel war. They depend on miscalculation, wishful thinking, and the will to self-deception. Such illusions are welcome because they spare us unpleasant insights, instead creating a sense of satisfaction. It was not so much propaganda as a need for self-deception that clouded the vision of the Allies and forced the pace of the war. Against their better judgement, they continued to believe in what they had persuaded themselves was true, proclaiming aims that the war soon left behind.

The 'double war' in Kosovo made ideas of a regular war between states appear obsolete. The air raids were more like a police operation on the periphery of imperial power, offering a show of determination without risk. The massacres and deportations carried out by the Serb side, on the other hand, were part of the familiar repertory of state-approved terrorist persecution. Despite the high intensity of violence, direct conflict was rare. No pitched battles were fought; little defence was put up to the bombardment, and any fighting on the ground was more in the nature of a skirmish. Poorly equipped and ignorant of infiltration techniques, the inexperienced Albanian irregulars of the KLA ran straight into minefields like living mine detectors and were shot down. Meanwhile the Allies remained at a safe distance 4,500 metres above ground level, leaving the lower airspace to the Yugoslav jet fighters and helicopters. The course of this 'war' was determined not by fighting but by terrorizing the defenceless population with destructive measures, manhunts and massacres.

For those in arms and their commanders this kind of 'warfare' came cheap. Losses among the 'combatants' were low. Rockets, laser bombs and Cruise missiles are ideal weapons for a society that believes in its moral mission but is not willing to pay a high price for it. They are suitable for punitive operations and demolition of the infrastructure, they demonstrate the putative vigour of those who use them, and they nourish moral pride. War in the air comes to look like a sacred mission in the service of civilization.

The destructive force of the barrage was obvious: the smoking ruins of factories, bridges, buildings and radio masts blown up, the skeleton of a bus, and ripped-off arms, blood, charred human bodies among the rubble. Yet the bombing achieved the opposite of what was intended. After the ceasefire the Serbian military power left the region without any losses of men and *matériel* worth mentioning. The despot's attitude was unbroken, the regime was reinforced, the loyalty of the population strengthened. The Allies' hopes of democratic resistance, assassination of the tyrant or a military putsch were pure wishful thinking. They had obviously forgotten the truism that pressure from outside usually strengthens cohesion within a society. Admittedly the enthusiastic defiance and sense of national elation felt by the populace in the early days of the bombing soon disappeared, but their despair and impotence did not lead to the hoped-for coup. Man's ability to endure even wretched circumstances should not be underestimated. Only when power relationships begin to change does the idea of revolution gain adherents. The air raids merely provoked fury – and a readiness to make sacrifices. The greater the suffering and destruction, the less the Serbs had to lose. And the less they had to lose, the greater their determination to hold out so that their sacrifices would not have been in vain. Another eighteen months had to pass before the dictator, after suffering electoral defeat, had to give way and resign under public pressure.

The personalist view of the enemy was equally mistaken. Terrorist persecution can never be laid at the door of a single despot. The number of perpetrators and accomplices usually runs into tens of thousands, and the number of accessories after the fact into hundreds of thousands at least. It cannot be said that the Serbian subjects were all mere unsuspecting victims of infamous deception, as if murder and exile had not been the official policy for years. As if atrocities had not happened nearby, outside their very doors. As if the warlords had not been acclaimed by the jubilant public as new national heroes. What evidence is there for the comforting assumption that the executioners did not come from the very society that supported them?

A calculated move in conventional warfare is to strike early in order to scatter the enemy army. However, this purposeful tactic fails if there are men on the other side who are ready to murder and burn, and will act instantly on their own initiative once they have been given licence to do so. A regular partisan army is trained for decentralized operation. The civil defence system makes every adult a potential soldier and encourages the change from citizen to warrior. The privatization of violence is inherent in the process of making national defence a democratic affair. An army quickly degenerates into a set of mobs when it knows that its ranks include uniformed marauders whose long-established profession or even vocation is the handiwork of slaughter. It is true that the air raids neither caused nor set off the systematic mass persecution, but they precipitated its terrors by freeing the war bands from the control of centralized power and giving them additional motives for murder: revenge and an urge to retaliate. The etatist illusion of a regular war waged between states lent encouragement and impetus to the 'ethnic cleansing'.

Terrorist expulsion does not call for a great deal of courage, ammunition or petrol. All it needs is a few sub-machine guns, knives, mobile phones, balaclava masks, routine habits and a certain amount of bloodlust. The Serbian troops acted on familiar lines that had been in practice since the beginning of the 1990s and were tolerated by the Western wait-and-see policy. Even intervention in Bosnia came only once moral standards had been breached in Srebrenica, by which time the ethnic cleansing had been successfully concluded. The air raids were only the continuation of the policy of *attentisme* by other means. There was no lack of knowledge, evidence or pictures of what was going on. Only the courage to understand it and draw the necessary conclusions in good time was lacking.

The methods employed in the raids were always the same. Strong feeling would be whipped up by meetings and demonstrations among the local population. Then the area was encircled, while masked troops searched house after house and drove the inhabitants out into the street. Spokesmen and those in official positions were executed immediately. Then the women, children and old people were separated from all the men between sixteen and sixty. If the time and opportunity were favourable the murderers would deal with their victims at once. The dead were perfunctorily buried or left to be eaten by wild animals, the survivors starved in the woods, were hunted across the border, or were held prisoner so as to avoid offering the other side a clear target. Finally the empty houses were looted, set alight, or blown up by gas explosions. The terrorists' cruelty brought them plenty of plunder and trophies. By the time the Allied ground troops finally arrived the Albanian society of Kosovo was a society on the run.

The Allies could not halt the work of terrorism. If theirs had really been a humanitarian operation to bring emergency aid, they would not only have set up field hospitals but also have started immediately on the work of clearing the bridgeheads, sniper zones and escape routes. But political determination, military preparation and social support for such intervention were lacking. Instead, the reaction to the failure of the air raids was to carry on with them, dropping bombs round the clock, giving destruction free rein. And as long as there was no phone call from the dictator – the call that would have solved everything, freeing the Allies from their straitjacket – they comforted themselves with new illusions.

These included calls for a unilateral ceasefire or moratorium, in order, it was said, 'to give diplomacy a chance'. The other side would have chalked up this ceasefire as a success, using the opportunity to reorganize and continue their terrorism with impunity. There were also dreams of future reconciliation, when the past would be forgotten; there was a belief in the omnipotence of agreement, consensus, politics without any enemies. Hopes were expressed that the exiles would soon return and everyone would live together peacefully and in multicultural harmony within the old borders, as if nothing had happened. To comply with reasons of state, there was a general readiness to expect that the survivors and refugees would go back to living on amicable terms with the murderers of their families, hand in their weapons and entrust themselves for better or worse to an international 'peacekeeping force' which so far had risked absolutely nothing to protect them. The 'peace' finally dictated by the great powers was built on mass graves and the silence of the survivors. As was only to be expected, multicultural peace is further away than ever, even after years of a protectorate run by foreign ground troops and police. The trauma of 'ethnic cleansing' cannot be undone by wishful thinking which disregards political facts. After a massacre, the only way out lies in secession.

Finally, apologists resorted to the high moral ground, which spared them the necessity of considering ends and using the requisite means to them. The dismayed remarks about genocide and the sudden collapse of civilization was a mirror image of the forceful rhetoric urging non-violence at any cost, even the cost of committing sins of omission. As usual, a concern for attitudes and feelings was put before any realization that the prime object of any policy was to protect human beings from their adversaries.

The only moral justification for violence is to bring emergency aid. The only justification for the violence of war is victory. Fine words are inappropriate in both cases. The higher the values, the higher the toll in blood will be. Those who enter into a war to bring emergency humanitarian aid without intending to fight for victory are naive, negligent and irresponsible. War presupposes not just a readiness to kill but the physical courage to risk your life for others, to suffer and if necessary to die. Societies which cannot summon up those virtues should withdraw as soon as possible and stop indulging in rhetoric about human rights. Nor should they act as if refraining from action out of cowardice were really a righteous act.

Terrorist warfare

Before the kerosene exploded in the tower, you could still see where the aircraft had crashed into the facade. The outline of the fuselage and both wings of the plane was clearly visible. Human bodies spun head first into the depths from the North Tower, legs kicking, arms flailing at the empty air. Their fall continued for endless seconds as gusts of wind blew the bodies away from the building. Suddenly the bright blue sky darkened. A wall of cloud consisting of lime and asbestos particles rolled through the chasms of the streets below, filling the air with dust.

We were not shown the dead, the crushed, charred bodies, severed limbs or shattered skulls. As in all the wars of recent history, pictures of physical destruction were not transmitted on TV. The remains of the corpses were taken away in body bags. There was no trace of most of the missing victims. They had been burned to ashes. A mountain of rubble remained behind, bent steel scaffolding, pulverized concrete, an empty place.

The scenario for the attacks on the World Trade Center on 11 September 2001 was familiar from films, books and articles. The well-informed secret services were expecting the worst. Ultimately, however, no one was prepared to believe it, and once again reality outdid imagination. No one had guessed at the silence that would lie over the great metropolis for a moment after the attack, to be followed by a hollow roar, the sound of a distant disaster. No one, probably not even the killers, had been able to imagine the darkness amidst the avalanche of dust, or the extent of the devastation.

Observers staring at those images from a safe distance were spared the panic and horror of those on the spot. They saw dreadful pictures, but did not experience the terrible reality or feel personal horror, which distinguished them from eyewitnesses directly affected by what had happened. Passers-by in south Manhattan were overcome by horror when chaos suddenly broke loose around them. Many turned pale as death and stood transfixed; others ran around screaming or whimpered quietly to themselves.

The horrified observers were also thousands of kilometres away from the horrors encountered day after day by the rescue squads. No danger menaced these distant viewers. Their reality remained unchanged. It is not true that the global media destroy distance. Even pictures shown in real time do not have a universal eyewitness. When the world far away is thrown out of joint, but nothing happens in your immediate vicinity, the foundations of your sense of security are not shaken. Despite a general vague anxiety, the will to preserve normality was unaffected. Trading continued on the European stock exchanges, sporting events were held as arranged, the annual Munich Beer Festival took place, although amidst high security. The sense of unreality lasted only a few hours, perhaps a day, before ordinary life reasserted itself.

Yet the attacks did leave behind a buried sense of anxiety. Terrorism is an imponderable danger with no name and address. A certain relief was felt when the first photographs of the terrorists were published, and there was talk of specific arrests. Governments showed their determination by expressing solidarity and taking hasty measures for the surveillance of society. The military were instantly put on standby; the presence of uniformed security forces everywhere was to some extent reassuring.

The emotional defences that were erected against anxiety matched the practical measures. All attention turned to a legendary, mysterious figure in a distant and mountainous land, as if a conspiratorial network of independent teams of terrorists were easier to understand if it was given a personal face. The automatic reflex, an appeal for the presumed causes to be carefully diagnosed, was another attempt to fit the destructive act back into familiar patterns of thought. Finally, people who had suffered no personal loss took refuge in gestures of collective mourning, displays of the kind that had proved their worth after technological disasters, or events such as the death of the Princess of Wales in a road accident. They gathered in churches or outside embassies, lit candles, sought to be in human company and indulged in tearful emotion. They believed they felt a breath of sublimity in procession and prayer. The communal mourning itself was less essential than the sense of being together in mourning, of a mood shared by the whole community.

Although everyday social life gradually reverted to its old course, the terrorist acts had after-effects. Unquestioning confidence in the peaceful continuance of one's own private world was undermined. Flights were cancelled; some people avoided public places. At first another attack was suspected behind any explosion or plane crash. Letters from unknown senders were viewed with suspicion. Even after the first shock had worn off, this new kind of war held the public spellbound. When the first attacks carried out with biological weapons were confirmed fear flared up again. This sudden dismay was also the result of forgetting, for it is surprising how short historical memory can be. There were earlier models for the attack. In March 1986 the Japanese terrorist Yu Kikimura was arrested on his way to New York on behalf of Colonel Gaddafi. Several fire extinguishers filled with explosives and large nails were found on the back seat of his car, mines which he meant to ignite outside a US Marines recruiting office in Wall Street during the midday break. Such a terrorist act would have mutilated countless victims. The bombers of 1993 intended to bring one of the twin towers of the World Trade Center crashing down on the other, at the same time liberating a poison cloud of natrium cyanide gas in the ruined tower to asphyxiate everyone in the vicinity. The number of injured on that occasion was over 1,000. Both plans misfired, but the scene of the crime was already set for the attacks of 11 September 2001.

Other warning signs too had been swiftly forgotten as time went by. In February 1993 thirteen car bombs set off almost simultaneously destroyed the city centre of Bombay; 400 people were killed and 1,000 injured. In December 1994 Algerian terrorists hijacked an Air France jet, planning to blow up the plane and its 283 passengers over Paris so that burning debris from the wreck would fall on the city. The project was foiled just in time. 224 people were killed and 4,500 injured in the attacks on the embassies in Nairobi and Dar es Salaam. The old truism to the effect that terrorism wanted more spectators, not more deaths, had long ago been disproved.

Thirty years ago terrorism moved away from its local spheres of influence to become an international activity. It extended its aims, its methods and the scenes in which it operated. Aircraft full of passengers were hijacked; discotheques, cafés, department stores and one of the Olympic villages served as the setting for bloody acts of violence. International cooperation saw the rise of the professional mercenary terrorist who killed to order for pay. In 1972 a Japanese Red Army commando squad armed with hand grenades and machine guns carried out a suicide attack on the Israeli airfield of Lod on behalf of the Popular Front for the Liberation of Palestine. Eighty people were wounded and twenty-six killed, including sixteen Puerto Rican pilgrims on their way to the Holy Land. The terrorists were well-educated students from highly regarded Japanese universities. The one Red Army man who survived felt so ashamed of it that during his trial he did all he could to get himself condemned to death after the event. He was sentenced to life imprisonment – the worst punishment he could have suffered.

Modern assassins no longer set their sights on tyrants, crown princes, industrialists or ambassadors. They prefer public places, public transport, road intersections where people can be found in large numbers. Such places are easily accessible and give the act of violence plenty of publicity. On their way to immortality, the Japanese Aum sect chose to test the destructive power of the nerve gas sarin in the Tokyo underground. Foreign tourists were slaughtered at Luxor; a Libyan commando ignited a bomb in a jet on a regular flight over the Scottish town of Lockerbie.

The series of attacks on New York, Washington and Pittsburgh in September 2001 united proven patterns of action in what is so far a unique act. The hijacked planes were steered to their targets like car bombs before them; the assassins sacrificed their own lives; the separate operations were precisely coordinated; the scenes were places of central importance; and the victims came from all over the world. The list of the missing contains people of sixty-two nationalities. Neither the scenes nor the atrocity itself were new, neither the camouflaging of the invisible enemy nor the sudden advent of horror. However, the extent of the devastation is unparalleled in the history of terrorism – the tenfold increase in the number of dead, the training of the perpetrators, the political consequences and the intensity of distress worldwide.

The massacre marks a watershed in the history of violence. It stands at the point of transition from terrorism to a new kind of war. The old logic of terrorism is not in force any more; the calculations of provocation have been superseded. The bloodbath is no longer a measure of political communication by other means. Terrorist acts used to serve as a signal, a beacon intended to rouse a movement's supporters from their impotence and strike terror into the enemy. The propaganda of the act gambled on paralysing the other side or inducing it to overreact repressively, so that its own weight would bring it down. Terrorist violence hoped to provoke disproportionate retaliation. Most criminal acts of symbolic violence were enough to do that: they were destructive operations with significance behind them.

This most recent act, admittedly, used symbols too. Its target was an emblem of the great international metropolis, the monument of the world market, the hubris of an urban culture that has built its edifices to God-like heights. The Pentagon is the symbol in stone of the *Pax Americana.* The aircraft itself stands for the end of a settled life and the omnipresence of the culture hated by the terrorists. But what was the destruction of the building and the death of so many supposed to prove? The fact that the superpower was vulnerable, its state, its economy and its lifestyle transient? Was the mass murder intended as an act of just retaliation in revenge for all the misdeeds ever committed by US governments? Was it a heroic act of resistance, a religious blow delivered in defence against globalization? Or just an evil manifestation of hatred for the USA as the strongest, richest and freest power in the world? There are no bounds to the imagination of those who try to interpret it.

A lack of obvious significance allows interpretations to proliferate. There have been many theories about the causes of the attacks. Especially popular was the idea that the terrorists were rebelling against poverty, powerlessness and suppression. According to this notion, their crimes were merely a reaction to the injustices of cultural and economic imperialism worldwide. If the murderers hate the West then the guilt must lie, at least in part, with the object of their hatred – thus runs the usual upside-down thinking which excuses the methods of the terrorist act by its alleged causes, holding the murder victims responsible for their own deaths. Since the perpetrators themselves had been terrorized by Western power and culture, this confused argument runs, they were bound to become hate-filled terrorists. For mankind, says this theory, is naturally good, and only the American policy of hegemony made the assassins what they were. There would be no terrorism if people were given hope and their living conditions improved. The fact that the terrorists came not from the slums of Algiers or Cairo but from well-to-do families troubled the spokesmen of social determinism as little as the fact that it is not usually real but perceived injustice that calls forth protest. Perception, however, can be influenced by a great many immaterial factors: anger, a rage to destroy, resentment, vengefulness, fanaticism.

Equally popular, therefore, was the argument from religion. But what does that explain? There is no direct path from religious fervour to the cockpit of a fully occupied passenger plane being steered to its target as a flying bomb. It takes more to make a terrorist than belief in a few sacred verses or maxims. There are millions upon millions of strict Muslim believers who would never dream of killing anyone. The imminent expectation of a place in paradise where the martyr can see the face of Allah and enjoy the repeal of prohibition does not cause anyone to blow himself up along with his victims out of religious enthusiasm. Presumably ritual prayers helped the terrorists to overcome the fear of death and anaesthetize themselves at the last moment. Yet fanaticism is neither necessary nor adequate to explain hatred and bloodlust. Even Islamic convictions are not required for anti-Western resentment. The killers did not have to account to anyone, least of all themselves. What inhibitions did they have to overcome before they acted? They needed no travesties of religion. The ascription of deep religious meaning to the attacks suits only the propaganda of enthusiastic supporters of such notions. Great crimes can be committed without any great ideas about God and the world behind them.

Stronger than any promises of salvation, experience tells us, are secular facts: the social pressure of loyalty among underground comrades in arms, reinforced by regular religious exercises; a conspiratorial climate controlling attitudes in the self-contained little world of the plotters; and in addition a fixation on the authority of a charismatic leader. Ultimately, on the day of the attack itself, there can have been no going back. The programme for the operation was worked out to the last second, the channel of events left no way out. As usual, the most effective counter-strategy lies not in enlightening blind activists but in destroying their social network.

The attack was not a statement of conflicting cultures, and to present it as a symbolic act of protest or fanaticism is simply to minimize it. The physical reality of mass death cannot be elevated to a culturally significant level. The accomplices of the terrorists deliberately refrained from making any comment, admission or appeal. The massacre was not provocation but mass destruction. No political aim could be discerned beyond that destruction. The attack made no statement; it was an act of annihilation without ulterior motives. The only thing it brought about was a *tabula rasa*, an empty space. Where something is, runs the watchword of destruction, there shall be nothing. Where there is life there shall be death. But terrorism bent on destruction leaves no trace behind. Anyone intent upon razing everything on earth to the ground has no interest in surviving personally to bask in his success.

Once violence is emancipated from any sense of purpose, nothing but destruction and cruelty is left. The principle of destruction is a feature of the new kind of warfare that has been current for some years now. The attack of 2001 was not a declaration of war but an episode in the history of a long war of terrorism. The USA had already reacted to acts of terrorism with air raids on Libya, Sudan, Iraq and Afghanistan in recent years. These acts of war were the preliminaries. The reciprocal and hostile violence that constitutes a war had been present for years, but the actual attacks and counter-attacks were sporadic events. In between there were periods of covert action none of which came to public attention. The inhabitants of Europe could continue to cherish the illusion of a secure peace. They regarded the attacks as isolated events to be quickly struck off the political agenda again. The attacks on Washington and New York have now taken that war to the metropolitan cities.

Terrorist warfare does not aim to occupy a country, conquer a state or extend the area of religious missionary activity. It does not want to topple a social order or take plunder. It does not aim for recognition or acknowledgement. It wants to kill large numbers of people, spread terror and paralyse life through fear. Its aim is purely death and devastation. Such a war is not the continuation of the political power struggle by other means. The weapons of mass terrorism cancel out any kind of politics.

Terrorist warfare is not war between states, cultures or religions. Its protagonists are agents, commandos, secret cells. They are not in the pay of any state but of a private warlord, and quite a number operate on their own account. Sometimes they are recruited by states as mercenaries and go underground again after committing their act. But their main bases are in regions where either a state will give them long-term shelter or the regime of warlords has already deprived the central state of power. From such bases their radius of action extends all round the world. Today the commandos act not just locally but globally. Under the shield of conspiracy they form a loosely connected network of small units coordinated only for a given project. This supranational 'underground army' uses everyday life as a cover. The fact that the enemy may be invisible does not mean that the enemy does not exist. The reconnaissance of enemy positions and the camouflaging of operations for the sake of surprise are part of all kinds of warfare.

The new war knows no fronts and no zones of safety. Anywhere can be the target. The dividing line between fighting forces and civilians has gone. The rules of war between states are repealed. We need not expect any conventions to be observed in terrorist warfare. Its tactics are not attrition, wearing the enemy down, making a breakthrough or encirclement, but the sudden surprise attack. The enemies of the terrorist commandos – state security agents and anti-terrorist units – observe the same principle. There are no battles in this duel in the dark. The resources of industrialized warfare count for little. The commandos draw on minimal technology with maximum powers of annihilation. Above all, they rely on the proven forces of destruction: secrecy, surprise, recklessness and unscrupulousness.

In the past terrorists would try to get away from the scene at once, but the suicide bomber, a prominent figure in modern terrorist warfare, breaks with the principle of self-preservation. At the moment when he leaves the darkness of anonymity and steps on stage, death hastens to meet him. His is one of the shortest appearances in the history of violence. Only the action itself confirms his social existence. Cold courage and pitiless cruelty, hatred and selflessness go hand in hand in the person of the suicide bomber. He shares with the war hero who fights to the last breath his rage for destruction and contempt for death; he shares with the martyr, who is ready to be killed for his convictions, the ardour of faith and blind confidence in God. And like terrorists of the old style he is in revolt against his own impotence. He is full of ill-will, but not a coward, and is therefore predestined to wage war with low intensity and simple technology. A wallpaper knife is enough for him, for his main weapon is himself.

The sacrifice of himself lends him unique destructive power. While the enemy calculates his risk on the chances of profit, the suicide bomber knows no such consideration, circumspection or care. While the soldier's courage goes as far as his hope of survival, the suicide bomber is giving his all from the start. He knows only the rationality of his purpose, not the means to it. He offers everything necessary for success, including his own death. He is strong because he knows no bounds. He relishes not having to care for anything or anyone. Intent on his aim, he can do everything. No deterrent alarms him. You cannot use the threat of death on someone who does not fear death.

There are no battles in terrorist warfare. Its warriors avoid fighting and prefer sudden attacks, assassinations, the mass murder of the defenceless. The New York terrorists have been wrongly described as kamikaze pilots. The Japanese pilots and infantrymen on Okinawa who charged the American tanks with explosives in their belts in the final attack were sacrificing themselves for their country; suicide bombers just want to ensure themselves a seat in the front row in paradise. The warrior tradition of ancient Japan felt only contempt for such illusions. Kamikaze pilots were fighting the superior force of the invading army; terrorists are not fighting at all but slaughtering thousands of innocent people. They bolster their sacrificial courage by taking as many victims as possible with them. Killing large numbers of other people decreases their own fear of death.

Two roads lead to the scene of such crimes. First there is the adolescent from a poverty-stricken background who undergoes months of preparation, first in a Koranic school, then in a training camp. He performs military and ascetic exercises and meditates. He is brainwashed and his brain is then stuffed with the maxims of the secret order. Tests of his courage and collective parades, everyone marching in time, integrate him into the community of the elect. Shortly before the operation the novice meets his commanding officer. This officer's authority promises protection and release. He tests the recruit's ability to take stress, his discipline and determination, accompanies him through the day-long prayers, primes his bomb and sends him out. Hair shorn, dazed by the monotonous rhythm of the chanting, the young man makes for his destination like a sleepwalker. Unknown helpers drive him over the border; he goes the last few steps alone. His vision is narrowed, sounds reach his ears muted, as if from beyond a sonic barrier. The smile of eternal bliss is on his face. At the moment of the explosion he will be in paradise. A young Palestinian suicide bomber who survived his own attack some time ago because only the detonator cap of his bomb went off thought he was already in heaven when he came round in hospital. He had a rude awakening when the secret service agents asked him if there were any Israelis in his paradise.

And there is the middle-class recruit who spends several months in a training camp and then lives an inconspicuous, ordinary life somewhere or other in the world. He studies, works as an interpreter, and gradually becomes an agent. He avoids the temptations of his environment by regular spiritual exercises in the circle of his brothers in the faith. A close companion helps him to overcome all doubts. With his comrades, he forms a sworn community in enemy territory. After years he hears the prophecy. It is not a command or an order, just the announcement of an event that the distant authority wishes to see happen. An unknown intermediary brings him his directions. He moves to another place, tests various possible ways of attack, goes through the necessary training. The night before the operation he tries to dull his fear of death with prayers. He bathes and shaves and goes through all the requisite details in his mind yet again. Even in the hire car going to the airport in the morning he quietly repeats the prayer. It helps him through any lapses in his concentration in the departure lounge, or later when he is sitting in the plane. When he and his accomplices enter the airport building to check in, they are all wide awake and concentrating, trying hard to freeze their sense of panic. They must react to any minor incident with presence of mind. At the moment of attack their tension threatens to become blind action, there is loud shouting, yelling, commands, threatening gestures; the hostages must be kept under control, the aircraft steered to the target. Utterly carried away by events, they follow the compulsion of the moment – up to the last call to prayer on impact.

Terrorist warfare is not a case for the criminal courts but for the army general staff. It comes somewhere between the areas of the military and the secret service. The police can reconnoitre and make arrests in their own country, but they are in no position to eliminate an elite troop of terrorists who operate across the globe, fear no punishment and will use any methods in the final engagement. Calls for the police to take action arise from the illusion of a world state, and confuse political crimes with terrorist acts of war against military command centres and the civilian population. Conversely, military operations undertaken as policing measures have so far regularly ended in disaster. The military machine is armed to fight military opponents, but Tomahawks are not suitable weapons against Kalashnikovs. Neither stealth bombers nor airborne troops can prevail against the contempt for death felt by assassins armed with carpet knives. Strategy according to the rules of air warfare misses its mark when there are no targets apart from a few oil tanks, radar masts, superannuated aircraft and abandoned training camps. Only defectors and native scouts know the way to the terrorists' caves and hiding places in the mountainous desert anyway. Retaliating to mass murder with deliberate area-bombing of civilian residential quarters is both unlawful and ineffective; it does nothing for justice but brings the terrorists mass support.

Social reforms may silence many sympathizers but have never prevented a war or an assassination. It is improbable, therefore, that a lengthy campaign will lead to the end of this war.

In any case, martial gestures against terrorists in their own country are useless, and merely make previously undiscovered 'sleepers' into rabid avengers. Attempts to control thoughts and attitudes are powerless against the destructive ingenuity of the human brain. Surveillance will miss spotting a neighbour who uses conformity as camouflage. Even a register of fingerprints can do nothing about people's ability to transform themselves. In the state of emergency that is global war, universal suspicion prevails: behind every face, conspicuous or inconspicuous, there could be someone busy preparing for the next attack.

IV

The Aftermath

10

Retaliation

The spirit of revenge is implacable. It rages with the lust for retaliation as it leaves the body of the dead victim, and seeks out accomplices. Its evil intent can assume many forms: snakes, vermin, poisonous insects, a storm submerging a whole valley in the waves, a plague visited on the entire countryside. Above all, the god of revenge haunts his victims in their sleep. Night after night he torments them with nightmares, images of horror, portents of future disaster. Those who can no longer bear it follow the call of ruin and end their own lives.

Revenge knows no forgiving or forgetting. Time may pass, but revenge keeps its target in view. It has a long memory and does not recognize the lapse of time. It waits patiently for its moment of fulfilment. Its memory of the deed is not extinguished; burned into the brain, it keeps bringing forth new and obsessive ideas of reprisals. Unlike punishment, which is a disciplined form of retaliation inflicted within limits and by the rules, fantasies of revenge are boundless. Past victors usually lull themselves into a false sense of security, while the defeated use the interim period to arm themselves. Then revenge suddenly comes out of a clear sky, striking its unsuspecting targets without warning, taking them back to the time when the wounds were still fresh. Revenge annihilates time and history. It obliterates everything that seemed to have been achieved in the meantime. When the hour comes centuries of armistice, peace and harmony are suddenly shattered. Revenge is so powerful that it can reverse historical time, casting the adversaries back to the beginning.

Revenge is a durable element in the flow of time. It keeps the past ever present: defeat, expulsion, oppression, crime, the murder of friends, relations and countrymen. Revenge remembers the dead and keeps faith with them. Its aim is to continue with what the dead no longer can. Not for nothing are solemn oaths sworn in catacombs or in front of tombstones and memorials. Revenge is not content with quiet mourning and pious proclamations, but calls for deeds. The defeat is to be reversed, counterbalanced, cancelled out by force of arms as the avengers move from impotent suffering to the pride of action.

The desire for vengeance links those involved to the third and fourth generation. Descendants merely continue what their ancestors began, always keeping the hatred their forebears felt alive. The dead are avenged by the hand of their children and grandchildren, and that inheritance weighs heavy as lead on their descendants. There is no waking from the nightmare of history. For the gods of vengeance, the past is never over. To abstain from retribution would be to betray one's own origins. Revenge forces enemies into irreconcilable positions and chains the later-born irrevocably to their dead.

Like gratitude, revenge is part of the moral memory of society. We are grateful to our friends for the kindness they have shown; we hate our enemies for the atrocities we had to suffer. Humanity has a long memory for good and evil alike. This moral quality has eluded modern analyses of revenge, which like retribution is poorly thought of today. It is considered a lower, atavistic instinct from the distant past when might was right, and we overlook its continuing force. For the universal principle of reciprocity that applies to barter and gifts also applies to revenge. In an exchange of goods we are in duty bound to give an item worth the same as the item we have received. In a vendetta it is the murderer's duty to pay for the life he has taken with his own. Revenge is the barter of death. However, while an exchange of goods is binding chiefly on the debtor, blood-guilt mainly affects the creditor, who can find no peace until he gets satisfaction. Only after he has struck his own blow is he as free as the debtor who has done his duty by returning a gift. But while an exchange of goods ends once and for all with payment, enmity persists, since bartering deaths, the creditor's revenge on his debtor, creates a new debt and a new desire for retribution.

The evil does not end with retaliation. Where the gods of revenge rule, a chain reaction comes into effect, and if it is not controlled by regulations or interventions it will go on indefinitely. The deed is followed by revenge, the act of revenge demands further retaliation; humiliation responds to humiliation, violence to violence, murder to murder. The adversary becomes a traditional enemy, war a permanent condition. All involved are bound to the chain of the first crime. History keeps returning to its roots. Where revenge reigns, time moves in circles, and revenge thus makes the dead immortal.

Nonetheless, revenge is a legal principle. Its point is not reformation, prevention or deterrence, but justice. Like is answered with like. This is the basis of the ancient law of an eye for an eye, a life for a life. In societies where there is no judge to pass sentence according to the law, punishment always takes the form of revenge. Retaliation is the duty of the injured parties, the clan of those who have been harmed and dishonoured.

They are in honour bound to retaliate, and will not shrink from doing their duty.

The more stable the institution of revenge, the less it requires emotional motives. It is the arrogance of civilization to imagine that revenge is only an outburst of blind fury. Where duty and honour are involved, retribution is never left to private inclination. The humiliated and injured man is obliged to avenge the wrong whether he wants to or not, either alone or in company with the group standing in for him. Revenge is not the act of a subjective, individual will which does justice only by chance. Moral law, not the law of the state, governs the rationale and extent of revenge. It is incumbent on the survivors to bury their dead and then immediately march against their opponents. Neglect of this duty inevitably brings contempt, for how can anyone respect a man who does not respect himself? Revenge is therefore a test of the group's inner coherence and moral standards. Revenge is a matter of honour, and just as honour is shown before the eyes of others it is lost before them too. A man who abstains from revenge loses his honour once and for all, a man who transgresses against the standards of the group stains the group's reputation. Similarly, a man insulted or injured by third parties is avenged by his group in all questions of honour, hospitality, the family, sexuality and physical existence.

The commandment of vengeance governs relationships between groups that are not subject to the rule of any state. The feuds of knights and warriors of the past were based on the duties of comradeship, the code of honour proper to their rank, and their pride in refusing to tolerate dishonour. In dealing with enemies of the same rank they usually observed the conventions, but the principle of annihilation applied to camp followers, infantry, peasants or unbelievers. The unauthorized warfare of marauders, war bands and ethnic groups owes its endless continuation not least to the culture of revenge. Among those fraternities of young men that determine the level of violence in a given region, greed for loot and group loyalty unite with a boundless desire for vengeance. But campaigns of retribution are no longer justified by such ancient values as clan and family honour; all the possessions of the community and its warlord, whether legally or illegally acquired, are tainted with blood. A bandit's status is determined by his wealth, prestige and the weapons he owns, not by courage, honour and principles. All strangers are enemies, their goods are regarded as loot, and every act of self-defence is interpreted as an attack on the war bands and calls for revenge.

Modern war between states and terrorist persecution are not unacquainted with vengeance either. A decline in ideas of personal honour brings with it a need for some collective substitute. The less one can take pride in oneself, the more worthy of veneration does the community or the nation seem. The cheapest kinds of pride have always been family and national pride. People with nothing to pride themselves on personally will end up as fervent adherents of the nation to which they happen to belong. Lacking character of their own, they will want a share of national honour and the national character, and will wish to be proud of the history of their people, their origins, their culture, the passport they hold. They will draw nourishment from the illusions of a community, which reinforce their self-confidence and strengthen their pliable backbones. Yet their self-respect will be based only on the collective minimum, on something they share in common with millions of others. While the patriot knows he is bound to his country and feels honest loyalty to it, the nationalist projects all his craving for honour on the fame of the nation. He pays homage to dazzling shows of national greatness, applauds martial parades of weapons, his breast swells with pride as he leaves the square dedicated to national heroes, and he cultivates a sense of vague resentment of the traditional enemies, who are 'traitors to the fatherland'. He is anything but harmless. He despises everyone who is different from himself. The lust for vengeance comes over him when he sees the country's banner besmirched or a national monument denigrated, when someone soils the nest, shabby as it may be, or when he so much as hears a mention of national crimes in the past. He waxes indignant and bitter, flares up with fury and feels that he is entirely in the right. The nation is a cause of honour to him, and for its sake he will walk the streets brandishing a club and march away to the next war with his comrades. One can never be sure that the ancient spirit of retribution will not revive sooner or later in nations that have been defeated in the past.

'The conquered,' says Virgil in the *Aeneid*, 'can be secure only in the knowledge that they can hope for no security.' It is up to the conqueror to decide whether or not he takes revenge, kills the defenceless or sells them into slavery, or alternatively shows mercy, burdens them with payments of tribute and enlists collaborators into his own ranks. The revenge of the victors can be terrible. After the triumphal procession, prisoners of war are executed, their women raped, their cities plundered and burned to the ground. The defeated can choose only between death and obedience. Once they surrender they have put their lives in the victor's hands, hoping for leniency, mercy or pity. They can make no claims, for unconditional surrender is not a treaty between equals but a gesture of submission. In return for renouncing further violence the defeated side receives – nothing.

The victor has almost unlimited freedom of action, restricted only by his interest in power. He can exercise mercy either so that the conquered can serve him or because generosity makes him feel more powerful. Amnesties granting the conquered freedom of thought or giving them aid place them under an obligation of gratitude. They are eternally in the debt of the victor who has magnanimously given them the greatest of all goods, life. On the other hand, the victor can feed his desire for revenge by imposing draconian retribution, but that will provoke fresh hostility. Now and then it is agreed that the conquered have shown courage – worthy opponents, after all, make the conqueror's victory shine even more brightly – but rebels, malcontents and partisans feel the full force of retribution. They have violated the proper order of things, have fought with malice and cunning, using despicable arms and methods. However, the ultimate reason for the conqueror's vengeance is not the underhand warfare practised by his opponent but to keep faith with his own dead. The conquered enemy must pay twice, three times, a hundred times over for every fallen man.

Revenge is not content with the principle of equivalence. The malefactor must not just suffer, he must suffer more than the victim. The traitor's tongue is cut out, the murderer's corpse desecrated and torn to pieces. Revenge is sweet, says the proverb. It brings a sense of pride and satisfaction. The avenger feels that he is in the right, and therefore increases the extent of the violence to such a degree that retribution is out of all proportion to the original offence. He ignores all the rites and rules of restraint. Revenge becomes excess; in the intoxication of victory he can give his desire for retribution free rein. Victory itself is sweetened by the joys of vengeance.

Terrorism leaves a desire for revenge behind it too, although the survivors of concentration camps and torture chambers are not so much eaten up by hatred as marked by injuries for which there is no compensation in the form of penitence, punishment or revenge. What measure of revenge can there be for a victim slowly dissected to death? It is true that many torture victims manage to survive because the thought of revenge keeps them going, but the constitution of many of the survivors is so shattered that the wounds inflicted on them never heal. The experience of helplessness robs them of the energy and confidence essential for acts of retribution. Quite a number of such victims find that if they are to go on living at all they must avoid even the memory of the horrors they suffered so long. Their dreams at night are memory enough. A past from which even revenge can no longer liberate them weighs them down.

But victims who have not reached the bottom of the abyss – and they alone – are capable of revenge. Revenge flourishes in refugee camps, the communities of the ethnic diaspora and political exile. This is where those who have escaped in time are to be found, those who still have enough of an idea of the future to arm themselves for their return. The exiles mourn for their lost homeland, their families, their comrades in battle, their companions who died in flight. Their mourning is mingled with anger at the injustice they have suffered and an urge to strike back as soon as possible. But if circumstances prevent a swift return, and they have no allies to smooth the way home, the expelled must readjust in exile. They draw up lists of perpetrators, collect accounts of the crimes that were committed, send petitions, call for action, swear oaths of loyalty at their meetings, even though they are impotent. In that case revenge is diluted to resentment, to the imaginary vengeance of the powerless denied the opportunity for the act itself. Since there can be no compensation for the injustice they have suffered, deep rancour sets in. Their bitterness lasts for decades. It is passed on to children and grandchildren who never saw the old homeland with their own eyes. Imagined as well as real revenge lasts for generations, binding the later-born to the dead.

The gods of bloodshed repeatedly break free of any peace that has been made. An armistice or the redefinition of borders does not mean an end to war and expulsion. The institutions of punitive justice are a poor substitute for the lust for revenge, since they take retribution out of the hands of the victims, condemning them to inactivity. Revenge, however, continues the violence. It ensures that there can be no peace. Even if the form of violence changes, the regime of the dead is still in force. Lustful ancestral dreams of retribution are the roots of history yet to come. The past offers no comfort, no home, no refuge, but casts its shadow over the present until it fades away. The usual historical ideas of a peaceful civil society present war and terror merely as episodes in the flow of time, accidental interruptions to the steady forward progress of peace. Seen from a greater distance, the opposite proves the case. Peace is only an interruption to the regime of the gods of war and vengeance. They are the true lords of history and always keep its wheels turning. If there were never any treaties, never a moratorium, blood feuds would end in mutual extermination. Revenge ensures the return of the ever-familiar. Turning points and watersheds seem to offer only the second form in which retribution manifests itself: punishment.

Punishment eliminates the crime. It is a reprisal, avenging the violation of the law. Whatever its intended or unintended consequences, an understanding that the aim of punishment is not to do good but to do justice must precede any arguments about prevention, deterrence or reintegration into society. Punishment is not intended to give the victim satisfaction or improve the criminal, let alone the world itself. Its purpose is to confirm the validity of the law and bring legal principles back into force. The act was unjust, contravening the law, the norm, the taboo. Punishment revises this situation, and is thus itself an aspect of the crime. Without crime there would be no punishment, and just as an answer is necessarily linked to a question, punishment is necessarily linked to a crime. Again, just as the question demands an answer, the commission of a crime rouses the goddesses of punishment, who sleep until the crime wakes them. Once their work is done, however, the case is closed. Punishment definitively puts an end to the wrong.

It is not for the victims of crime but for the court to judge and pass sentence. The representative of the law, not the injured party, reconciles the law with itself. He turns the retaliation of revenge into the retaliation of punishment, satisfies the demands of justice and restores legal peace. At the same time, the nature and degree of the punishment must be in proportion to the crime, so that in injuring another the criminal has injured himself. The principle of equal retaliation thus determines the extent of legal punishment, for if the two cannot be seen as comparable, then a suspicion that the judgement is arbitrary and merely does more wrong will immediately arise. We should not of course see them as literally comparable; the criminal need not suffer exactly the same fate as his victim. The murderer does not have to be killed to satisfy the demands of justice. Nor does the nature of the crime have to be precisely reflected: tearing out a liar's tongue, hacking off a thief's hand, burying adulterers alive together are all punishments which obey the principle not of equivalence but of analogy, deterrence, purification or defilement, and such punishments are morally unjustified. Punishment should never be merely a means of promoting another value, and the person of the criminal cannot be used as a means to a meritorious end. Punishment is inflicted because a crime has been committed, not for any other purpose.

But how does one punish war and terrorism? Punishment comes into the equation only if war is considered a crime. The first question is: who was guilty of starting the war? Historically, it is usual for each side to blame the other. But since the war itself always begins not with attack but defence, with resistance to aggression, it follows that the defender is responsible for the fighting. The attacker can be held solely responsible for the attack but not for the war itself. If the party attacked had not put up any defence, then there would have been no war. But when both parties wage war they have both abandoned their legal foothold and are operating outside the law. War is an instrument not of the law but of power, and violence, not the legal process, decides the course of the fighting. Victory goes not to the just but to the strong. As a result, the defeated side is always considered the guilty party whether or not it started the war, since ultimately the power of the victor decides the question of justice or injustice. The victor and not the law calculates guilt and punishment, drawing no distinctions between might and right, victory and innocence, guilt and defeat. And here lies the structural dilemma of punishing war. At best, a neutral tribunal might offer a way out of the dilemma, but it would have to be empowered to punish the victors should their guilt for the war be irrefutable.

In wars between states the states themselves are responsible, not individuals. Punishment must therefore be inflicted on the collective agent, that is to say the state and its citizens, independently of whether they welcomed, supported or opposed the war. But it is next to impossible to punish the entire population of a state, and furthermore the majority of them would see such a verdict as unjust and reject it on the grounds of bias.

Both verdict and penalty would thus lose any legal and legitimate basis, and consequently many victors are content to consider the defeat punishment enough in itself.

War crimes are different. Cases of guilt *in* the war, not *for* the war are on trial. There are plenty of instances of war crimes: the use of despicable or banned weapons, cruel treatment of prisoners, the massacre of innocent parties, acts of terrorism against the civilian population. Although custom and convention have generally been ignored in emergency, the distinction between war and war crimes is not of recent date. Long-range weapons were regarded as contemptible long before the invention of gunpowder. The mere existence of unwritten laws of warfare provides a basis for punishment. Only if the war is waged from the first as a war of total annihilation or terror are war and war crimes one and the same. While the question of war guilt aims at a verdict on one side or the other, war crimes affect both sides. Furthermore, the defendants on trial are not states but the individuals who actually committed the crimes. The prospects for the punishment of war crimes are better than for the punishment of war guilt, and as the war criminal has also offended against the norms of his own state there is not even any need for an international tribunal. The criminal is not left to the victims or handed over to a neutral tribunal of arbitration, but judged by the society from which he comes. The basis of the structural dilemma of punishment for war is removed only when both sides, victors as well as vanquished, call the guilty in their own ranks to account.

Retaliation for terrorism raises other problems. The punishment for terrorist persecution presupposes a reversal of power, for in the very nature of terrorism the victims can do nothing for themselves. Terrorism is entirely one-sided, so outside help is needed to restore the law. Social and state terrorist institutions must be destroyed, the leaders and their accomplices arrested. A fundamental reversal of power structures is essential to bring the law into force at all. Half-hearted changes of elites usually leave the personnel of despotism alone and do not risk conflict with the old order. Truth commissions like those set up in South Africa and Latin America for purposes of national reconciliation decreased the number of lies told but had no powers of retribution. On the contrary: criminals who made full confessions got off scot-free. Earlier terrorist associations survived investigation with little loss of legitimacy. Their power remained unimpaired and there was no atonement for the injustice they had done. Truth alone is clearly no guarantee of justice. In so far as terrorism and mass murder are practised for the sake of the state, national loyalty raises obstacles to the prosecution of tyrants and their henchmen. The torturers are often honourably pensioned off, are not stripped of their decorations, and can live unmolested in retirement. Those who replace them react indignantly to outside accusations even decades later. National honour is always put before any official admission that a terrorist crime on a large scale has been committed at all.

Criminal proceedings have the advantage of individualizing guilt. Particular offenders, not the state or the nation, are in the dock. Guilt rests on individual shoulders. But some collective crimes go far beyond infringement of the law. The organization of concentration camps, mass murder and genocide is much more than a legal offence, and from the first the extent of the crime exceeds that of any possible punishment. It is impossible to imagine equal retribution. There can be no fitting atonement for such acts. The idea of just retribution, like the principle of equivalence, fails before the extent of the crime. Even the maximum penalty merely signals that the criminals cannot get away with their crimes with complete impunity.

Mass terrorism not only has countless victims but requires a large number of perpetrators. Only a collective, whether state-organized or not, is in a position to imprison, torture and kill human beings in their hundreds of thousands, or indeed in their millions. The destructive power of the collective exceeds the sum of the destructive powers of all the individuals concerned, for cooperation is a destructive force in itself. Consequently, the concept of 'collective guilt' is by no means unjustified. It does not depend on the idea of the existence of a collective national soul, nor does it imply that the entire population of the state deliberately and intentionally decided on a course of persecution and eradication. In Germany the concept was rejected not on objective grounds but for reasons of political expedience. Soon after the end of the Second World War, the Western Allies and the German elites reached an agreement. They were in great haste to blame collective crimes on a radical minority that apparently represented no one else. But the negation of collective guilt is not collective innocence. Given that not all members of the collective German state were guilty, or were accomplices of the guilty, it does not follow that no one was really guilty. The laws of political representation apply to crimes committed by the state too. The patrons, followers and sycophants of the guilty, and those who voted for them, are responsible for the misdeeds of their elected representatives. If representation is institutionalized, then those representing state subjects will include some to whom those subjects did not give a vote, let alone a mandate. So to reject the term 'collective guilt' cannot neutralize the guilt that could have been offset only by the protest, resistance, and aid of every individual member of the national collective.

The guilt of the collective results from the sum of the guilty conduct of individuals with a combination of crimes of commission and omission, guilty utterances and guilty silence. The number of 'normal' mass murderers in the Second World War runs at least into tens of thousands, the number of those directly and indirectly involved runs into millions. They include the neighbours, companies and banks that enriched themselves from Jewish property; the 'People's Comrades' next door who denounced victims of persecution; the civil servants who organized deportations; the spectators who applauded when a column of prisoners was driven through their home town; the villagers who helped to hunt down fugitives; the police officers and soldiers who, even if they did not fire a gun themselves, cordoned off the area marked out for a police or military raid. In short, without the participation of countless Germans and European accomplices in East and West alike, the murder of the Jews would never have taken place. How can we fail to speak of collective guilt if only a few thousand just men and women are to be found among millions? The chances of a wanted Jew finding refuge with a Gentile on the continent of Europe during the Second World War were about one to 70,000. In Germany, the land of those who invented, planned and perpetrated genocide, the chances were of course even smaller.

Not every guilty act, of course, is a breach of the legal code. Not every sin of omission, morally reprehensible as it may be, is grounds for retribution. Pure passivity, deliberate ignorance, enjoyment of the misfortunes of others or obdurate silence are not criminal offences. However, they constitute the environment for a collective of murderers, their henchmen and profiteers which deserves punishment as a whole. Active membership of a criminal state association which directly commits murders is a criminal offence too. Most of the legal proceedings, however, never came to court. Instead of punitive retaliation, first there was collective silence and then – in several phases –

the expression of a certain horror, now and then a scandal, finally a well-meant appeal to everyone's duty to remember, and a retreat into introspection. When the gods of retribution sleep the benign goddesses of memory reigns. For the war criminals and those who followed them, the condition of cultivating memory is a cheap offer. Justice is replaced by the truthfulness of self-examination – which no one else can check. Memory costs nothing and atones for nothing. And there is no point in urging the victims to remember. They cannot forget anyway.

11

Forgetting

Some people are said to live entirely in the present. Only those of their contemporaries who happen to be with them at a given moment seem to attract their attention, and once a conversation is over they waste not a single further thought on it. An infallible instinct tells them to turn their minds away from everything that could distract them from their present occupation. No memory disturbs their concentration. They dislike the repetitive, reliable monotony of habit. For these virtuosos of oblivion, every episode is a new beginning, every appearance a debut. Their lives resemble a series of leaping musical intervals.

The art of such unconditionally literal presence of mind exerts a curious power of attraction. Those who shake off their memories have clear ground before them. The burden of experience is cast away. Of course no one can govern the course of memory entirely. Ultimately, neither remembering nor forgetting is voluntary. But those who have the gift of forgetting are free of the compulsion to be always consistent. Just as the past eludes them, they transform and forget themselves: they do not wonder who they are or where they come from. They are not checking up on anyone, least of all themselves. No doubts, sadness or self-consciousness trouble them. It is hard to tell whether such people are aware of themselves at all at any given moment.

There is something uncanny about such a mode of existence. People usually comfort themselves with the idea that what is forgotten can be recalled to mind, that it is stored in a kind of internal archive and can be reawakened by reflection. But forgetting, if we understand it in a suitably radical way, is not a rift in the memory, a temporary flaw, a mental shift or suppression. It is extinction. What has been entirely forgotten cannot be remembered any more. Even the smallest trace of memory has been obliterated. The imprint in the sand has disappeared.

In forgetting, mankind lives outside time. Memory loss does not just extinguish the awareness of history but obliterates all temporal consciousness. Without memory there is no idea of the future, without a basis of past experience there is no expectation. It is true that forgetting takes time. The impression of the moment fades gradually, becoming fainter with every passing hour. For time itself is the gravedigger of memory. It turns traces of events into dust and ashes, and in the end it too is cancelled out. In a condition of true oblivion there is no before or after, no earlier and later, no yesterday and tomorrow, not even a Now linking different aspects of time together. Someone without memory lives entirely in the moment, surrounded by a chasm of timelessness. He does not know who he is, he knows nothing of his present or past nature or his mortality. Because he does not relate to himself at all he feels no fear of his end either. He is free of the fear of death. Lethe, the river of oblivion, does not divide the realm of the living from the world of the dead, but flows along the borders of paradise. Those who drink from that river forget pain and guilt, pleasure and suffering, grief and death.

Some people are inclined to regard this condition as a

misfortune, but what do they know of the inner world of those who have lost the habit of memory, their lack of inhibition, their folly, perhaps their cheerfulness? Do we not secretly envy them and crave that other condition? To those who like a systematic way of life, forgetting is generally suspect. There is sometimes talk of the 'flight into oblivion', of forgetting honour and duty, of the deplorable thoughtlessness of those with no memory, of the 'unreal existence' of someone who forgets himself – as if the whole point of existence were to be constantly within ourselves, storing up all experiences in the memory instead of closing the chapter. Contrary to much well-meant advice, surely the aim of knowing ourselves when we cannot avoid it is not to remember what we have suppressed, but to be able to shake off experiences reiterated in the memory. The way out of compulsive repetition is through the memory – but it is only a roundabout route to final oblivion.

Some injuries, however, cannot be forgotten. Their scars in the body's memory do not heal over. The experience of violence has broken through the barrier of the skin and penetrated the core of the self. Even time cannot heal this trauma. The pain returns, the overwhelming moment, the sense of impotence, the sight of the dead, the screams of the dying. These previous experiences spontaneously breach the protective dam of oblivion in nightmares and waking dreams. A slight, chance cause is enough to release the tide of remembered images that suddenly floods the conscious mind. It can wash over the injured even years later, sweeping them back to the past they have never escaped. They feel as they did then, helpless and abandoned, bones aching, hands numb and rigid, fingers and eyelids trembling, until at last the black void spreads again and all sensation freezes over.

The physically injured do not shake off their history. The

cripple whose leg has been torn off in an explosion is reminded of his misfortune at every step he takes with the aid of a crutch or an artificial limb. The survivor whose face is disfigured is surrounded by surprised and sympathetic looks, or people who avert their eyes. Every glance in the mirror shows him yet again what he has become. The mutilated man cannot move as he would like; his body, his self is always in his way. He can no longer act unselfconsciously and out of his physical core. The injury is far more than a 'handicap' that merely slows down the usual course of action. It is a visible stigma, a rift that runs through the body and will not close up. Unquestioning existence in the world is gone for ever. The disaster is lodged within his body.

The past weighs heavily on the present of the victim of violence. Mind and senses are no longer free to face the future. While the violence was still going on he had to limit his sense of time in order to survive. Dreaming of the future, thinking beyond the present, would have impaired the need to concentrate on the day's demands. When a man's life is in danger he must be able to forget quickly, but once the danger is over the victim's altered perception of time casts a shadow over his future life. The over-alertness of the senses endures and will now control all perceptions. The merest hint of danger sets off a prompt attack of terror, which is why many war veterans appear intemperate and aggressive to their contemporaries. There is no way back from the jungle to the moderate zones of civilian society. The survivors are still held in the dungeon of constant watchfulness. They do not sleep, they hear every sound in their drowsy state, they are worn down, fretful, tired to death.

People who live in the present come and go but do not linger. They tell us nothing and refrain from inflicting their life histories on others. They are free of melancholy and pride, resentment and ambition. Since they lack any idea of death they waste no time wondering what will make them immortal. They need not be expected to produce great works, memorable contributions to the cultural heritage of mankind. They require no future and no utopias, nor do they want to go down in history. They are not thinking of leaving anything behind, and in that they undermine the foundations of society, tradition and morality.

All social morality is ultimately based on memory. Gratitude links human beings together, conscience protects them from each other. A sense of good and evil, however, does not spring from spontaneous inspiration but from arduous, painful experience, and it is engraved afresh on the minds of every generation. To speak of educating or moulding the conscience is simply to gloss over reality. It is pain that inscribes morality on the memory. The conscience is forcibly aroused by the tyranny of education, and militates against the inclination to forget. Human beings are expected to remember their misdeeds, take conscientious note of their faults, pay their debts on time. Every project to improve the human species demands an energetic campaign against the moral failure of memory, the metamorphoses of the self and the temptations of the present.

Power, the written word and religious ritual are the strongest bulwarks against oblivion. Ritual calls upon the dead and reminds human beings of their origins. As an institutionalized form of repetition, ritual shores up the fragile connections within the collective. It is performed at regular intervals; forgetting to observe it is like sacrilege. Irrespective of the object of veneration, the form of ritual is a kind of remembering in practice. The mourning ritual of farewell averts oblivion and preserves the memory of the dead even though life goes on.

Long before the invention of the written word, ritual was a way of linking the present to the past.

The first written records were financial accounts, lists of goods, and laws. Accounts are reminders of the debtor's duty to pay what he owes, legal decrees are reminders of the subject's duty to obey authority. Government and the barter economy do not tolerate forgetfulness, and writing is one of their tools, a defence against oblivion. Words and thoughts are set down, the spoken word is no longer transient. It has been said that something recorded in writing is part of the world for all eternity. Thoughts written down can of course be set aside and ignored for a while, but they are on record and can be retrieved at any time. Recorded history is permanently rescued from oblivion and need no longer be retold. Memory acquires material substance in writing.

Power has made use of the written word too. Power forgets nothing. It suspects contradiction, rebellion and treachery everywhere, and consequently seeks to know everything about its subjects. The tendency towards surveillance is by no means peculiar to totalitarian dictatorships, but is a basic element in every form of power. Government authorities kept files on their staff, faithfully documenting praise and blame. Monitoring institutions have countless amounts of data and lists of omissions at their disposal, since only complete knowledge guarantees complete security. Suspicion will not tolerate oblivion. The dream of power is an all-embracing archive recording all inclinations and actions.

Power seeks to prevent offences against the norm by means of threats and punishments. It therefore aims to punish misdeeds and deter future malefactors. Admittedly punishment does not usually improve anyone; it is more likely to put the malefactor on his guard, let him feel that he has been victimized and reinforce his lack of conscience. But it shows very clearly that guilt will meet with retribution and will not be ignored. It is true that penal atonement does not undo any evil that was done, let alone its consequences. It cannot compensate for the victim's suffering. Punishment is not a personal settlement of accounts but retribution for breaking the law. However, the brand remains indelibly marked on the criminal's body, as a lasting reminder of the law's long memory to anyone who sees it.

A society that never forgot anything would be intolerable. If human beings were not so made that most of what they experience disappears from their minds for ever, they would be bound to an endless chain of the balancing of accounts, setbacks and retribution. They would be entirely occupied to the last with paying each other back for their actions. Not the smallest new beginning would be possible. Since nothing done in the past can be reversed or undone, their existence would be eaten up by continuing the consequences of the past into the future. Resentment and irreconcilability would poison social relationships. Everyday life would be determined by discord and the desire for vengeance. Forgetfulness frees us from all this, releases us from the consequences of our actions and keeps us from looking back at the unhappy experiences of our lives. And it spares us having to keep forgiving each other. Forgiving often calls for magnanimity, generosity and will power; forgetting requires only a short memory.

But some things cannot be forgiven. The venial sins, oversights and misdemeanours of everyday life are worth forgetting; crime is not. Minor sins of omission are the result of the thoughtlessness, carelessness and failure to pay attention of the person who has forgotten something. Crime, on the other hand, is planned and carried out deliberately. The criminal knows in advance that his action is prohibited. He is not a man who lives in the present, but acts with full knowledge and memory. Murder, finally, will tolerate no absolution. Its guilt is never invalidated by time. Death breaks the continuity of social life. Murder breaks the taboo on which all social intercourse depends, the taboo on killing.

What is true of individual conduct is applicable only in part to public life. Collectives do not remember in the same way as people. One person's memories cannot be transferred to someone else's mind. In spite of recitation and ritual, in spite of narrative, memorial or funeral ceremonies, every memory ultimately remains individual. At the most we can speak of common memory or collective forgetfulness in the sense of an analogy or a social commitment. The norm of opinion which prescribes that we should all have certain memories and ideas acts as a generally binding social compulsion. Whether everyone really remembers in the right way, of course, cannot be ascertained. All the same, rules are always being made to militate against oblivion and prevent the failure of moral memory.

In earlier times peace treaties usually provided for a general amnesty to prevent blood feuds and make it possible for social life to continue. The injured party was to accept the malefactor's atonement, forgive him, and consider the war over. No more thought was to be given to the preceding evils for all eternity. The treaty ending the butchery of the Thirty Years' War invoked the idea of 'eternal oblivion and amnesty' for all hostile acts on both sides. Refraining from punishment was intended to encourage mutual forbearance. The hatchet was buried, the treaty cancelled out the war as if it had never been. People were supposed to behave as if they had forgotten the violence and treat their enemies as if there had been no war. There was no question of 'reappraising' or 'coming to terms with' the past. It was taken into account – and then forgotten. No one thought it could catch up with you again. Of course the negotiators were aware that war and violence cannot simply be forgotten to order. The peace treaty, however, promised a kind of fictional oblivion with very real consequences, for by acting as if they had never harmed each other people could more easily make further agreements and do business together.

Public oblivion presupposes that both parties recognize each other's equal rights. A peace treaty which leaves one side subject to the other is not a treaty but a diktat. However great the material inequality between victors and vanquished, the form of a peace treaty demands absolute equality. Oblivion calls for equality because inequality opens the gates wide to memory. The victors decide on the guilt of the vanquished and make them pay for it. The vanquished, in turn, are full of resentment, which makes them keep thinking of vengeance to come. Peace diktats with clauses allotting guilt date from the old days of royal and foreign rule. They were issued by monarchs dictating to their vassals, or colonialists dictating to rebellious natives. The model of a peace between nation states which did not forget the preceding war was not adopted until the twentieth century, and since then memory has prevailed over oblivion.

The case of collective terrorism is quite different. No equality, either formal or material, exists between the surviving victims and the terrorists. Here there is neither a treaty to be concluded nor a hatchet to be buried. There has been no struggle. Any talk of reconciliation glosses over this structural bias. There can be no reconciliation between the murderer and the victim. An outstretched hand offered by the killer to the survivor is an insult. No, we terrorists and our children bear the victims no grudge. The gesture assumes that the criminal has a right to forgive. Even worse: it requires the survivors to disown their dead and forget them instantly. In fact all the author of injustice can do is beg forgiveness and ask leniency for the unforgivable, and he cannot avoid the risk of rejection. But flying in the face of all that is just, he can expect that ultimately his request will be granted, for the commandment of equivalency applies to the communication of reconciliation. A man asking forgiveness is confessing to a crime. The apology admits guilt and is a voluntary if cheap gift, positively demanding forgiveness whether out of forbearance or goodwill, complacency, magnanimity or mercy. Those who forgive are enhancing themselves, giving themselves a sense of moral superiority, and the malefactor's humble request counts on that fact. On the other hand, the injured party who remains implacable and frowns on the surreptitious attempt to win immunity from punishment offends against society's rules of exchange and is making himself awkward. Social reconciliation is thus a proven method of glossing over suffering and putting the victim in the wrong. The survivor who prefers to keep faith with his dead can only reject the apology, refuse to be reconciled, and thus exclude himself from society. For him, the offered gesture of reconciliation is nothing but a social trap.

Material 'compensation' also has the odour of injustice about it. Blood-guilt cannot be financially discharged. Business deals are concluded after the final payment is made, but compensation ends nothing. The moral account remains open for ever. Morally it should be taken for granted that wages for slave labour are paid, at least after the event, and that bargaining over them is beneath anyone's dignity. But financial compensation for years of painful imprisonment transforms the price of a damaged life into the most abstract of values, one that means nothing, and payments in compensation for the loss of relatives reckon up death in terms of cash, changing the dead into goods for sale and then haggling over their number and their price. The degree of relationship determines the amount paid. But how high is the price of a grandfather's death, or a mother's, what is the life of an uncle worth, the life of a sister or a nephew? It shows the moral level of modern society that we think a few banknotes can settle the bill of suffering and death, and indeed it is evidence of the nature of the crime that it still eludes conversion into the most common medium of social life, money. The victims, most of whom are not interested in what is a low level of compensation anyway, are thus forced to apply for money simply so that people will understand what happened to them.

Collective murder cannot be expiated or atoned for, even in the collective mind. In the case of Germany, the society of the killers ignored the dead for a while and tried to elude unwelcome memories. This was not psychological 'suppression' but oblivion through avoidance of memory. Something suppressed is not available to the conscious mind and will come to the surface only after arduous effort. There was never any question of that. Many Germans knew perfectly well what had happened in the past but avoided thinking about it. Forgetting took the form of escape, flight, a wish not to know, a deliberate policy adopted towards the past.

However, since memory was by no means extinguished, public ceremonies could be held after years of silence, traces could be discovered, memorials erected. In the society of the perpetrators of crimes, remembrance was declared a duty and commemoration a state act. At the same time consciences were cleared by admissions of guilt that cost only a few words. To this day much effort has been expended on countering the sin of forgetting. Fulfilling the duty to remember is regarded as a test of moral integrity and finally promises release from the debt. In this the society of the perpetrators has appropriated a saying that belongs to the history of the victims. 'The secret of deliverance is memory, for oblivion lengthens the period of exile,' was originally the insight of a Hassidic rabbi of the Diaspora. Remembrance and memory were to ensure the continuity of their tradition for all the Jews dispersed around the globe, and it is as presumptuous as it is meaningless for the well-settled society of their persecutors to adopt the maxim. A murderer is not 'delivered' from his guilt by remembering, nor does his identity as a murderer permanently enable him to understand and acknowledge himself.

Since there was no punishment at the right time the guilt remained unatoned for. Instead, a curious language of public conscience has developed among the belated plethora of commemorations, a rhetoric of moral feelings which tries either to 'internalize' the question of guilt or to shift the blame. The old craving for forgiving and forgetting can be sensed beneath the talk of shame, guilt and disgrace, although no one dares express it openly. Public speeches on the theatrical stage of memory do not deal with crimes and guilt but move between empty appeals, hypocrisy, sentimental confessions and clichés of self-accusation.

Even to speak of 'deeply felt shame' is absurd in the face of mass murder and war crimes. Shame forces itself on us when our own actions or ideas fall far below our ideal image of ourselves. Shame means seeing ourselves devalued by comparison with our own social group or personal ideal. Someone who feels ashamed experiences a sense of his own inadequacy, set off by a sudden change in his view of himself. He lowers his gaze so as not to be seen or noticed. Suddenly he recognizes himself as the author of his own misdemeanours, the cause of offence. Shame is not something unloaded on him by others but is like an attack from within, overwhelming him, permeating and paralysing his whole person. He would like to conceal himself, hide, disappear into the earth, become invisible, but there is no way out. The instinct of flight is blocked, he is chained to the situation.

Shame eludes display. It seeks expression but cannot be represented, so it cannot be ritually staged. Shame is totally unsuitable for public confession. A man ashamed feels no urge to reveal himself to all eyes and ears. On the contrary, he avoids any occasion that might bring the blush of shame to his face. Shame isolates him, and witnesses usually try, politely, to overlook it. In shame a human being is thrown entirely back on himself and his own failure. He is on his own; shame is not a feeling that can be shared with others. A grief shared, it is said, is a grief halved; a joy shared is a double joy. But shame can never be material for a common emotion. People can feel ashamed side by side with each other, but not *with* other people. Shame is therefore inappropriate and insignificant as a reaction to a collective crime. It is transient, an emotion subject to oblivion. The tide of shame ebbs again as suddenly as it came flooding in. Above all, however, shame is a private, indeed an egocentric feeling. It is not concerned with the suffering of others but solely with our failure to live up to our own ideals, with the damage to our image of ourselves.

Nonetheless people can feel ashamed on behalf of others, people close to them, people to whom they feel they belong, or with whom they share something else in common. No very close bond is necessary for us to feel ashamed of the poor conduct of others. This second-hand shame is often felt when the person concerned is obviously *not* ashamed although he has every reason to be. Someone feeling shame on behalf of another relieves that other person of the rigours of remorse. Children can be ashamed of their parents in this way, parents can be ashamed for their children, and similarly state representatives can be ashamed of the crimes of their society. Those born later can feel ashamed at second hand for the indifference, murderous feelings or shamelessness of their forebears. It is part of the unwanted legacy of ancestors that they pass on to their descendants the remorse and shame they refused to feel themselves.

There is much talk of shame in memorial speeches; consequently the speaker himself never expresses personal shame. At most he deplores the shamelessness of others. Anyone who makes out that he is publicly confessing shame is really presenting himself as someone who knows he occupies the moral high ground. What looks like inner remorse is actually a sign of secret pride. The man bowed down by shame shows that he has diligently learned his lesson from history, and thus the public show of shame is really the opposite of what it claims to be. Anyone who utters the word 'shame' is either trying to appeal to the conscience of others or to take refuge from guilt in the ardour of his sentiments. Even worse: the rhetoric of shame encompasses an outrageous redefinition of the misdeed. For shame strikes involuntarily, after unintentional misdemeanours, and speaking of shame in connection with a mass murder thus implies that collective crime was not committed intentionally but was like a blow of fate, an accident, a misfortune, a deplorable historical mishap.

The sense of guilt shows itself differently. Shame arises from injuring one's own ideals, guilt from harm done to others which we wish undone, or for which we would like to make amends. Guilt visualizes the victim's suffering in quite a different way from feelings of shame. Guilt always relates to others, it recognizes our own misdeeds with reference not to private ideals but to social norms. However, guilt and the sense of guilt may be clearly distinguished. We judge whether someone is guilty by the normal criteria and by what he did or failed to do. It makes no difference whether he himself feels guilty. The fact that most perpetrators of mass crimes and their accomplices displayed notoriously clear consciences and tried to talk their way out of their predicament, making all kinds of threadbare excuses, does not decrease their guilt in the least. Conversely, confessions of guilt by people who did nothing personally seem to be far too cheap. They cost nothing, and only serve the speaker employing the rhetoric of guilt to polish up his own self-image. Moral confusion is evident when those who are entirely blameless tell each other how guilty they feel, while the real criminals show not the slightest sign of remorse. Yet this confusion has a psychological function: if you feel guilty you can also feel morally cleansed. Narcissistic German guilt has less to do with the remorse of true guilt feelings than with an apparent demonstration of improved moral standards.

Human beings can also feel guilt on behalf of others, those who themselves lack insight into their guilt. They feel as if they themselves were responsible for the crime, or even as if they had personally committed it. It is obvious that this has nothing to do with a rational view of the facts. The vague, insistent sense of guilt stokes up resentment and prevents independence of judgement. There is no escape into autonomy, for the only way out lies in maintaining a distance from the collective that committed the crime. Nothing but distancing themselves will enable those born after the event to act logically. Responsibility can be assumed without an attitude of penitent remorse or a sense of personal guilt. Those taking on the guilt of others will partly discharge their guilt, feeling responsible for mitigating the consequences of the crime. Such retrospective expiation does not undo or compensate for anything, nor does it shore up hopes that a time will come when everything is forgiven and forgotten. Even if the passage of time closes the account some day, guilt for collective crime cannot be settled. Reparations are not a punishment that eliminates the crime or a way to reach the realm of oblivion. They merely ease the burden on the author of the misdeed, and guarantee survivors at least a minimum of recognition and support.

While the rhetoric of shame tries to shift the real guilt inwards, into the mind and the heart, the rhetoric of disgrace operates in the other direction. The rancour of guilt feelings makes itself felt here too. The idea of 'disgrace' comes from the vocabulary of a society based on notions of honour. Malefactors were banished from the social circle 'in disgrace'. Individuals can bring disgrace on a collective, a family, a clan, a social class or a nation if they contravene its standards. However, it is impossible for a group or a nation to disgrace itself deliberately. Disgraceful conduct is ascribed to it, and the dishonour is felt in so far as an individual's image of himself is based on membership of the group. To describe genocide as a 'disgraceful act' presupposes an idea of national honour that was discredited either by the accusations of survivors or the crimes of a radical minority from among its own ranks. The rhetoric of disgrace seeks to diminish the fact that the collective of perpetrators numbered hundreds of thousands and was supported by a majority in society. It repudiates guilt by association and complicity, and turns the society of the perpetrators into a society of supposed victims. As with shame, it remains entirely fixed on the side of the perpetrators, and even more – it asks sympathy for injustice apparently done to them. Anyone making himself out the victim of a disgraceful act that he himself has committed is bent on reversing the roles and unloading his guilt on others.

It is doubtful whether a collective crime can be approached at all with the moral feelings of which individuals are sometimes capable. Feelings of shame or disgrace are inadequate, deceptive and insignificant in view of real collective guilt and its consequences. The inner law-court of the conscience is not a substitute for moral judgement, political action, and the assumption of responsibility in retrospect. Treblinka, Babi Yar and Auschwitz are not matters of German shame or honour but of German guilt. The public rituals of mourning and lamentation with which the survivors and their descendants remember their dead are not appropriate for the moral relief of non-Jewish Germans and their European accomplices. Shared memory cannot be acquired by devious means, and still less can shared oblivion, for there is no such thing.

12

The fading of the horror

Dense green thickets of vegetation hide the old fortress. A troop of soldiers have set up a radio station on the forecourt, camouflage nets are draped over their vehicles, the men are lounging around their campfire, open knives at their belts, clean-shaven young faces, shorn heads. It is a safe place for manoeuvres, since the old fort provides plenty of cover. A stone bridge crosses the dried-up moat, the iron gate stands ajar; in the courtyard, doors covered by grilles peer out from under green mounds, entrances to the empty underground storerooms. On the left a footpath runs along the castle wall, a spiral staircase winds its way down the corner tower. It is dark and damp there, smelling of mould and violence, and sparse rays of sunlight fall through narrow loopholes. You cautiously seek a footing on the slippery trodden earth floor, water drips from the walls. This could be the abode of bats, spiders, rats, nocturnal creatures. The faint light of an electric bulb flickers in the distance at the end of the long battlement walk. Somewhere, in one of the niches, there is a table made of rough wooden planks nailed together, and two stout benches. Numbers are painted over the passageways down to the vaults: eight, nine, ten, thirteen, the casemates are numbered, each niche is a self-contained dungeon, a crypt.

This German fortress on the Upper Kuhberg in Ulm was originally built as a defensive bulwark against France. However, the mighty citadel was never used for defence, only as an ammunition depot and underground prison. In 1870 prisoners of war, the Moroccan auxiliaries of Germany's traditional enemy, were thrown into its cold and draughty vaults. Then the military withdrew and let the walls fall into ruin, until the Brownshirts rediscovered the abandoned fort in November 1933 and brought it into use as a penal camp for political prisoners. A concentration camp in Ulm? The first inmates arrived from Württemberg in two open trucks, their guards were recruited from the army of local unemployed farm labourers and craftsmen, eighty men for 200 prisoners, a concentration camp as a job creation measure, terror as a way of earning your living. They could do as they liked on the Kuhberg; no screams penetrated the metre-thick walls. A discreet, secret scene for crime on the outskirts of the city. Hermetically sealed off from the world above, the executioners were alone with their victims.

On Sundays, when the citizens relax after their week's work, power holds sway underground. The yell of the guards echoes through the vaults, it is the day for calling the register, counting the eating implements, cutting hair, cleaning clothes. The rusty tin bowls are scoured for hours on end. A blunt machine takes the hair off the men's heads, shorn in sign of disgrace, all cut to the same length, close to the scalp. Next door uniforms that have been scraped clean are brushed down, then it's out to the checkpoint, there's always something to object to, a missing button, a mark on the trousers, followed by punishment drill in the snow and mud – 'Lie down, get up, jump, quick march!' – to the point of exhaustion, back to the crypt at a run to scrub the mud off, cleanliness is a prisoner's first duty. Water comes from the well where two one-armed men work the pump. It is brackish, contaminated water. Black worms wriggle at the bottom of the tin cans. Urine and faeces seep straight into the groundwater from the latrines.

No one dies on the Kuhberg. Anyone about to perish of cold, starvation and beating is discharged early or sent on to Dachau. No one wants any deaths yet because of the foreign press, no one is yet struck down at work. There is nothing to do in this camp. The prisoners wait for weeks and months, stand around in the cramped casemates four metres underground day after day, each day like the next, reveille at six, breakfast at seven, chicory coffee and black bread, at twelve a litre of watery stew, at four in the afternoon a bit of bread and margarine. Now and then a guard comes in, picks a man out and amuses himself shouting, beating, kicking him in the groin and the belly, satisfying a brief desire for violence. No laws restrict his tyranny; this endless condition is officially known as protective custody for the prisoners, none of whom knows what still awaits him. The memory of freedom pales, evaporates, they are buried alive in these caverns. What is the precise duration of eternity, a year, a day, a minute, the second when the blow falls?

The history of the German concentration camp system began on the Kuhberg. It was a place of disorganized, random terror. As yet the prisoners did not wear striped pyjamas but discarded Berlin tramline uniforms, black uniforms marked in red lead on the sleeves and trouser legs. The jailers were still members of the SA, the lansquenets of the Brownshirt revolution, a guard of amateur thugs soon to be deprived of power by the professional terrorists of the SS. No written camp constitution yet existed, nor did the intricate system of punishments, the division of power, forced labour and the death factories. In 1935 the Wehrmacht took over the fortress, the prisoners were moved to Dachau, the inspection centre in Oranienburg gradually closed the unofficial camps and concentrated its slave army in new, modern camps built above ground: cities of huts behind barbed wire, watchtowers, stone quarries, factory sheds, crematoria. Withdrawal from the darkness of limbo led straight to the upper world and the inmost circles of hell.

Hundreds of studies and reports have tried to convey the truth about the world of the camps. A few criminal trials were held, a few executioners hanged; most, in the usual phrase, were acquitted for lack of evidence: years of membership of a terrorist association did not count. German justice simply failed in the face of the moral demands of the Nuremberg trials. The further the pen-pushing criminals had sat from the mountain of corpses, the milder was their punishment. The commandant of the Kuhberg camp near Ulm grew old with honour, covered by the merciful cloak of the post-war amnesty. He drew his well-earned pension. His period of service in the concentration camp had counted towards it.

The successor state of East Germany rid itself of collective guilt by simply ranging itself on the side of the victims and explaining the barbarism of the Nazi regime as a late consequence of capitalism, thus keeping its own view of the world straight. The West German Republic employed the methods of the money economy. It turned guilt into debts and made payments in 'reparation', liquidating the damage, one could say, by loan conversion. The big privately owned companies on whose factory sites countless camps stood proved less generous. Over the decades they refused to pay meagre compensation to the survivors for the exploitation of their lives.

A curious conflict is typical of the social consciousness. We have the unspeakably empty phrases of soapbox oratory, emotional talk of tragic guilt and involvement, of forgiveness and reconciliation, where in reality there is nothing to be reconciled. Every year we see the mourning rituals of commemoration, well-meant duty exercises on the national timetable. We get the threadbare condemnation of suppressing memory, as if those terrible deeds were not real but a psychological trauma, as if anyone could ever 'come to terms' with murder and violence. We get the ingenuous assurance that lessons have now been learned from history, for even the merciful dispensation of being born after the event is no protection against folly. And finally many people, old and young alike, play an obscene numbers game, counting up the historical quotas of murder, setting Auschwitz off against Dresden, Dachau against Katyn. The scale of reaction ranges from the persistent lies of fellow-travellers to the demonization of ordinary executioners, from moral self-anaesthesia to the official confession of guilt, from helpless appeals not to forget to physical attacks on those who would at least like to put up a memorial plaque.

The well-meaning intelligentsia do not escape this dilemma either. Historians endlessly debate who ultimately gave the orders, although the machinery of the concentration camps could function smoothly only because the many small cogs in it went along with the system and did their duty, because the middle ranks of henchmen and the torturers on the spot had full powers of decision, because the population looked stonily away in the streets and on the railway stations.

Teachers officially entrusted with the work of 'coming to terms' with the past try in vain to instil historic awareness into the grandchildren of the perpetrators, while the school classes they take round the memorial sites fool around, Walkmans plugged into their ears, at most asking where the gas chamber is. No sightseeing excursion is complete without its sensation. Local historians of the younger generation industriously search the archives for documentary records and come up with many stories from the camps, bring buried pieces of evidence to light, mentions of the camp on the corner of the street and of those unknown concentration camps whose names read like a gazetteer of place names from Central and Eastern Europe.

Whence comes this awkward position somewhere between denial, the appeal to memory, and industrious work on the details? They are helpless responses to a terror that leaves all nightmares far behind. Reality exceeds the power of imagination. Who does not remember the pictures of the camps being liberated? Here the verminous, emaciated, bony figures in grotesque zebra-striped rags, their dull glances looking as if they were already dead this side of the grave, the heaps of skeletons, the bundles of fleshless arms and legs being thrown into the trucks.

And there the comfortable German living rooms of those who did the deed, flower-patterned wallpaper, a heavy oak desk, a lampshade made of tattooed skin taken from the dead, a shrunken head with long, matted strands of hair in a display case, a trophy of cannibal savages. But the faces of the executioners are normal faces, not monstrous masks, the faces of well-nourished German fathers and mothers, neighbours like you and me. The transports always came early, the work was usually done by eleven, when we came off duty we would go into town to the café where the band was playing, it cheered us up . . . Which of us have not found ourselves looking through such pictures and swiftly drawing in our breath, shaking our heads, shrugging our shoulders, cracking a cynical joke, wanting to look away, thinking of retaliation until the chill sets in, freezing the shock over and letting us return to the normal business of the day?

But the shock of these horrific images rests on an erroneous perception. The heaps of skeletons do not represent the meaning of the concentration camps. The system was never intended to leave corpses both living and dead behind. They were only unplanned remnants left by the murderous machinery because the capacity of the incinerators was inadequate. It proved possible to get rid of most of the dead in time, blow up the crematoria and dispose of the records. The system served to show that anything is possible, that human bodies can be slaughtered and destroyed leaving no trace behind, as if they had never been. Only sporadic traces are still left, a memorial tablet here and there, the accounts of survivors. But what are we to do but go on looking at what happened, keep the images before our eyes, seek out the unknown places where these horrors took place?

You will not have to go far. Take a large-scale map of Central Europe and unfold it on the table. Now draw in large dots, preferably in ink, on the big cities: Munich, Linz, Vienna, Hanover, Hamburg, Berlin, Danzig, Warsaw and Riga. Then look for the major industrial centres: Nuremberg, Mannheim, Essen, Salzgitter, Leipzig, Kattowitz, and then the holiday areas: the Vosges Mountains, the Black Forest, the Swabian Alps, the Upper Palatinate, the Harz mountains, the Thuringian forest. Finally, add the centres of intellectual life: Weimar and Jena, Göttingen and Krakow, Salzburg and Bayreuth. Big black dots all over the paper, the sites of German concentration camps. You don't believe your eyes? You still have to add the villages and small towns, Überlingen on Lake Constance, for instance, Michelstadt in the Odenwald, Goslar, Papenburg, Husum. You will end up with over 1,200 dots, 1,200 concentration camps, not counting the assembly and transit camps, the camps for foreign slave labourers and prisoners of war, or the countless

'Jewish camps' in the east, staging posts on the way to Treblinka, Chelmno and Auschwitz. These were 1,200 concentration camps: they were not labour camps for convicts, as so many of the earnest city fathers would like to fool us into believing today, they were concentration camps in our own neighbourhoods, on busy main roads, in the woods near our home towns, in requisitioned schools, on the sites of privately owned armaments firms. The map is sprinkled all over with ugly dots; Central Europe is covered by a close-meshed network of camps.

The central point of the Greater German Reich was to be in neither Berlin nor Munich. Heinrich Himmler, head of the SS and in charge of the camps, had chosen another cultural location for the headquarters of his Death's Head units, the castle of Wewelsburg near Paderborn. He planned to build a gigantic palace for the Führer here with a castle wall eighteen metres high, mighty gate towers, a barracks for the men and a colony of villas for the officers, as well as a railway viaduct, a ceremonial avenue for parades, and a direct link to the new autobahn, all architecturally focused on the central point of this little world, the north tower of the old castle. The village that stood in the way of the architectural plans was to be moved, its inhabitants resettled as pioneers in the east, and their farms appropriated.

And so that the knights of the Round Table would want for nothing here in their Grail castle, treasures were looted from occupied Europe: valuable paintings, antique furniture, the finest porcelain for table use and decoration, carpets, silver and gold. Occult festivals of consecration were to be held here, meetings of the Death's Head order, conferences and discussions to reinforce the noble generals' *esprit de corps.* But none of these grandiose plans came to anything. The Wewelsburg remained a grotesque torso, witness to the new Middle Ages, a historical masquerade, a farce that cost 1,285 prisoners their lives.

From the castle moat you go down a narrow stairway to the sanctum of the north tower. Your footsteps echo gloomily through the circular vaulted cellar. Twelve empty stone plinths are arranged round the wall, the empty thrones of the group leaders. If you stand right beside the wall you can make yourself heard all over the room in a whisper. There is a multiple echo in the centre of the hall. Up above, at the top of the monumental dome, turns the grey sun-wheel, the swastika, the hooked cross of four gallows, in endless motion. Does it not remind us of the limbs of victims of the past broken on the wheel? Directly below, a shallow stone basin with a gas pipe in the middle is let into the floor. According to the tale told in the village, this was where the eternal flame was to burn the wooden coats of arms of dead SS knights. This gloomy domed hall, a hall for the dead, was carved out of the rock by the prisoners. It is the crypt of the twelve companions, the Valhalla of the Nordic order.

Before the slaves could begin converting the castle they first had to dig out their own camp. It was the familiar architecture of the German concentration camp: wooden huts, watchtowers, an electric fence with a death zone just outside it, accommodation for the guards, attractive detached houses for the camp officers, a crematorium and a gatehouse with a raised platform for a machine gun. The SS paid over 600,000 Reichsmarks to have the German cultural monuments of their own concentration camp tended. The 3,000 workers, however, came free; more could be brought in at any time if they died. Russian slave labourers and prisoners of war were brought here, Poles, Czechs and gypsies, German convicts from Sachsenhausen marked with the black or green chevrons of the 'work-shy' or 'professional criminals', as the jargon of the camps put it. Many of them were promoted to administrative tasks and became block wardens and Kapos, a privileged troop of assistants who relieved the executioners of work. They were both victims and perpetrators, functionaries who passed on orders to those below them and freed themselves from the threat of death by goading, tormenting and killing their fellow prisoners.

Only one group resisted the enticements of power: Jehovah's Witnesses, members of whose sect were valued by the SS as reliable servants. While a relentless struggle for survival went on between Germans and foreigners, between wearers of the black and green chevrons, the faithful believers with their mauve chevron held firmly together. They had been sent to the camps ever since 1935 because of their steadfast refusal to do war service or give the German salute. Three hundred of them were taken to Wewelsburg as good labourers to work on the sites of the pagan cult there. They protected each other from attacks, looked after comrades who had been beaten, and shared their meagre rations without ever rebelling against the superior power. They conscientiously kept the camp rules, cleaned their block and showed exemplary morale in their work. It was unnecessary to guard them; the Jehovah's Witnesses would not try to escape. None of them had ever picked up a cudgel or wanted a position of power. Religious principle welded the group together, a rare example of fraternity and peaceable conduct inside the concentration camp. They survived because they endured the violence that confirmed them in their faith.

Silence lies over the empty parade ground today. The asphalt is scarred, the holes in it mended. The village fire brigade's equipment is now stored in what was the prisoners' kitchen, and a joiner's workshop has been set up in a garage. But the watchtowers and blocks are gone; the last hut was demolished twenty years ago. A young woman is just leaving the old gatehouse carrying her shopping: meat, vegetables, chocolate. The villagers now buy their groceries where the starving columns of prisoners were once inspected as they marched out. It is the same building, the walls are the same, but the arch of the gateway has been walled up, the tower demolished, the machine-gun placement torn down. Fresh plaster covers up memories, and the windows have been altered too, internal partitions have been removed, the rooms are converted, the roof re-tiled. The present moved in here long ago. The gatehouse has been altered and rebuilt until it is almost unrecognizable; the work of oblivion has been thorough indeed. Whether by means of demolition or conversion, memory loss has a practical foundation based on the removal of material traces. But how does anyone live in the rooms where the masters of the camp once relaxed; how can anyone sit comfortably in a corner where they used to prop their rifles?

The village has rolled over the old camp, churning it into the ground. If you want to know what happened here you must visit the concentration camp museum in the former castellan's service apartment. Here a model of the camp has been built to scale, small low-built huts on a silver-grey base, little watchtowers, tiny red-brown buildings, the gate, the kitchen, the bunker, the crematorium, all made of cardboard, precisely lined up, a conscientious, loving reconstruction reduced to the format of a toy. All the model lacks are the little characters waiting in the wings, and then the drama of the camp could begin. This bright, clean miniature is attractive, more memorable than copies of documents and written records, a teaching aid for visitors which turns reality into an illustration, prettifies and neutralizes it.

All that can still be tracked down has been meticulously assembled: the deranged architectural plans for the palatial complex, photographs of an SS conference, generals in cheerful mood joking with the castle maids; newspaper cuttings, a written application for permission to cut down trees; express letters, post-war pictures of the camp, a permit for corpses to be sent out. It has all been carefully sorted and explained, a mosaic of local history which for a long time was ploughed underground by the local inhabitants themselves. The museum has indeed brought memories to the light of day, has broken down the collective wall of silence, but how can the horror be exhibited, shown in images, mounted and displayed on white walls? All you can see is a dry substrate; memory fails before this monstrous absurdity. Behind glass, you can read a prisoner's handwriting, the account of a Jehovah's Witness, the only one that has been preserved:

> 'They brought in a pretty girl. She had to work long hours ironing laundry. The German head of the section was molesting the girl, who was said to have belonged to a partisan group. She resisted the man's attempts to get close and hit him on the forehead with the iron, striking so hard that he died. They hanged the girl secretly here in the camp. Those present were only Commandant Haas and some SS officers, and Stolle the executioner [. . .]. The girl was handcuffed. Stolle was going to put the noose round her neck, but then everything happened very fast. The girl spat right in Stolle's face and pushed him away hard with her fists. She got the noose round her own neck, put her tongue out at the senior SS officers and jumped off the platform. Commandant Haas laughed. "Good Lord, what a wildcat!" Then Stolle said, "She'll pay for that!" In the crematorium Stolle took an iron hook and mutilated the dead girl's genitals with it.'

The wooden locomotive rattles cheerfully over the playground. Puffs of smoke rise to the sky. The children perch on the trunks of oak trees, whistling a song about a long journey. The train ride goes past the steep wigwam, the balancing pole, the car tyres, the climbing frame, right down to the tower on the palisade beyond the birch trees. The adventure ends at the fence; this is where the school grounds begin. The school is an ordinary building, three storeys high, monotonous rows of windows without a touch of colour, no posters or pictures, the barracks of urban youth. The years have left black streaks on the walls. The place was built in 1950 when the huts of the old secondary school would no longer do. Generations have gone to school on this hill near the old town hall, even during the war, when over 900 Jewish women were interned in the nearby blocks. At break, when the children left their classrooms to play on the climbing frame, the women would drag themselves over to the barbed wire fence and beg for bread.

The women had been travelling for weeks before they reached Lichtenau in Hesse early in August 1944. Eichmann's men had dragged them from their homes and forced them into the ghettos, and a few days later they were put into cattle trucks and sent to Auschwitz on one of the many 'Jewish trains' from Hungary. They were unloaded on the ramp at Birkenau. 'Everyone out, good morning, ladies, please hurry up and get out, everything will soon be better.' They were lined up two by two and herded to the selection point. The brief movement of a finger pointed them to the right, their parents and siblings to the left as useless, unfit for work, it was mass murder depending on your appearance, slavery to the right, gas to the left. Their heads were shaved, their bodies dressed in coarse linen sacks and loaded into the cattle trucks again three weeks later. The Reich needed slave workers, even Jewish slave workers, to build bombs and aircraft. The journey in the gloomy half-twilight of the barred trucks went on for days without food and drink, a journey into the unknown, until at last the locomotive stopped at Hessisch-Lichtenau.

> 'We could see at once that the camp was much better equipped than Auschwitz. We thought the huts were clean, we had bunks, and most important of all we had water. We could drink and wash ourselves. Our own equipment was dreadful: ragged clothes, wooden shoes, no underclothes at all. The food was very bad too, thin soup with fifty grams of bread a day. On that, we had to work hard for ten to twelve hours daily.'

Their way to work every day passed right through the town. The road slopes slightly downhill outside the camp gates, on the right the old fire station and its tower to protect the town. On the left a mural of a zoo paradise showing brightly coloured parrots in the jungle. A little further comes a butcher's shop – one of the SS men always helped with slaughtering the animals – down on the corner stands the new green savings bank building, you turn right up the road with the post office, past a shoe shop – most of the women wore only rags round their feet, many went barefoot in the icy slush – next comes a dry cleaner's, thank you for your custom, a ladies' hair salon with smartly coiffured heads in the window, and the supermarket, fresh deliveries every day, cheap food every day, every day an okay day! Next to the railway station where the women once boarded the special train to the factory every morning there's a yellow sign saying 'Kassel 25 kilometres', a play oasis showing shimmering sand dunes, poplars, a blue southern sky, next to it a transit store catering for long-distance travellers from the east, an articulated truck stopping for a rest, huge letters on its yellow tarpaulin: Hungarocamon Budapest, Telex 5488.

Day after day, morning and evening, the townsfolk saw the Jewish women walk down their streets – no, don't look, child, that's not for your eyes – the women SS guards armed with switches, sticks and cudgels going along beside the marching troop, a procession of wretchedness and violence. They stood gaping curiously, perhaps indifferent, perhaps frightened, some of them enjoying the sight. Who can still excuse themselves by saying they saw and knew nothing? It has taken the town over forty years of reflection to put up a memorial outside the school. When the procession turned into their street, some of the townsfolk turned away quickly and sought the nearest way indoors, swiftly shut their windows and drew the curtains – no, there's nothing to see – but they pricked up their ears until it was all over. No one could have failed to know about the camp, no one would have taken it for a sanatorium. Even then it was beginning, the Germans' lifelong illusion about their own frenzied enthusiasm, the craven brutality that never admits to what it has done, the grovelling submission to the stronger. They did not suppress memories after the event; they just refused to look at what they were doing.

The ruins of the old explosives factory are curiously busy. Beside the burnt-out skeleton of the boiler house a forklift truck is stacking machinery on a lorry; a steel saw is screeching in a derelict storehouse, opposite an old man is mowing his lawn. He has moved into the empty office bunker. Ferns, birches and dwarf spruce grow on the flat concrete roof with its jagged corners. Forty gardeners were employed at the time planting up the factory site, a huge area of 230 hectares, as camouflage against air raids. The siren in the wooden watchtower has fallen silent; a black mastiff on a chain barks furiously in the kennels. In a backyard, someone is hosing down a brightly painted bus, wooden pallets stand around, rusty metal drums, selected iron girders, a broken bunker ceiling sticks out of the earthworks at an angle. House number 402 is still for sale and has a board with a phone number outside it; a family has converted the dilapidated building on the other side of the street into a bungalow. The network of streets dates from wartime: Dieselstrasse, Siemensstrasse, Liebigstrasse, the munitions factory in the Hirschhagen woods was the third largest in the Reich and the main shareholder was IG-Farben, the Auschwitz company.

A Federal Railways freight truck is waiting at the loading ramp. The doors of the storehouses are walled up, the broken windows covered with cardboard, the original muddy brown paint shows through the grey plaster. This is where the women loaded grenades into the trucks. Now a green poster is advertising an ecological firm of builders. Thirty-five kilometres of railway tracks are laid on the site. The post office has taken over the porter's lodge, the old administrative offices house a firm selling marble, another firm selling ventilators occupies the premises where bombs were filled with explosives, there are new windows, a second storey has been added, the car park is spick and span. It was heavy work scraping surplus explosive off the filled bombs for eleven hours on end, screwing the tails into place; the poisonous vapours corroded the lungs, stained the skin yellowish green. The moulding works are abandoned, the concrete pillars of the cooling tunnel are gradually emerging from the churned earth, the black rust of an explosion is eating at the empty windows.

> 'When I came back to camp from the night shift early on Sunday morning I had to go straight to the parade ground for rollcall. All the prisoners were there. The camp commandant told us that one group was being taken to

Auschwitz for medical care. They were prisoners who were sick and unable to work. He read out their names from a list, and those whose names were called had to step out from the rest of us. There were 200 women in all, as well as the sick. After that we left the parade ground. Since my shift changed on a Sunday I left the camp at eleven in the morning, and when I came back from work that night the group had already gone.'

Cheerful laughter rings out from the table next to mine. The little girl there almost spilled her cocoa over her pale pink jacket, there's a reproachful glance from her mother – can't you be more careful? – young mothers are always the same. The child's little brother is bent over his plate shovelling large scoops of ice cream into his mouth, we'll have to order him another, a promise is a promise. The father drinking beer, a full-flavoured Alsace brew, is a deliberate, robust man not much older than thirty with a thick moustache, green huntsman's shirt, walking boots. He sits stolidly on the rickety plastic chair, enjoying the clear view of the tree-grown mountain peaks. Ideal hiking weather today, not too hot, not too cold, pretty place up here, good clean air, none of the smells you get in town.

Do we have to go and see it, he had asked before the expedition, surely not, I mean there's nothing to see, after all, this is my day off. But he left the car down in the valley and walked up here with his family. Rooms still vacant in the hotel, a nice clean place, a bit run-down, sure, but a fresh coat of plaster sometimes works wonders. Good choice on the menu, something for everyone: spaghetti napolitaine, couscous, ham omelette. Guests once travelled fifty kilometres from Strasbourg to come here for the skiing in the winter and the walking in the summer. After that the hotel was reserved exclusively for the gentlemen from the camp. The commandant often came, it's not far, only 500 metres up the mountain. If my wife hadn't said we ought to see the place I wouldn't have come, it's no place for children.

The gas chamber stands a few metres from the hotel. The guide in his blue museum uniform has left the metal door open, entry is free. No, there's nothing to see, the cold, dim light of an electric bulb, the barred windows are covered with gratings, nailed up, bleak and empty rooms, cracked concrete floor, old plaster peeling off the walls, reddish brown streaks of dirt. Pale green walls in the changing room next door, distempered like an operating theatre, three deep basins tiled in clinical, aseptic green in the back room. The lids over the basins, made of rough wooden boards, are lifted. Here the dead were not burned but preserved in formalin, the lower abdomen separated, arms in one trough, legs in the other. The stink has gone, medical cleanliness leaves no traces behind. A wooden door is covered with newspapers to hide the cracks between the planks, old newspapers, yellowed with age, shabby, tattered.

> '*Frankfurter Zeitung*, 1 June 1943. The Berlin Philharmonic in Madrid. Just a year ago the Berlin Philharmonic was in Madrid with Clemens Krauss. This time Hans Knappertsbusch was conductor of the concerts that for the people of Madrid were the conclusion and high spot of the orchestra's tour. Germans do not need to advertise in Spain; no sooner does word get around that a German ensemble or even just a German conductor is giving a guest performance than everyone tries to get a ticket, whether they are the music-loving Spanish people of Madrid or those Germans who feel deeply bound to their homeland on such occasions.'

Who was reading the arts section of the *Frankfurter Zeitung* in the gas chamber of Natzweiler concentration camp? Probably not the commandant, more likely one of the doctors and professors from Strasbourg carrying out experiments here with mustard and phosgene gas, dissecting selected skulls for their collection of ancestral types. There were Germans of culture and education in the middle ranks of the SS, one was called Fleischhacker [literally 'flesh hacker'], his superior was Hirt ['shepherd'], doctors with dissecting knives, butchers armed with scalpels and romantic souls, perhaps fervent Wagnerians. In the evening you went to the opera, in the morning you put on your white coat in the University Institute, tied your rubber apron round you, the corpses from the camp were waiting, their vacant eyes open and shining, encrusted blood round their noses and mouths, a cross section, the head is separated from the body, preserved in liquid, stacked in tin containers. Your now familiar work with the knife is to remove the flesh, in your break you glance at the paper, Germans in Madrid, first the Condor Legion, now the Berlin Philharmonic. The commandant had spared these scientists the act of murder itself in the camp one mild August night. Eighty Jews had been sent from Auschwitz to Natzweiler for their purposes, thirty women and fifty men, a consignment of skulls for the race researchers. Here is the meticulous account of the commandant, an accountant in civilian life:

> 'One evening about nine I drove to the gas chamber for the first time with about 15 women in a small truck. I told these women that they must go into a disinfection room, but I did not say they were to be gassed. With the help of some SS men I made them take all their clothes off and when they were entirely naked pushed them into the gas

> chamber. Once the door was closed they began screaming. I then introduced a certain amount of the salts through a pipe fitted to the right of the peephole. Next I added water and turned the tap that closed the opening. [. . .] I then switched on the light and looked through the peephole to see what was happening inside the chamber. I observed that the women went on breathing for about half a minute before they fell to the ground. When I had switched the air on in the ventilation shaft I opened the door. I found the women lying dead on the floor in their own excreta.'

The gas chamber is a quiet place, a small box-like room two and a half metres both wide and high, three and a half metres long, with cold, dirty white tiles, a round hole for the porcelain basin set into the concrete floor. At the back of the room, in the corner, lies a bunch of flowers. There is a chain over the entrance; the open door is covered on the inside with a lacquered metal plate, it has three bolts and a locking screw, there is fine-meshed wire netting over the peephole. The room was once used as a refrigerator for the hotel. Converting it cost 236 Reichsmarks. No, there is nothing to see, it is a silent, odourless place, no formalin, no disinfectants. The horror lies beyond the perception of the senses. Only the banality of the place is terrifying, its shabby, overpowering ordinariness.

The Natzweiler-Struthof concentration camp in Alsace has been described as Auschwitz in France. It was a death camp in the west, with no ramp or death factory but organized along the same lines and with the same aims. Opponents of the regime were to be rapidly annihilated without trace: such was the secret order issued by the Wehrmacht High Command. Prisoners from the occupied countries, the Luxembourgers, French, Dutch, Norwegians, had the two letters NN for *Nacht und*

Nebel, 'night and fog', marked in bright yellow oil paint on their striped rags. Arrested in dawn raids, they had vanished behind the veil of the terror. No relatives discovered where the Gestapo was taking them; they were interned in a camp on the northern slope of a peak in the Vosges, 800 metres above sea level, a concentration camp in the mountains. No one knows exactly how many they numbered. In August 1944 7,000 were evacuated, but how many died before that in the nearby stone quarry, the gas chamber, the infirmary, the doctors' laboratory, on the gallows?

The tricolour flies at the gateway of the camp. The two clocks on the watchtower have gone. A double row of barbed wire surrounds the site; the terraced fields where the huts once stood are empty. Red granite gravel covers the bare surfaces, white marble blocks remind us of the places where mass murder was committed: Dachau, Buchenwald, Bergen-Belsen, Stutthof, Gross-Rosen, Majdanek. The gallows stand on the upper parade ground with a wheelbarrow beside the structure, a cart tipped over, a heap of stones. Each stone contains the weight and toil of countless tormented journeys. The heap is to stay there for ever, through eternity. The road leads from the museum down the steep slope of the mountainside to a dark blue wooden cabin from which a slender chimney emerges. Four cables hold the chimney upright, anchoring it. There's only one way out of here, the guards used to tell the prisoners on arrival, and that's through the chimney.

Someone has left a bunch of immortelles by the grate of the heavy cast-iron stove. The hooks still hang on the wall opposite the pulley of the block and tackle that brought corpses up from the cellar. When the storeroom was full to the ceiling the bodies were stacked outside. Where were they all to be put? The fire burned in the stove day and night, stinking plumes of smoke drifted over the camp. First the flames dried the bodies out, then they burned like torches. That way you saved fuel. Ashes and remains of bones were mingled with clinker and sweepings to be fertilizer for the cabbages in the commandant's kitchen garden. The heat of the oven was piped to a gigantic boiler to heat water for the showers, thus ingeniously recycling the corpses. There are no graves, no crosses, not even a grass-grown mound above the dust and ashes, the economy of the concentration camp left no traces of any kind, only smoke, the stink of burnt fat, fertilizer, and water for the showers.

At the foot of the stone quarry a narrow paved path leads to the new housing estate. The mountainside rises steeply, hundreds of metres high; the bed of the mountain stream has dried up. Mighty steps are carved out of the black rock, a staircase for Cyclopean giants, platforms for excavators and dump trucks. No work is going on today, it is Sunday, a fine Sunday, yellow roses are in flower in front gardens. Bedding hangs out of open windows to bleach in the sunny air, women are doing the housework indoors, a suspicious glance darts from behind a curtain. The streets are empty, silence lies over the asphalt, the supermarket in the middle of town is closed, there is a telephone kiosk, a wall of posters, ads for a fair in Ebensee, best beer tent in the Salzkammergut, three days of fun and frolic, music in the tavern, a tourist rally, dogs to be kept indoors in case of rabies. Nearby is the village youths' football field, with goalposts made of rusty steel piping. It is an old playground, desolate and empty, older than the new buildings round it, with tall undergrowth spilling over the edges. Is this where the roll-calls were held, those mass occasions lasting for hours when the guards displayed their unassailable power to the full assembly of camp inmates? Beside the field stands a dense wood of spruce trees, slender trunks side by side, a garbage heap in the undergrowth, dented tin cans, beer, Coca-Cola, the sole of a shoe, the remains of an oilskin jacket, No Dumping, says a dirty notice, beside it is a paved car park, and the grating over the gate to the concentration camp cemetery.

What draws strangers to a cemetery? Is it the devout silence in which they suddenly find themselves, a silence of mourning and memory, the sense that time has stopped and is held motionless? They walk reverently among the graves, look at the gravestones, seeking names and inscriptions, perhaps people of their own age who are now out of the race. Is there not a secret satisfaction in being alone among the dead? There they lie at your feet, close together, side by side, carefully arranged in ranks, a motionless society. You alone come and go as you please, strolling among them, relaxed and upright, a free visitor.

But where are the dead in this cemetery, the familiar stones of family graves, the wreaths and lanterns, letters carved in the stone telling of the lives of those buried here? A stone memorial stands beside the entrance gate, the sturdy tower of a fortress. A blood-red cross is nailed to the inside wall, the fire in the basin has gone out. The little space in front of it is covered with grey gravel, on the left there is another cross, behind it level areas of turf with narrow paths running between them. These are the mass graves, grass cut short and even, fields of the dead enclosed in rough stones the size of a fist, the grassy foundations of huts, each block just like the next. The heaps of corpses have been flattened, pressed down below the earth. On every green area stands a pink marble stone, no name, no year of birth, just the Christian cross, fifty metres away the Star of David, numbers, 295, 428, 1341, the mass graves of about 1,000 concentration camp victims. How many are laid to rest here? Are there 5,000, 10,000, in the middle of the new village that has buried all traces of the camp beneath it? They died en masse and are buried en masse, stacked in blocks, in rectangular spaces, as they were stacked in life. Bulldozers pushed the haphazard heaps of bones into the pit.

'Let not the worms my flesh devour, the pure flame shall consume me. I loved the warm and sunlit hour, so bury me not but burn me.' These lines were to be read on the notice that the SS executioners put up in the crematorium, German verse in Ebensee concentration camp, the last major German camp to be liberated by the Allies on 6 May 1945, three weeks after Bergen-Belsen, two days before Germany surrendered. Over 18,000 inmates were found crowded together here in the woods on the southern bank of Lake Traun, where German visitors go for their summer holidays today. Ebensee was the last camp in the Ostmark, as Austria was then called, the final destination of the death marches. The columns came in from all directions, from the camps in Salzburg, Vienna and Melk, Steyr and Linz, Gusen and Mauthausen. A transport bringing 2,700 prisoners came from Gross-Rosen in Lower Silesia; 650 of them died immediately of starvation and exhaustion. Others came from Nordhausen in the southern Harz mountains, from Sachsenhausen, even from as far away as Neuengamme near Hamburg. Their odyssey through the concentration camp system ended here, where the last survivors were to disappear for ever, so that no witness should be able to tell posterity what had happened in Germany.

A narrow arcaded walk runs along the wall at the far end of the cemetery. Moss and ivy cover the chalky white stone, the paved path wends its way past the names. Medallions with little photographs are fixed to the walls, pictures to fend off oblivion, photographs to vanquish the past. Marble tablets are memorials to the dead, Tito Arfaioli, Sergio Fanceni from Florence, among them Tadeusz Milka, a Polish architect born 1916, registration number 128721, Jean Hay of La Rochelle, deputy for the Départements Charente Maritime, a bunch of fresh violets, the picture of a young man in a crumbling wooden frame, a soft face, thick black hair combed back from his forehead, his name was Ezio Maranghi and he was nineteen years old when they killed him on 5 May 1945, a day before the camp was liberated. His bones lie somewhere, perhaps in one of the mass graves, or in the galleries of the stone quarry. But here is a picture of him, the young man in the grey suit, smartened up for the photographer, tie correctly knotted. Did he go into the mountains when the Germans came, did someone give him away as he unsuspectingly crossed the street where the pursuers were lying in wait for people to fill their camps?

The regime in Ebensee needed an army of slaves. A gigantic development was to arise here, under the cover name of 'Zement', to build Germany's largest weapon of mass destruction. Up in the stone quarry at the entrance to the new housing estate, prisoners drove galleries as high as houses into the rock. The labyrinth of underground passages goes down to a depth of 250 metres, and each tunnel had its siding, the walls of the halls were clad with cement three storeys high, the niches were furnished as offices, a factory within the mountain, unassailable, bomb-proof. The testing and pumping bays were ready in the catacombs, the oxygen system had not been fitted yet, there were tools for the production of mammoth rockets, intercontinental rockets with single explosive heads that were to fly to America and reduce New York and Washington to rubble. But the network of tunnels remained unfinished, the quota unmet; instead of building rockets the prisoners fitted ball bearings and distilled petrol. The chief designer took the rocket plans to America with him after the war.

Early on Monday, when the siren goes off, work in the stone quarry begins again. The yellow diggers are already waiting behind the steel gates that close off the galleries. A dump truck stands in front of the first steep level of the rock, a monstrous vehicle with tyres as tall as a man, beside it a bulldozer pushing rubble in front of the empty hole in the wall. Oil drums lie around, a porous car tyre, a piece of railway track forgotten in the undergrowth. New sheds have been built, a workshop, an office for the management, a recreation room for the workers. The old concrete bunker still stands, a shapeless colossus, half ruined by falling rocks, and to this day is used as a shelter when the rock up above is blasted. The work goes on day after day, year after year, like life down in the village. History disappears, level after level is exploded and carried away. No one now strays in the labyrinth of abandoned shafts, no one is hurled down the slope or carried to the nearby oven in the wheelbarrow.

No dead lie in the mass graves, no legs and skulls, no remnants of bone or urns of ashes. They do not rest easy, they do not lie peacefully on their backs, teeth fallen out, open mouths full of dirt. They do not complain, they do not whimper. They did not die, they were slaughtered, annihilated, burned to dust. Nor do soldiers lie here with their identity tags, a cross of honour or at least a stone slab for each, arranged in ranking order as they stood on the parade ground at roll-call. They have vanished entirely, there is no place left for them, not a stone to mark their graves.

Sources and notes

On killing

The Biblical quotations are from Genesis 8:21 and Genesis 9:1–6. For the links between giving, sacrifice and the ritual of death, an essential work is Walter Burkett: *Homo Necans. Interpretationen altgriechischer Opferriten und Mythen* (Berlin 1977) and ibid.: *Kulte des Altertums. Biologische Grundlagen der Religion* (Munich 1998). On the fascination of violence for spectators, see a fuller discussion by Wolfgang Sofsky: *Traktat über die Gewalt* (Frankfurt am Main 1996). There is a survey of the history of martyrs in Lacey Baldwin Smith: *Fools, Martyrs, Traitors. The Story of Martyrdom in the Western World* (New York 1997). Death, survival and immortality are at the centre of Elias Canetti's *Masse und Macht* (Hamburg 1964; Eng. *Crowds and Power*, London 1962), a radical work of unsurpassed insight. The quotation is from this book. I am also indebted to Zygmunt Bauman: *Tod, Unsterblichkeit und andered Lebensstrategien* (Frankfurt am Main 1994).

The paradise of cruelty

On the significance of the power of imagination for violence, see in particular Heinrich Popitz: *Phänomene der Macht* (Tübingen 1992). On the limits of research into violence cf. the introduction by Trutz von Trotha (ed.): *Zur Soziologie der Gewalt* (Opladen 1997). I take the theme of 'transgression' from Georges Bataille: *Die Erotik* (Munich 1994; Eng. *Eroticism*, San Francisco 1986) and Roger Caillois: *Der Mensch und das Heilige* (Munich 1988). Elias Canetti's analysis of the giving of orders in *Masse und Macht* (Hamburg 1964), emphasizes them as a thorn in the flesh more than as the granting of licence to commit violence. The best study of provocation is by Rainer Paris: *Stachel und Speer. Machtstudien* (Frankfurt am Main 1998).

Actions

I have reconstructed the details of the amok phenomenon from archival researches in the *New York Times*, *Der Spiegel*, the *Süddeutsche Zeitung*, the *Sunday Times* and the *Independent*. The acount of Java in 1516 is given in *The Book of Duarte Barbosa* (London 1921), to which my attention was drawn by Hans-Joachim Neubauer's excellent article 'Der verdunkelte Blick' in the *Frankfurter Allgemeine Zeitung* (20 November 1999). The 'Wagner case' has been meticulously documented in Bernd Neuzner and Horst Brandstätter: *Wagner. Lehrer, Dichter, Massenmörder* (Frankfurt am Main 1996). The following works are informative on the ethnopsychiatric aspect: W.M. Pfeiffer: *Transkulturelle Psychiatrie* (Stuttgart 1971), and Thomas Knecht: 'Amok. Transkulturelle Betrachtungen über eine Extremform menschlicher Aggression', in: *Kriminalistik* (10/98). The activities of hooligans during the European football championships of 2000 caused considerable uneasiness among state authorities. In England the severe measures taken by the Belgian security forces against episodes of violence were seen in some quarters as an attack on the national honour. I am drawing here on accounts in the *Independent*, *The Times*, the *Observer*, *Der Spiegel* and the *Süddeutsche Zeitung* in June 2000. On the history of football fans cf. Eric Dunning et al.: *The Roots of Football Hooliganism: A Historical and Sociological Study* (London 1989). An inside view of mob actions is provided by Bill Buford: *Among the Thugs* (London 1989) *Geil auf Gewalt. Unter Hooligans* (Munich 1992). Ritual battles are only a form of archaic warfare. Even before the existence of nation states, societies organized persecution campaigns and what amounted to wars of annihilation. Cf. on this subject J. H. Turner-High: *Primitive War, its Practice and Concepts* (Columbia 1971), and J. Haas (ed.): *The Anthropology of War* (Cambridge 1990). For the incidents in Paulsgrove in August 2000 I have consulted reports in various British newspapers and journals, including *The Times*, the *Independent*, the *Observer* and the *Daily Mirror*. On the lynch murder of Eamon Collins, the most detailed accounts are those in the *Irish Times* and *Irish News* of January and February 1999. I found the fullest documentation of the anti-Christian burning in the *Hindustan Times*, *Statesman* and the *Times of India* of January 1999. The attack on Reçak was reported by the entire international press, and served not least as the justification for NATO intervention in Kosovo. As usual, the most detailed accounts were in the *New York Times*, *Le Monde*, the *Neue Zürcher Zeitung*, the *Süddeutsche Zeitung*, the *Frankfurter Allgemeine Zeitung*, *Newsweek* and *Der Spiegel* in January and February 1999.

The modern world and barbarism

I take the points quoted here on the relationship between civilization and barbarism from Norbert Elias: *Studien über die Deutschen* (Frankfurt am Main 1990; Eng. *The Germans*, Cambridge 1996), Max Horkheimer and Theodor W. Adorno: *Dialektik der Aufklärung* (Frankfurt am Main 1969; Eng. *Didactics of Enlightenment*, London 1973), Zygmunt Bauman: *Dialektik der Ordnung. Die Moderne und der Holocaust* (Hamburg 1992), and Hans-Peter Duerr: *Obszönitat und Gewalt. Der Mythos vom Zivilisationsprozess*, Vol. 3 (Frankfurt am Main 1997). The quotation from Carl von Clausewitz: *Vom Kriege* (Frankfurt am Main 1980; Eng. *On War*, Harmondsworth 1968) is taken from Book I, ch. 1.28. The model of the rational bureaucracy that lies behind romantic criticism of modern society and most historical studies of the Shoah was long ago replaced by more realistic structural and environmental models in research on organizational structures done during the last fifty years. We have to accept that politics and terrorist persecution cannot be ascribed to the intentions of a charismatic leader. On the significance of local and decentralized initiatives for the radicalization of terrorism, cf., for instance, the studies by Dieter Pohl: *Nationalsozialistische Judenverfolgung in Ostgalizien. Organisation und Durchführung eines staatlichen Massenverbreaches* (Munich 1996) and Thomas Sandkühler: *'Endlösung' in Galizien* (Berlin 2996). On the power structure of concentration camps cf. Wolfgang Sofsky: *Die Ordnung des Terrors. Das Konzentrationslager* (Frankfurt am Main 1993). On the totalitarian potential of the modern state cf. Zygmunt Bauman: *Moderne und Ambivalenz. Das Ende der Eindeutigkeit* (Hamburg 1992). Helmuth Plessner was already studying the destructive dynamic in communities in 1924, in an early manifesto against the tyranny of intimacy: *Grenzen der Gemeinschaft. Eine Kritik des sozialen Radikalismus*, in: *Gesammelte Schriften*, vol. V (Frankfurt am Main 1981). For the idea of the nation I am drawing on Max Weber: *Wirtschaft und Gesellschaft*, ch. VIII, § 3 (Tübingen 1972; Eng. *Economy and Society*, Berkeley and London 1979), and most of all on Ernest Gellner: *Nations and Nationalism* (Oxford 1983) and ibid.: *Nationalism* (London 1997).

Auschwitz, Kolyma, Hiroshima

The quotation from *The Gulag Archipelago* (Reinbek 1978) by Alexander Solzhenitsyn is from part 3, ch. 3. The most important account of Kolyma, on the same high level as Primo Levi's account of Auschwitz: *Ist das ein Mensch?* (Frankfurt am Main 1961; Eng. *If This is a Man*, Harmondsworth 1979) is still Warlam Schalamow: *Geschichten aus Kolyma* (Frankfurt am Main 1983). A brief and concise survey of the Soviet system of terrorism by Markus Wehner: 'Stalinismus und Terror', may be found in the volume edited by Stefan Plaggenborg: *Stalinismus. Neue Forschungen und Konzepte*

(Berlin 1998). A longer work on the institutional history of the Gulag is Ralf Stettner: *'Archipel GULag': Stalins Zwangslager. Terrorinstrument und Wirtschaftsgigant* (Paderborn 1996). I owe information about the numbers of victims to Stephan Merl: 'Das System der Zwangsarbeit und die Opferzahl des Stalinismus', which appeared in: *Geschichte in Wissenschaft und Unterricht* (46/1995). Also very useful was the solidly based study by Nicolas Werth: 'Ein Staat gegen sein Volk. Gewalt, Unterdrückung und Terror in the Sowjetunion', in the otherwise controversial *Schwarzbuch des Kommunismus* (Munich 1998), initiated by Stéphane Courtois. During the debate on the 'Schwarzbuch', instant expressions of indignation confused analytical comparison with historical equivalence or moral relativism. Instead of studying the crimes committed under Communist rule more closely, commentators turned at once to the problem of the singularity of Auschwitz. In familiar chauvinist manner, German critics emphasized the alleged cultural advance Germany has over Russia – as if Bach and Goethe alone represented cultural levels and Tolstoy and Tchaikovsky did not. According to these ideas, Auschwitz was unique because the crime there was committed by Germans, whereas apparently nothing else was to be expected of Russians. We can see that endeavours to observe political correctness in historical studies do not shrink from resorting to the old stereotypes. On comparative studies of mass murder and genocide cf., however, R. J. Rummel: *Death by Government* (New Brunswick 1997), Levon Chorbajin: *Studies in Comparative Genocide* (Basingstoke 1999), and Israel W. Charny (ed.): *Encyclopedia of Genocide* (Santa Barbara 1999). A well-known example of a military engagement where the outcome was certain from the start is the Battle of Omdurman (in the Sudan) on 2 September 1898. The Mahdi's army had only muskets with a firing range of about 100 metres, while the Anglo-Egyptian troops under Kitchener had gunboats, field-guns, machine guns and rapid-firing arms available, weapons that could hit a target with relative accuracy at a distance of over 500 metres. Of the Mahdi's 40,000 men around 10,000 were killed, another 10,000 wounded, and 5,000 taken prisoner. The British lost about 500 men, most of them during the old-fashioned cavalry pursuit after the battle. Winston Churchill, then a war reporter, describes the engagement in *The River War* (London 1899), not without a sportsman's admiration for the pointless courage of the dervishes. Cf. also the collection of letters, photographs and diaries by Peter Harrington and Frederic A. Scharf: *Omdurman 1898: The Eyewitnesses Speak* (London 1998). Wars of annihilation or total destruction are neither a German invention nor a modern development. Archaic wars between tribes or peoples could lead to the complete eradication of another ethnic troop. All the men were killed, while the women were enslaved or absorbed into the population of the victors. Among the most important studies of labour in the 'death factories' is Richard Glazar: *Die Falle mit dem grünen Zaun. Überleben in Treblinka* (Frankfurt am Main 1992), and the conversations held by Gideon Greif with survivors of the 'special commandos': *Wir weinten tränenlos . . . Augenzeugenberichte der jüdischen 'Sonderkommandos' in Auschwitz* (Cologne 1995). For Hiroshima, I have drawn on Gar Alperovitz: *Hiroshima: die Entscheidung für den Abwurf der Bombe* (Hamburg 1995) and Dennis D. Wainstock: *The Decision to Drop the Atomic Bomb* (Westport 1996).

Time and terror

On the modes of time experienced in a state of fear, cf. Martin Heidegger: *Sein und Zeit* (Tübingen 1971). On clarification of the concepts of 'the sudden' and 'the moment' see Karl Heinz Bohrer: *Plötzlichkeit. Zum Augenblick des ästhetischen Scheins* (Frankfurt am Main 1981). An instructive survey of the history of political assassination is provided by Franklin L. Ford: *Political Murder. From Tyrannicide to Terrorism* (Cambridge, Mass. and London 1985). *Der politische Mord. Von der Antike bis zur Gegenwart* (Hamburg 1990). On the change in modern terrorism, cf. Peter Waldmann: *Terrorismus: Provokation der Macht* (Munich 1998). Detailed accounts of raids by the German occupying powers and their accomplices in the occupied countries can be found in Louis Begley: *Wartime Lies* (London 1991). *Lügen in Zeiten des Krieges* (Frankfurt am Main 1994) and Alexander Tišma: *Das Buch Blam* (Munich 1995). For a historical monograph, a still exemplary model is the study by Christopher Browning: *Ordinary Men: Reserve Police Battalion 101 and the Final Solution in Poland* (London 1992). *Ganz normale Männer. Das Reserve-Polizeibataillon 101 und die 'Endlösung' in Polen* (Reinbek 1993). On the death marches under the Nazi concentration camp system, cf. most recently Daniel Blatman: 'The Death Marches, January–May 1945: Who Was Responsible for What?' in: *Yad Vashem Studies* XXVIII (Jerusalem 2000). Death marches were not confined to the final phase of the Nazi concentration camp system. Many deportations in the Soviet Gulag system also resembled death transports. It was not unusual for there to be no camp in the north of Siberia that could take in the exhausted prisoners at the end of their voyages or marches. They were simply exposed in the taiga and left to their own devices. The transports along the rivers Ob and Yenissei were notorious, and so were the transports by sea from Vladivostok to Magadan, the port of the Kolyma region. During the First World War the Turkish authorities and their Kurdish accomplices drove hundreds of thousands of Armenians into the Mesopotamian desert. Many columns were taken round and round in circles until everyone was dead. In October 1904 the German colonialists in south-west Africa drove the indigenous Hereros out of their reservations into the Namibian desert and then closed the border. Months later patrols found skeletons in dry holes twenty metres deep which the Hereros, dying of thirst, had dug with their bare hands. Some 80,000 people died in the desert. On this episode see also Woodruff D. Smith: *The German Colonial Empire* (Chapel Hill/NY 1978).

Societies of war

The *Daily Mirror* photograph is in the catalogue of the Imperial War Museum compiled by Malcolm Brown: *The Western Front* (1993).

The background to the armistice in the winter of 1914 is studied in Modris Eksteins: *Tanz über Gräben. Die Geburt der Moderne und der Erste Weltkrieg* (Reinbek 1990). The social transformations that occur during violence in battle are not studied in most historical writings on war and society, and even the operational history of the movement of tactical bodies, as demonstrated by Hans Delbrück in his classic *Geschichte der Kriegskunst* (4 vols, Berlin 2000), does not study them on this level. Among the few studies that do focus on a microanalysis of military encounters are Richard Holmes: *Acts of War. The Behavior of Men in Battle* (New York 1989), John Keegan and Richard Holmes: *A History of Men in Battle* (London 1985), Gerald F. Linderman: *Embattled Courage. The Experience of Combat in the American Civil War* (New York 1987) and *The World Within War. America's Combat Experience in World War II* (New York 1997), S. L. A. Marshall: *Men against Fire* (New York 1947), and S. A. Stouffer et al.: *The American Soldier* (Princeton 1949). I also owe important insights to the Falklands veteran Hugh McManners: *The Scars of War* (London 1993). The search for assumed 'causes of war' does not even approach an analysis of the societies of war. Cf. Michael Howard: *The Causes of War and other Essays* (London 1984) and Bernd Wegner (ed.): *Wie Kriege entstehen. Zum historischen Hintergrund von Staatenkonflikten* (Paderborn 2000). The essential causes of and reasons for wars are to be found in a short passage in Jonathan Swift: *Gulliver's Travels*, part 4, ch. 5. Fortifications and sieges are as old as war itself, and have existed since the Neolithic revolution. The cities of Mesopotamia were fortified, and so were Jericho and Troy. Useful works on the history of siege warfare are Paul B. Kern: *Ancient Siege Warfare* (Bloomington 1999), Ivy A. Corfis (ed.): *The Medieval City under Siege* (Woodbridge 1995), Christopher Duffy: *Siege Warfare* (London 1979), S. Pepper and N. Adams: *Firearms and Fortifications. Military Architecture and Siege Warfare in Sixteenth-Century Siena* (1986), Geoffrey Parker: *The Military Revolution: Military Innovation and the Rise of the West 1500–1900* (Cambridge 1988). *Die militärische Revolution. Die Kriegskunst und der Aufstieg des Westens 1500–1800* (Frankfurt am Main 1990). The horrors of Sebastopol are impressively described by the first modern war reporter, William Howard Russell: *Meine Sieben Kriege* (Frankfurt am Main 2000). On the siege of Paris cf. Victor Debuchy: *La vie à Paris pendant le siège* (Paris 1999). On the siege of Leningrad by the German Wehrmacht much information can be obtained from Harrison E. Salisbury: *The 900 Days: The Siege of Leningrad* (London 1969). *900 Tage. Die Belagerung von Leningrad* (Frankfurt am Main 1970) and *Blockade Leningrad 1941–1944. Dokumente und Essays von Russen und Deutschen* (Reinbek 1992), as well as Lidia Ginsburg: *Aufzeichnungen eines Blockademenschen* (Frankfurt am Main 1997). On Sarajevo cf. Zlatko Dizdarević: *Der Alltag des Krieges. Ein Tagebuch aus Sarajevo* (Frankfurt am Main 1995) and Ivana Macek: *War within. Everyday Life in Sarajevo under Siege* (Uppsala 2000). On occupied societies I found it particularly profitable to read Gerhard Hirschfeld: *Fremdherrschaft und Kollaboration. Die Niederlande unter deutscher Besatzung, 1940–1945* (Stuttgart 1984), Mark Mazower: *Inside Hitler's Greece: The Experience of Occupation 1941–1944* (New Haven 1998), Bernhard Chiari: *Alltag hinter der Front. Besetzung, Kollaboration und Widerstand in Weissrussland 1941–1944* (Düsseldorf 1998), Christian Gerlach: *Kalkulierte Morde: die deutsche Wirtschafts- und Vernichtungspolitik in Weissrussland 1941–1944* (Hamburg 2000) and Keat Giu Ooi: *Rising Sun over Borneo. The Japanese Occupation of Sarawak, 1941–1945* (Basingstoke 1999).

The violence of war

The first hours of the Battle of the Somme are described by Martin Middlebrook: *The First Day on the Somme* (London 1971) and John Keegan: *The Face of Battle: A Study of Agincourt, Waterloo and Somme* (London 1976). *Die Schlacht. Agincourt, Waterloo, Somme* (Munich 1981). The idea of the *agon*, the 'extended duel', is based on the concept of war proposed by Carl von Clausewitz: *Vom Kriege* (Frankfurt am Main 1980). For an understanding of human conduct under fire this idea is as unfruitful as referring back to the political aims of war. For general accounts of the First World War I found the following useful: Marc Ferro: *Der grosse Krieg 1914–1918* (Frankfurt am Main 1988; Eng. *The Great War* London 1973), Hew Strachan (ed.): *The Oxford Illustrated History of the First World War* (Oxford 1998), Wolfgang Michalka (ed.): *Der Erste Weltkrieg. Wirkung, Wahrnehmung, Analyse* (Munich 1994), Roger Chickering and Stig Förster (eds.): *Great War, Total War. Germany, France, Great Britain, and the United States, 1914–1918* (Cambridge 2000), and John Keegan: *The First World War* (London 1998). *Der Erste Weltkrieg. Eine europäische Tragödie* (Reinbek 2000). On the tactics of battle I learned most from Timothy Travers: *How the War Was Won* (London 1992), Paddy Griffith: *Battle Tactics of the Western Front. The British Army's Art of Attack 1916–18* (New Haven 1994), and M. Samuels: *Doctrine and Dogma: German and British Infantry Tactics in the First World War* (Westport 1992). The most precise descriptions of barrage fire, the storming of trenches and wounds are found not in historical but in literary works which all provide greater detail: Robert Graves: *Goodbye to All That* (London 1982), Reginald H. Roy (ed.): *The Journal of Private Fraser, Canadian Expeditionary Force* (Victoria 1985), Siegfried Sassoon: *Memoirs of an Infantry Officer* (London 1965), Ernst Jünger: *In Stahlgewittern* (Stuttgart 1978), Henri Barbusse: *Le Feu* (Paris 1916), Erich Maria Remarque: *Im Westen nichts Neues* (Berlin 1991; Eng. *All Quiet on the Western Front*), J. P. Campbell: *In the Cannon's Mouth* (London 1979), Ludwig Renn: *Krieg* (Reinbek 1988), Frank Richards: *Old Soldiers Never Die* (London 1983). The account of the future deserter Dominik Richert: *Beste Gelegenheit zum Sterben. Meine Erlebnisse im Kriege 1914–1918* (Munich 1989) shows that accounts of battle hardly differ at all with the narrator's politics or nationality.

Unauthorized warfare

The epoch-making significance of war outside state policies and discipline is illustrated by Martin van Creveld: *Die Zukunft des Krieges*

(Munich 1998), and the essays and reportage of Ryszard Kapuściński: *Afrikanisches Fieber* (Frankfurt am Main 1999) and Robert Kaplan: *The Ends of Earth. A Journey at the Dawn of the Twenty-First Century* (New York 1996), also ibid.: *The Coming Anarchy: Shattering the Dreams of the Post-Cold War* (New York 2000). The first interim balance sheet has been drawn up by Herfried Münkler: 'Die privatisierten Kriege des 21. Jahrhunderts', in: *Merkur* No. 63 (3/2001). The readable essays of Michael Ignatieff: *The Warrior's Honour: Ethnic War and the Modern Conscience* (London 1998). *Die Zivilisierung des Krieges. Ethnische Konflikte, Menschenrechte, Medien* (Hamburg 2000) are concerned with the moral problems of intervention. On the difference between the marauder and the partisan as figures in society cf. Herfried Münkler (ed.): *Der Partisan: Theorie, Strategie, Gestalt* (Opladen 1990). I found comprehensive accounts of the massacres in Algeria in *Le Monde*, *Libération*, and the *Neue Zürcher Zeitung* in January 1998. On the slaughter in Chenalho there were detailed reports in December 1997 and January 1998 in the *New York Times*, *Le Monde*, the *Neue Zürcher Zeitung*, *Der Spiegel* and the *Süddeutsche Zeitung*. For Srebrenica I used Jan Willem Honig: *Srebrenica: A Record of a War Crime* (London 1996) and David Rohde: *A Safe Area: Srebrenica, Europe's Worst Massacre Since the Second World War* (London 1997). *Die letzten Tage von Srebrenica* (Reinbek 1997). For the storming of the tomb of Joseph and the lynch murder in Ramallah I consulted the *New York Times*, BBC News, *Le Monde*, the *Neue Zürcher Zeitung*, the *Jerusalem Post* and *Ha'aretz* in October and November 2000. For the terrorist attacks on 11 September 2001 and the subsequent events I drew most of my information from the *New York Times*, CNN News, BBC News, the *Guardian*, the *Neue Zürcher Zeitung*, *Der Spiegel*, the *Süddeutsche Zeitung* and the *Frankfurter Allgemeine Zeitung*. On the prehistory of the attacks I consulted Bruce Hoffman: *Inside Terrorism* (London 1998) *Terrorismus. Der unerklärte Krieg. Neue Gefahren politischer Gewalt* (Frankfurt am Main 1998), Robert Jay Lifton: *Destroying the World to Save It: Aum Shinrikyo, Apocalyptic Violence and the New Global Terrorism* (New York 1999). *Terror für die Unsterblichkeit.*

Erlösungssekten proben den Weltuntergang (Munich 2000) and Jessica Stern: *The Ultimate Terrorists* (Cambridge 1999).

Retaliation

On the universal nature of revenge cf. Peter Waldmann: 'Rache ohne Regeln. Zur Renaissance eines archaischen Gewaltmotivs', in: *Mittelweg 36* (6/2000). There is a comprehensive survey in the three volumes edited by Raymond Verdier: *La Vengeance. La vengeance dans les sociétés extra-occidentales* (Paris 1981). On the critique of national honour all that need be said will be found in Arthur Schopenhauer: *Aphorismen zur Lebensweisheit*, ch. IV (Frankfurt am Main 1976). The quotation from Virgil is in the *Aeneid* Book 2, line 354. The retaliatory principle in punishment occurs in G. W. F. Hegel: *Grundlinien der Philosophie des Rechts*, sections 99–104. On the limitations of truth commissions for punishing state crimes cf. Stanley Cohen: 'State Crimes of Previous Regimes. Knowledge, Accountability and the Policing of the Past', in: *Law and Social Inquiry*, vol. 20 (1/1995). By now rejection of the thesis of collective guilt has become almost an automatic defensive reflex. At first the accusation still encountered arguments; I will mention only Karl Jaspers: *Die Schuldfrage. Von der politischen Haftung Deutschlands* (Heidelberg 1946) and the major articles by Eugen Kogon in the *Frankfurter Heften*, collected in Kogon: *Ideologie und Praxis der Unmenschlichkeit* (Weinheim 1995). Forty years later, during the Goldhagen debate, it was enough to state that someone represented the thesis of collective guilt to discredit him publicly. Well-founded reservations about this over-swift reflex were expressed by Jean Améry: *Jenseits von Schuld und Sühne. Bewältigungsversuche eines Überwältigten* (Stuttgart 1977; Eng. *At the Mind's Limits*).

Forgetting

I am particularly indebted here to the famous literary history of forgetting by Harald Weinrich: *Lethe. Kunst und Kritik des Vergessens*

(Munich 1997) as well as the phenomenological study by Paul Ricœur: *Das Rätsel der Vergangenheit. Erinnern – Vergessen – Verzeihen* (Göttingen 1998). For praise of forgetting one may read Friedrich Nietzsche's poem *Die Sonne sinkt* from his *Dionysos-Dithyramgen* cycle, printed in vol. VI of the *Sämtliche Werke* compiled by Colli/Montinari (Munich 1980). On the proper relationship of forgetting, forgiving and punishment I owe important insights to Hannah Arendt: *Vita activa oder Vom tätigen Leben*, section 33 (Munich 1981). On the history of peace treaties cf. Jörg Fisch: *Krieg und Frieden im Friedensvertrag. Eine universalgeschichtliche Studie über Formelemente des Friedensschlusses* (Stuttgart 1979). On the precise nature of the concept of shame I am indebted to the perceptive study by Hilge Landweer: *Scham und Macht. Phänomenologische Untersuchungen zur Sozialität eines Gefühls* (Tübingen 1999).

The fading of the horror

Quotations and historical data on the various camps mentioned are taken from Sylvester Lechner: *Das KZ Oberer Kuhberg und die NS-Zeit in der Region Ulm/Neu-Ulm* (Stuttgart 1988), Julius Schätzle: *Stationen zur Hölle* (Frankfurt am Main 1974); Karl Hüser: *Wewelsburg 1933–1945 – Kult- und Terrorstätte der SS – Eine Dokumentation* (Paderborn 1982); Dieter Vaupel: *Das Aussenkommando Hess. Lichtenau des Konzentrationslagers Buchenwald 1944/45* (Kassel 1984); Jürgen Ziegler: *Mitten unter uns – Natzweiler-Struthof: Spuren eines Konzentationslagers* (Hamburg 1986), Wolfgang Kirstein: *Das Konzentrationslager als Institution totalen Terrors. Das Beispiel des KL Natzweiler* (Pfaffenweiler 1992); Hans Marsalek; *Die Geschichte des Konzentrationslagers Mauthausen* (Vienna 1980) and Florian Freund: *'Arbeitslager Zement'. Das Konzentrationslager Ebensee und die Raketenrüstung* (Vienna 1989).

Acknowledgements

The present volume brings together several essays written for various different occasions in the last few years. For book publication they have been thoroughly revised, cut or extended, rewritten or fitted into a wider context as a subsection. The following acknowledgements give the place of first publication, although many sections have been entirely rewritten, especially in chapters 2, 4, 5 and 9.

1. 'On killing', previously unpublished.
2. 'The paradise of cruelty', earlier version in the *Frankfurter Allegemeine Zeitung*, 2 February 1999.
3. 'Actions'
   'Running amok', in: *Das Magazine/Tages Anzeiger*, 8 April 2000
   'The mob', in: *Das Magazine/Tages Anzeiger*, 1 July 2000.
   'The pillory', in: *Die Weltwoche*, 7 September 2000.
   'Masks and fire', in: *Die Weltwoche*, 4 March 1999.
4. 'The modern world and barbarism', earlier version entitled 'Zivilisation, Organisation, Gewalt', in: *Mittelweg* no. 36, 2/94, pp. 57–67.
5. 'Auschwitz, Kolyma, Hiroshima', earlier version entitled 'Formen absoluter Gewalt' in: *Mittelweg* no. 36, 5/93, pp. 36–46.
6. 'Time and terror', extended version under the title 'Gewaltzeit'

in: T. von Trotha (ed.), *Soziologie der Gewalt.* Special publication 37 of the *Kölner Zeitschrift für Soziologie und Sozialpsychologie,* Opladen 1997, pp. 102–121.

7. 'Societies of war', previously unpublished.
8. 'The violence of war', previously unpublished.
9. 'Unauthorized warfare'

   'The return of the marauder', in: *Das Magazine/Tages Anzeiger*, 4 April 1999.

   'The massacre', earlier version entitled 'Das Gesetz des Gemetzels' in: *Die Zeit,* 2 April 1998; also in Danish: 'Nedslagtninger', in: *weekendavisien,* 8 April 1998.

   'The weapon of desecration', in: *Die Weltwoche*, 19 October 2000.

   'Kosovo, the double war', under the title 'Krieg und Illusion' in: *Die Zeit,* 22 May 1999.

   'Terrorist warfare', published in parts in: *Literaturen* 11/2001; *Focus* 42/2001; the *Süddeutsche Zeitung* 19 September 2001; and the *Neue Zürcher Zeitung* 25 September 2001.
10. 'Retaliation', previously unpublished.
11. 'Forgetting', previously unpublished.
12. 'The fading of the horror', in: *Neue Rundschau* 4/88, pp. 19–40.

Index